Junge Schweizer Archit

Carmen Humbel

Junge Schweizer Architekten und Architektinnen
Young Swiss Architects

Valentin Bearth
Andrea Deplazes

Ueli Brauen
Doris Waelchi

Raffaele Cavadini
Michele Arnaboldi

Jean-Pierre Dürig
Philippe Rämi

Rolf Furrer
François Fasnacht

Nick Gartenmann
Mark Werren
Andreas Jöhri

Christian Gautschi
Marianne Unternährer

Dieter Jüngling
Andreas Hagmann

Claudine Lorenz
Florian Musso

Meinrad Morger
Heinrich Degelo

Pierre-André Simonet
Yvan Chappuis

Birkhäuser
Basel · Boston · Berlin

Übersetzung/Translation: English Experts, Munich
Publiziert mit Unterstützung von / Supported by:
Walter Ambrosina Oertli Stiftung
Eternit AG

A CIP catalogue record for this book is available from the Library of Congress, Washington D.C., USA

Deutsche Bibliothek Cataloging-in-Publication Data
Humbel, Carmen:
Junge Schweizer Architekten und Architektinnen : Valentin Bearth ...
= Young Swiss architects / Carmen Humbel. – 2., unveränd. Nachdr. –
Basel ; Boston ; Berlin : Birkhäuser, 1996
   ISBN 3-7643-5548-4 (Basel...)
   ISBN 0-8176-5548-4 (Boston)

This work ist subject to copyrigt. All rights are reserved, whether the whole or part of the material is concerned, specifically the rights of translation, reprinting, re-use of illustrations, recitation, broadcasting, reproduction on microfilms or in other ways, and storage in data banks. For any kind of use, permission of the copyright owner must be obtained.

Erster, unveränderter Nachdruck 1996
First uncorrected reprint 1996

© 1995 Birkhäuser Verlag, P.O. Box 133, CH-4010 Basel, Switzerland
Printed on acid-free paper produced from chlorine-free pulp. TCF ∞
Gestaltung/Design: Heinz von Arx
Printed in Germany
ISBN 3-7643-5548-4
ISBN 0-8176-5548-4

9 8 7 6 5 4 3 2

Inhalt / Contents

- 7 «Treize points» –
  Auf der Suche nach einer neuen Schweizer Architektur
- 11 "Treize points" –
  In Search of a New Swiss Architecture
- 15 Valentin Bearth · Andrea Deplazes
  Chur
- 29 Ueli Brauen · Doris Waelchli
  Lausanne
- 39 Raffaele Cavadini · Michele Arnaboldi
  Locarno
- 57 Jean-Pierre Dürig · Philippe Rämi
  Zürich
- 67 Rolf Furrer · François Fasnacht
  Basel
- 79 Nick Gartenmann · Mark Werren · Andreas Jöhri
  Bern
- 93 Christian Gautschi · Marianne Unternährer
  Zürich
- 103 Dieter Jüngling · Andreas Hagmann
  Chur
- 113 Claudine Lorenz · Florian Musso
  Sitten
- 123 Meinrad Morger · Heinrich Degelo
  Basel
- 137 Pierre-André Simonet · Yvan Chappuis
  Freiburg
- 147 Mitarbeiterinnen und Mitarbeiter / Collaborators
  Auswahlbibliographie / Selected Bibliography
- 152 Bildnachweis / Illustration Credits

Einführung

«Treize points» – Auf der Suche nach einer neuen Schweizer Architektur

Nichts kennzeichnet das ausgehende zwanzigste Jahrhundert in den Industrienationen mehr als unsere pluralistische Zeit des totalen Überflusses und deren fatale Konsequenzen. Dieses uns immer mehr bedrohende Phänomen beschreibt der französische Philosoph Paul Virilio in seinem apokalyptischen Buch «Rasender Stillstand» (Wien 1992) auf sehr treffende Weise: Er diagnostiziert diesen Zustand als «Leichenstarre der Bewegungslosigkeit» oder als «mediale Ghettoisierung». Sich von diesem lähmenden Zustand zu befreien, bedeutet, alle vorgefaßten Meinungen abzubauen. So ist die Suche nach dem Ursprung, nach dem Fundamentalen eines der wichtigsten Gegen-Momente im heutigen Gesamtprozeß. Diese generelle Erkenntnis läßt sich gut auf die junge Schweizer Architektur beziehen.

Richten wir in der vorliegenden Monographie den Blick auf die zeitgenössische Schweizer Architekturszene, die weit über die Landesgrenzen hinaus auf ein wachsendes Interesse stößt: Nicht die bekannten Größen sollen für einmal zur Darstellung kommen, sondern elf exemplarisch ausgewählte Büros der jungen Generation aus allen Kulturregionen der Schweiz werden mit ihren interessantesten Bauten und Projekten vorgestellt. Dieser Dokumentation ist eine Vortragsreihe am «Architektur Forum Zürich» vorausgegangen, bei der die Büros ihre Arbeiten einer breiteren Öffentlichkeit – oft zum ersten Mal – präsentiert haben und die durch eine Artikelserie in der Beilage «Bauen Planen Wohnen» der Neuen Zürcher Zeitung begleitet wurde. Die Resonanz war allgemein so positiv, daß eine Bestandesaufnahme in Buchform sinnvoll erschien. Die vielleicht nicht immer spektakulär anmutenden Beispiele weisen nicht unbedingt revolutionäre Innovationen und aufsehenerregende Erneuerungen auf. Ihnen allen gemeinsam ist aber – auch den Projekten, die (noch) nicht verwirklicht wurden – eine überdurchschnittlich hohe architektonische Qualität. Gemein ist diesen 23 Architekten und Architektinnen ferner das Alter. Sie sind, mit wenigen Ausnahmen, unter vierzig Jahre alt. Damit haben sie, wenn auch mit individuellen Wurzeln, teil an gewissen verbindenden, prägenden Erfahrungen.

Um das Phänomen faßbarer zu machen, ist versucht worden, diese jüngste Architekturentwicklung in kennzeichnende, charakteristische Elemente zu unterteilen. Dabei sind eine durchgehend zutreffende Gemeinsamkeit (Universelle Betrachtungsweise) und zwölf auffallende Merkmale (Sensible Wahrnehmung bis Wirksame Traditionslinien) auszumachen. Diesen «treize points» zur neuen Schweizer Architektur sind exemplarisch ausgewählte Projekte angefügt, um die aufgestellte These zu veranschaulichen.

Universelle Betrachtungsweise

Gemein ist ihnen allen das Interesse am allgemeinen Weltgeschehen, das sich in einer offenkundigen Neugier in politischen und gesellschaftlichen Bereichen manifestiert. Ihnen allen gemeinsam ist, daß sie ihre Architektur weder auf einem ideologischen Ansatz noch auf einem stilistischen Glauben aufbauen. So ist in zahlreichen Büros eine weitgespannte, offene, gleichsam universelle Betrachtungsweise – frei von belastenden Konventionen und Ideologien – auszumachen. Es wäre deshalb unangebracht, nach regionalen Tendenzen zu suchen oder gar über stilistische Fragen zu debattieren. Pragmatisch beurteilen beispielsweise die in Chur arbeitenden Dieter Jüngling und Andreas Hagmann ihre Architektur selbst als von einer bewußten Stil-losen Haltung geprägt.

Sensible Wahrnehmung

Im Alltäglichen liegt der Stoff, aus dem wir das Material für unsere Denk- und Arbeitsweise beziehen, betonen die beiden in Chur wirkenden Valentin Bearth und Andrea Deplazes. In eine ähnliche Richtung zielt der Ausspruch: «Es beschäftigen uns [...] die Formen, in denen ein alltäglicher Gebrauch seine Bedeutungen abgelagert hat.» (Marcel Meili, Ein paar Bauten, viele Pläne, in: Peter Disch, Architektur in der Deutschen Schweiz, 1980–1990, Lugano 1991) Eine sensible Wahrnehmung für das Beachtenswerte im Üblichen gekoppelt mit einer gesunden Offenheit für das Besondere ist eine wichtige Voraussetzung dafür, daß Architektur wieder zu berühren vermag.

Kontextuelle Haltung

Eine bei Architekten und Architektinnen in allen Regionen der Schweiz festzustellende Eigenschaft ist eine intensive kontextuelle Haltung, das heißt eine besondere Neigung, sich mit dem Kontext im weitesten Sinne zu befassen. Ausgehend von der Modulierung der gegebenen Topographie, der Struktur der umliegenden Bauten und dem charakteristischen Ausdruck der näheren Umgebung werden Lösungen gesucht, die dem zu bebauenden Ort seine ihm gebührende Identität geben. In der französischen Schweiz waren es beim Wohnhaus Suter in Montblesson von Ueli Brauen und Doris Waelchli die verschiedenartigen umliegenden Nutzungen der Parzelle – Feld, Wald und bestehendes Wohnhaus –, die maßgeblich den Entwurf bestimmten. Deutlichen Bezug auf die Umgebung, insbesondere auf die einmalige Sicht des Lago Maggiore, nehmen die Wohnungen Quattrini in Minusio, die Michele Arnaboldi entwarf. Aber auch in der Deutschschweiz sind ähnliche Bestrebungen sichtbar. Beim Röntgenareal in Zürich versuchten Jean-Pierre Dürig und Philippe Rämi den Charakter der nahegelegenen Röntgenstraße präzise in ihrem Projekt wiederaufzunehmen. Der Ort gehört eigentlich zum Ursprung jeder Architektur. Und da jeder Eingriff, so insbesondere das Bauen, eine Zerstörung bedingt, postuliert Luigi Snozzi: «Zerstöre mit Vernunft.» Ebenso ist er bezüglich des Kontextes der Auffassung: «Es gibt nichts zu erfinden, alles ist wiederzufinden.» (Progetti e architetture 1957–1984, Mailand 1984) Es ist daher wichtig wahrzunehmen, was bewahrt, was umgestaltet und was zerstört werden darf.

Konzeptionelle Aspekte

Architektur, die konzeptionelle Aspekte aufweist, meint eine Architektur, die ihren entwerferischen Prozeß als ein akribisches Suchen nach einem übergeordneten Thema – einem persönlich formulierten Konzept – begreift, dem alles unterzuordnen ist. Als herausragendes Beispiel sei das Schulhaus und die Mehrzweckhalle in Tschlin von Valentin Bearth und Andrea Deplazes genannt, dessen Thema, das Licht, die einzigartige atmosphärische Stimmung im Unterengadin, nachhaltig den Entwurf bestimmte. Weitere Beispiele dieser Arbeitsweise sind: das Sportzentrum in Yverdon-les-Bains von Ueli Brauen und Doris Waelchli, bei dem die besonders flache Topographie, die Horizontalität, zum Thema des Entwurfes gewählt wurde; oder das Schulhaus und Gemeindezentrum in Mastrils von Dieter Jüngling und Andreas Hagmann, bei dem es ebenso die markante Topographie war, die ausschlaggebende Impulse für das Festlegen des Entwurfsthemas gab.

Kompositorisches Verhalten

Zahlreiche Projekte zeichnen sich durch ein klares kompositorisches Verhalten aus, das heißt, durch die Gestaltung von verschiedenen, mindestens jedoch von zwei Baukörpern. Um diese in ihrer Identität zu stärken, gehen die Architekten und Architektinnen oftmals von deren Funktion aus. Da die Wahrnehmung der Teile vom Ganzen bedingt wird, ist beim Ökumenischen Begegnungszentrum Au in Wädenswil von Christian Gautschi und Marianne Unternährer die als Ganzes gelesene Anlage in verschieden große Volumen mit unterschiedlichen Nutzungen komponiert. Ähnlich reagiert das Projekt für den Kontrollturm des Flugplatzes in Sion von Claudine Lorenz und Florian Musso; die zusammengehörende Anlage besteht aus zwei, durch ihre Funktion bedingt verschiedenen, aneinandergebauten Volumen. Sie werden aber mit denselben Materialien errichtet, im Sinne, daß Ähnlichkeit die Voraussetzung für das Wahrnehmen der Unterschiede ist.

Experimentelle Erkundungen

Ein weiteres gemeinsames Betätigungsgsfeld zeigt sich im bewußten Erkunden und Ausprobieren von konventionellen Materialien, das über die rein technische, konstruktive Anwendung und über den taktil-sinnlichen Aspekt hinauszielt. Von besonderem Interesse ist dabei nicht nur das Erfassen der eigentlichen Grenzen eines Materials, sondern auch das Aufspüren des Dahinterliegenden. So erzeugt beispielsweise die aus naturbelassenen Kupfertafeln gefügte Fassade der Höheren Technischen Lehranstalt in Chur von Dieter Jüngling und Andreas Hagmann eine schwer faßbare, geheimnisvolle, beinahe mystische Atmosphäre. Wie der Baustoff Beton experimentell angewendet werden kann, ist bei der roh belassenen Fassade des Wohnhauses Chappuis in Corpataux von Pierre-André Simonet und Yvan Chappuis besonders gut ersichtlich. Mit faserzementgebundenen Platten sind Valentin Bearth und Andrea Deplazes beim Wohnhaus Werner in Trin ein besonderes Experiment eingegangen, indem nämlich Dach und Fassade mit dem gleichen Material und in derselben Verlegungsart eingekleidet wurden. Die Hülle des Baukörpers erscheint als Schleier und ist damit besonders artikuliert: gleichsam als Objekt des Begehrens.

Innere Bilder

Auf der Suche nach adäquaten architektonischen Lösungen stoßen viele Architekten und Architektinnen auf Erfahrungen und Ereignisse, die sie in ihrem bisherigen Leben gemacht haben, sowie auf persönliche Neigungen. Diese abgelagerten Bedeutungen werden in Form von inneren Bildern gefaßt, die in ganz bestimmten Situationen als Bruchstücke der Erinnerung an die Oberfläche dringen. Bildhaft oder schemenhaft, auf jeden Fall Fundstücke – «des objets trouvés» –, wie dies die Churer Valentin Bearth und Andrea Deplazes äußern, oder wie André Malraux, der sie treffend als unser «musée imaginaire» bezeichnet. Ein Bilder-Arsenal, das beim Entwerfen unter Umständen wirkungsmächtig werden kann.

Einfache Konstruktion

Besonderes Augenmerk legen zahlreiche Büros in der heutigen wirtschaftlich rezessiven Zeit auf eine einfache und damit oftmals auch preisgünstige Konstruktion. Gefragt sind zweckmäßige und beständige sowie vermehrt auch ökologisch und energetisch bewußte Lösungen. Die Kombination der Grundrißdisposition, des gewählten Holzrahmenbaus, der Trockenbauweise sowie des großen Anteils an vorfabrizierten Bauteilen beim Wohnhaus Roethlisberger in Langnau von Nick Gartenmann, Mark Werren und Andreas Jöhri ließ (als Resultat der hohe technische Anforderungen stellenden Konstruktionsphase) ein ästhetisch anmutendes, einzigartiges Bauwerk entstehen.

Handwerkliche Präzision

Einfache und klare Konstruktionsweisen erlauben und verlangen einen höheren Perfektionsgrad, so daß die fertiggestellten Details oft eine erstaunliche handwerkliche Präzision aufweisen. Der sorgfältigen, soliden Ausführung gerade bei kleinsten Realisationen wird größte Beachtung geschenkt, so beispielsweise bei den Wartehallen für die Verkehrsbetriebe in Basel von Rolf Furrer und François Fasnacht.

Sinnliche Materialpräsenz

Immer deutlicher wird das Material in seiner ganzen Gegenwärtigkeit gezeigt. Die sinnlichen Eigenschaften, die das Material besitzt, werden offenbart, es wird in seiner absoluten Nacktheit präsentiert. Jacques Herzog und Pierre de Meuron: «Das Material ist dazu da, den Bau zu bestimmen, aber der Bau ist in gleichem Maß da, um zu zeigen, aus was er gemacht ist.» (El Croquis, Heft Herzog & de Meuron 1983–1993, Madrid 1993) Diesem Aspekt tragen etwa das Schulhaus und die Mehrzweckhalle in Alvaschein von Valentin Bearth und Andrea Deplazes besonders Rechnung.

Farbliche Akzente

Auffallend ist, daß die junge Generation der Farbe wieder viel mehr Beachtung schenkt, als das vor einiger Zeit noch der Fall war. Historisch gesehen hatte die Farbigkeit ihren festen Platz beispielsweise in den Siedlungen der zwanziger Jahre von Bruno Taut, der die durch die Typisierung hervorgerufene Eintönigkeit mittels Verwendung von Farbe zu überwinden suchte. Mehr und mehr jedoch wurde dieses Gestaltungsmittel verdrängt und gegen Grau und Weiß ausgetauscht. Bei der neuen Schweizer Architektur sind keine eigentlichen Farbpräferenzen auszumachen, vielmehr werden bewußt farbliche Akzente gesetzt, die verschiedene Aussagen beinhalten können. So gibt es Projekte, die durch die Farbe architektonische Intentionen verstärken und unterstreichen möchten; zum Beispiel beim Bootshaus in Murten von Pierre-André Simonet und Yvan Chappuis, das mit seinen braunrot angestrichenen Holzlatten an die Tradition der in unmittelbarer Nähe sich befindenden Bootshäuser anknüpft. Anders ist es beim Schulhaus und der Mehrzweckhalle in Tschlin von Valentin Bearth und Andrea Deplazes, bei der die leicht auskragende, massive Betonkiste rot lasiert wurde. Damit hebt sie sich von ihrer Umgebung ab und erscheint als völlig entmaterialisiertes Volumen.

Minimale Notwendigkeit

Es fällt auf, daß tendenziell eine einfache, klare, präzise, ehrliche, minimale, aber notwendige Architektur stets oberste Devise bleibt. Über allem steht, so propagieren es die in Basel tätigen Meinrad Morger und Heinrich Degelo mit Nachdruck, der sinnvolle Gebrauch materieller wie geistiger Ressourcen. Ziel sei es, die Architektur auf ihre notwendige Substanz zu reduzieren, auf das Wesentliche zu beschränken. Ihrer Meinung nach ist Sinnlichkeit – Form, Material und Farbe – erst möglich nach dem Besinnen auf das Notwendige. Exemplarisch und mit aller Deutlichkeit ist dies am kommunalen Wohnhaus in Basel von Meinrad Morger und Heinrich Degelo oder am Wohnhaus Cavadini in Brissago von Raffaele Cavadini ersichtlich.

Wirksame Traditionslinien

Auch die neue Schweizer Architektur steht deutlich in den Traditionslinien der klassischen Moderne, die mit Le Corbusier, Mies van der Rohe oder Walter Gropius ihre wichtigsten Exponenten aufweist. Hinzu kommen wichtige Einflüsse von zeitgenössischen Architekten wie zum Beispiel Luigi Snozzi in Locarno, Peter Zumthor in Haldenstein (Graubünden) oder Herzog & de Meuron in Basel, bei denen zahlreiche Nachwuchskräfte der jungen Generation ihre ersten Erfahrungen sammeln konnten. Nachdrückliche Anstöße vermitteln auch Erkenntnisse oder Erfahrungen aus der bildenden Kunst mit Arbeiten von Edouard Hopper oder Donald Judd als Vertreter der Minimal Art sowie anhand von Werken, die sich mit dem Phänomen des Wahrnehmens befassen. Zu nennen ist der amerikanische Videokünstler Gary Hill, der sich besonders auf das Thema der Differenz zwischen Sehen und Anschauen konzentriert: Das bloße Sehen deutet nicht, Anschauung hingegen vermag zu deuten.

Introduction

"Treize points" –
In Search of a New Swiss Architecture
The last years of the twentieth century are characterised more than anything by a pluralistic period of absolute affluence and its fateful consequences. This ever more threatening phenomenon is described very aptly by the French philosopher Paul Virilio, in his apocalyptic book "Rasender Stillstand" (Vienna, 1992): he diagnosed this condition as "a rigor mortis of immobility" or "medial ghettoisation". To free ourselves from this paralysing state means tearing down all preconceived notions. Thus the search for the origin, for the fundamental, is one of the most important counter-movements in the overall trend today. This view is particularly true when applied to young Swiss architecture of today.
In this book we direct our attention to the contemporary scene in Swiss architecture, one which is attracting growing interest far beyond the borders of the country. This time our gaze is not directed towards the big names, but to the interesting buildings and projects of eleven selected architectural offices exemplary of the young generation – from all cultural regions of Switzerland. The idea for this publication came as a result of a lecture series at the "Architektur Forum Zürich", in which these architects presented their work to a wider public – often for the first time – and following a series of articles in the supplement on building, planning and living in the "Neue Zürcher Zeitung". The very positive response to these two series led to the creation of this book. The examples shown here may not always be spectacular, or contain revolutionary innovations and exciting new developments, but all of them, including the projects which have not (yet) been carried out, have one thing in common – their above-average architectural quality. Another common feature of these 23 architects is their youth – with but a few exceptions they are all under 40. This, despite their individual roots, gives them certain links in terms of key experiences. To aid comprehension of this phenomenon we have divided this most recent Swiss architecture into its characteristic components: against a shared background ("Universal Approach") twelve striking aspects (from "Sensitive Perception" to "Effective Tradition") can be distinguished. These "treize points" on new Swiss architecture are each supplemented with a selected list of projects which illustrate the individual theses.

Universal Approach
All of these architects share an interest in general world affairs, witnessed by their obvious concern for political and social developments. A common feature is also the fact that they base their architecture not on ideology, nor on a particular philosophy of style; they are characterised instead by a broad-based, open and at the same time universal approach – unburdened with convention or ideology. For this reason it would be inappropriate to look for regional tendencies, or even to debate questions of style. Dieter Jüngling and Andreas Hagmann, for example, working in Chur, state pragmatically that their architectural approach is consciously free of any particular style.

Sensitive Perception
The basis for our thinking and our work is to be found in the everyday, according to the Chur-based architects Valentin Bearth and Andrea Deplazes. Or, similarly: "We are concerned [...] with the forms in which everyday uses have deposited their meanings." (Marcel Meili, "Ein paar Bauten, viele Pläne", in: Peter Disch, Architektur in der Deutschen Schweiz, 1980–1990, Lugano 1991). A sensitive perception of the noteworthy in the usual, combined with a healthy openness for the special is an important precondition for meaningful, moving architecture.

Contextual Attitude
An ever-recurring theme with architects in all parts of Switzerland is an intense awareness of context, in other words a marked concern with the question of context in the wider sense. Starting with the local topography, the structure of nearby buildings and the typical features in the immediate surroundings, solutions are sought which give the site to be developed an appropriate identity. In French-speaking Switzerland, for example, in the case of the Suter residence in Montblesson built by Ueli Brauen and Doris Waelchli, the various different uses

of the surrounding lots – field, woods, and an existing house – were a major factor in the final design. A clear reference to the environs, in particular the unique view of Lake Maggiore, is evident in the design by Michele Arnaboldi for the Quattrini apartments in Minusio. In German-speaking Switzerland, too, the same tendencies can be seen. On the Röntgen site in Zurich Jean-Pierre Dürig and Philippe Rämi's project reflects very precisely the attempt to incorporate the particular character of the nearby Röntgenstrasse. The location is a fundamental aspect in all architecture. And as every intervention represents destruction, especially in building, Luigi Snozzi postulates: "Destroy with care." On the question of context he believes: "Nothing has to be invented, everything has to be rediscovered". (Progetti e architetture 1957–1984, Milan 1984) It is therefore important to perceive what may be preserved, what redesigned and what destroyed.

Conceptual Aspects

Architecture which displays conceptual aspects is one which sees its design process as a meticulous search for a generic theme – a personally formulated concept – under which all else is subsumed. An outstanding example of this is the school building and multipurpose hall in Tschlin, by Valentin Bearth and Andrea Deplazes; here the theme of light and the unique atmospheric mood of the Lower Engadine is an unmistakable element in the design. Further examples of this method of working are: the sports centre in Yverdon-les-Bains by Ueli Brauen and Doris Waelchli, in which the particularly flat topography, the horizontality, have become the selected themes in the design; or the school and community centre in Mastrils by Dieter Jüngling and Andreas Hagmann, in which the striking topography had a decisive influence on the chosen design theme.

Compositional Treatment

A clear treatment of composition is evident in many designs incorporating at least two different building volumes. The architects often strengthen the individual identities of these buildings by concentrating on their different functions. The perception of the parts is determined by the whole – an example of this is the "Au" Ecumenical Meeting Centre in Wädenswil by Christian Gautschi and Marianne Unternährer; here, the building group is composed of differently sized volumes with different uses. A similar approach is taken in the project for the control tower of Sion airfield by Claudine Lorenz and Florian Musso; their building ensemble consists of two adjoining volumes distinguished by their different functions. They are, however, built in the same materials, similarity being a precondition for perceiving differences.

Experimental Investigation

A further, shared area of activity is a conscious investigation and testing of conventional materials, beyond purely technical and constructional or sensory and tactile concerns. A focus of this experimentation is not simply testing the actual limits of the material, but also seeking out what lays behind it. Thus, for example, the untreated copper cladding on the façade of the College of Technology in Chur, by Dieter Jüngling and Andreas Hagmann, creates an inaccessible, mysterious, even mystic atmosphere. A particularly good example of the experimental use of concrete is shown in the exposed concrete façade of the Chappuis residence in Corpataux by Pierre-André Simonet and Yvan Chappuis. Fibrated concrete panels were used in an unusual way for the Werner residence in Trin by Valentin Bearth and Andrea Deplazes; here the same material was used in the same way for both roof and façade cladding. This gives the building skin a distinct, veil-like appearance, temptingly concealing the structure behind.

Inner Images

In the search for appropriate architectural solutions, many architects fall back on experiences and events in their own lives, as well as personal preferences. These stored meanings take the form of inner images which, in certain specific circumstances, emerge to the surface as fragments of memory. Whether as clear images or sketchy outlines they represent a veritable treasure chest, or "objets trouvés", in the words of the Chur architects Valentin Bearth and Andrea Deplazes; or, as André Malraux aptly notes, these are our "musée imaginaire". An arsenal of pictures which, during the design process, can become a real force.

Simple Construction
A particular concern of many of the architectural offices in these times of economic recession is an emphasis on simple and, as a result, often lower cost constructions. Demand is high for solutions which are durable and appropriate, as well as ecological and energy-conscious. The Roethlisberger residence in Langnau by Nick Gartenmann, Mark Werren and Andreas Jöhri is exemplary in this respect: the combination of the chosen ground plan, a timber frame, dry construction techniques and the use of a large proportion of prefabricated elements (as a response to the high technical requirements during the construction phase) has resulted in an aesthetically pleasing, unique building.

Craft Precision
Simple, precise methods of construction demand and permit a higher level of perfection; details often display astoundingly high quality craftsmanship. Much attention is devoted to careful, solid construction, whatever the size of the project. An example is the various tram waiting halls for Basle Public Transport designed by Rolf Furrer and François Fasnacht.

Sensory Presence of Material
Ever more immediate use is made of the actual materials themselves. The sensory qualities inherent in them are revealed; the materials are displayed in their naked, unveiled form. In the words of Jacques Herzog and Pierre de Meuron, "The material is there to determine the structure, but the structure is no less there to show what it is made of." (El Croquis, Issue on Herzog and de Meuron 1983–1993, Madrid 1993) This aspect is particularly clear in the school building and multipurpose hall in Alvaschein by Valentin Bearth and Andrea Deplazes.

Colour Accents
It is noticeable that the younger architects pay more attention to colour than previous generations. From a historical point of view colour was a feature of, for example, the 1920s estates by Bruno Taut, who tried to use colour to relieve the monotony resulting from the juxtaposition of many buildings of the same type. Over the years this device has faded more into the background, and grey and white have come to dominate. In this new Swiss architecture there is no one particular colour preference, but rather a tendency to use colour accents which can make different statements. Some projects use colour to emphasise certain architectural intentions, such as the boathouse in Murten by Pierre-André Simonet and Yvan Chappuis; here the architects painted the wooden planking a red-brown colour, in line with the more traditional boathouses nearby. A different approach was taken in the school building and multi-purpose hall in Tschlin by Valentin Bearth and Andrea Deplazes; here the slightly cantilevered, "solid" concrete box was scumbled in red, to distinguish it from its surroundings, and in doing so it gives the impression of being a completely dematerialised volume.

Minimal Necessity
There seems to be a general tendency to give priority to architecture that is simple, clear, precise, honest, minimal but necessary. Above all else, in the opinion of the Basle-based architects, Meinrad Morger and Heinrich Degelo, is the sensible use of material and intellectual resources; the aim is to reduce architecture to its basic essence. They believe that a consideration of sensory aspects – of form, material and colour – is only possible after full reflection on the essentials. This is seen to good effect and very clearly in the local authority-owned housing in Basle designed by Manfred Morger and Heinrich Degelo, and in the Cavadini residence in Brissago by Raffaele Cavadini.

Effective Tradition
New Swiss architecture also stands clearly in the tradition of the classical modern movement, which encompassed such leading exponents as Le Corbusier, Mies van der Rohe and Walter Gropius. To this are added important influences from the contemporary architectural scene, from such people as Luigi Snozzi in Locarno, Peter Zumthor in Haldenstein (Canton of Grisons) and Herzog & de Meuron in Basle; in their offices many of the architects in this new generation were able to gather first experiences. Strong influences also come from encounters with contemporary art, in the works of Edward Hopper and Donald Judd, as representatives of minimal art, and from works which deal with the phenomenon of perception. The American video artist, Gary Hill, is one such artist who concentrates on the difference between seeing and perceiving: mere seeing is not understanding, perceiving, however, can be.

Valentin Bearth · Andrea Deplazes, Chur

Vielschichtige Reduktion

Die Architektur von Valentin Bearth und Andrea Deplazes basiert weder auf einem philosophischen Ansatz noch auf einem stilistischen Credo. Als entscheidenden Faktor für ihr Schaffen bezeichnen die beiden Bündner die täglich anfallenden Wirklichkeiten. Ihrer Meinung nach liegt gerade darin das Besondere. In ihren Arbeiten versuchen sie das Geheimnis der Selbstverständlichkeit zu ergründen, das Besondere im Alltäglichen auszuloten, um das Unfaßbare, Unsichtbare freizulegen. Aus der Unmöglichkeit, sich von vorneherein «richtig» entscheiden zu können, wählen sie zur Interpretation der gestellten Aufgabe ein Thema, das eine persönliche Wahl ist – eine Bandbreite, innerhalb derer Entscheidungen stattfinden können. Hinzu kommen individuelle Neigungen und Erfahrungen, nebelhafte Fetzen oder scharfe Fragmente, «des objets trouvés», wie sie selber betonen. So wird ein Thema auf der konzeptionellen Ebene bis zur Essenz destilliert, Überflüssiges weggelassen, dabei aber der Spielraum der Rezeption und Interpretation weit belassen. Diese architektonische Haltung bezeichnen sie als ein Paradoxon: eine vielschichtige Reduktion. Ihre Bauten zeigen eine Vorliebe für das Detail, für das beständige, gewöhnliche, einfache Material.

Multi-Layered Reduction

The architecture of Valentin Bearth and Andrea Deplazes is based neither on a philosophical approach nor on a stylistic credo. The two Grisons architects name day-to-day realities as the decisive factor affecting their work. In their view, it is precisely in the quotidian that we should look for the remarkable. In their works they try to penetrate the mystery of what is taken for granted, to sound the depths of the familiar, to bring to light the unfathomable, the invisible. Given the impossibility of taking any "correct" decision at the outset, they make a personal choice in interpreting the given task – they select a theme, a waveband within which their decisions can be taken. To this are added their individual inclinations and experiences, nebulous residues or clear fragments, "objets trouvés", as they themselves emphasise. In this way a subject is distilled down to its essence on the conceptual level, superfluous matter is eliminated while the scope for receptive interpretation is kept wide. This architectural attitude they call a paradox: a multi-layered reduction. Their buildings show a predilection for detail, for simple, ordinary, durable materials.

Biographie

Valentin Bearth

1957
Geboren in Tiefencastel.

1977–83
Architekturstudium an der ETH-Zürich.

1983
Diplom bei Professor Dolf Schnebli an der ETH-Zürich.

1984–88
Mitarbeit im Büro Peter Zumthor in Haldenstein, Graubünden.

1988–89
Lehrauftrag an der HTL (Abendtechnikum) in Chur.

1990–92
Vorsitzender des Schweizer Werkbundes, Sektion Graubünden.

Seit 1988
Gemeinsames Büro mit Andrea Deplazes in Chur.

Andrea Deplazes

1960
Geboren in Chur.

1982–88
Architekturstudium an der ETH-Zürich.

1988
Diplom bei Professor Fabio Reinhart an der ETH-Zürich.

Seit 1989
Dozent an der HTL (Abendtechnikum) in Chur.

Seit 1994
Mitglied der SIA-Wettbewerbskommission.

Seit 1988
Gemeinsames Büro mit Valentin Bearth in Chur.

Auszeichnungen

1992
Eidgenössisches Kunststipendium.

1992
Internationaler Architekturpreis für Neues Bauen in den Alpen (Schulhaus und Mehrzweckhalle in Alvaschein).

1994
Auszeichnung guter Bauten im Kanton Graubünden (Schulhaus und Mehrzweckhalle in Alvaschein, Schulhaus und Mehrzweckhalle in Tschlin).

Ausgewähltes Werkverzeichnis

1988

Wohnhaus Wegelin in Malans (Kanton Graubünden; 1988–89)
Mostgasse
Ausgeführtes Projekt.

Schulhaus und Mehrzweckhalle in Alvaschein (Kanton Graubünden; 1988–91)
Wettbewerb, erster Preis.
Ausgeführtes Projekt.

1989

Schulhaus und Mehrzweckhalle in Tschlin (Kanton Graubünden; 1989–93)
Wettbewerb, erster Preis.
Ausgeführtes Projekt.

Wohnhaus Iten in Chur
Braunsches Gut
Ausgeführtes Projekt.

Wohnsiedlung für Feriengäste in Laax (Kanton Graubünden)
Wettbewerb, zweiter Preis.
Überarbeitung, zweiter Preis.

Gestaltung Seeufer in Flüelen (Kanton Uri)
Wettbewerb, zweiter Preis.

Erweiterung Schulhaus in Malans (Kanton Graubünden; 1989–90)
Wettbewerb, dritter Preis.
Überarbeitung, zweiter Preis.

1990

Gemeindezentrum, PTT und GKB in Sent (Kanton Graubünden)
Wettbewerb, Ankauf.
Überarbeitung, erster Preis.

Höhere Technische Lehranstalt in Chur
Wettbewerb.

Gestaltung Areal «Oberer Quader» in Chur
Ideenwettbewerb, fünfter Preis.

Wohnhäuser der Kantonalen Pensionskasse in Schiers (Kanton Graubünden)
Wettbewerb, vierter Preis.

Industriehalle mit speziellem Klärverfahren bei der ARA in Chur
Ausgeführtes Projekt. Zusammenarbeit mit dem Kantonalen Hochbauamt und Amt für Umweltschutz.

Renovation und Restauration Marienkirche und Friedhof in Lenz (Kanton Graubünden; 1990–93)
Ausgeführtes Projekt. Zusammenarbeit mit der Kantonalen Denkmalpflege.

Wohnsiedlung «Im Sunniga» in Chur-Masans (1990–95)
Kirchgasse 68/70
Ausgeführtes Projekt.

1991

Schweizerische Holzfachschule in Biel
Wettbewerb, zweiter Preis.

Renovation Wohnhaus Meerhafen in Chur (1991–92)
Hegisplatz 4
Ausgeführtes Projekt. Zusammenarbeit mit der Kantonalen Denkmalpflege.

Wohnsiedlung «In den Lachen» in Chur (1991–unbestimmt)
Wettbewerb Variante 1, erster Preis.
Wettbewerb, Variante 2, erster Preis.
Quartierplan.

1992

Schul- und Gemeindezentrum in Duvin (Kanton Graubünden)
Wettbewerb.

Schul- und Gemeindezentrum in Molinis (Kanton Graubünden)
Wettbewerb.

Gestaltung Regierungsplatz in Chur
Wettbewerb. Zusammenarbeit mit Valerio Olgiati, Chur, und Maya Vonmoos, Zürich.

Gemeindezentrum mit PTT und Volg in Sufers (Kanton Graubünden)
Wettbewerb.

Schulhaus und Kindergarten in Malix (Kanton Graubünden; 1992–94)
Dorfstraße
Ausgeführtes Projekt.

Wohnhaus Werner in Trin (Kanton Graubünden; 1992–94)
Tignuppa
Ausgeführtes Projekt.

1993

Gewerbeschule in Bulle (Kanton Freiburg)
Wettbewerb, dritter Preis.

Schulhaus und Mehrzweckhalle in Fanas (Kanton Graubünden)
Wettbewerb, vierter Preis.

Gestaltung und Beratung Au-Brücke in Landquart (Kanton Graubünden; 1993–94)
Umfahrungsstraße ins Prättigau.
Ausgeführtes Projekt. Zusammenarbeit mit dem Kantonalen Tiefbauamt.

Wohnhaus Hirsbrunner in Scharans (Kanton Graubünden; 1993–94)
Palidetta
Ausgeführtes Projekt.

Schul- und Gemeindezentrum mit Kursaal in Flims (Kanton Graubünden; 1993–etwa 97)
Wettbewerb, erster Preis.

1994

Umbau und Erweiterung Atelier und Wohnung Balzer in Haldenstein (Kanton Graubünden)
Oberplätzli 9
Ausgeführtes Projekt.

Casino, Erweiterung Hotel Kulm und Badrutt's Palace sowie Parking Serletta in St. Moritz (Kanton Graubünden)
Wettbewerb, sechster Preis.

Schulhaus und Mehrzweckhalle in Vella (Kanton Graubünden)
Wettbewerb, erster Preis.

Schulhaus und Mehrzweckhalle in Thusis (Kanton Graubünden)
Wettbewerb, zweiter Preis.

Kur- und Golfzentrum in Alvaneu (Kanton Graubünden)
Wettbewerb, zweiter Preis.

Biography

Valentin Bearth

1957
Born in Tiefencastel

1977–83
Studied architecture at the ETH Zurich

1983
Graduated with diploma under Professor Dolf Schnebli at the ETH Zurich

1984–88
Worked at the Peter Zumthor architectural office in Haldenstein, Grisons

1988–89
Teaching appointment at the HTL (college of technology) in Chur

1990–92
Chairman of Swiss Werkbund, Grisons section

Since 1988
Joint architectural office with Andrea Deplazes in Chur

Andrea Deplazes

1960
Born in Chur

1982–88
Studied architecture at the ETH Zurich

1988
Graduated with diploma under Professor Fabio Reinhart at the ETH Zurich

Since 1989
Lecturer at HTL in Chur

Since 1994
Member of SIA Competitions Committee

Since 1988
Joint architectural office with Valentin Bearth in Chur

Awards

1992
Swiss state art scholarship

1992
International architectural prize for New Architecture in the Alps (school and multipurpose hall in Alvaschein).

1994
Award for good buildings in the Canton of Grisons (school and multipurpose hall in Alvaschein, school and multipurpose hall in Tschlin)

Selected list of work

1988
Wegelin residence in Malans
(Canton of Grisons; 1988–89)
Mostgasse
Completed project.

School and multipurpose hall
in Alvaschein (Canton of Grisons;
1988–91)
Competition, first prize.
Completed project.

1989
School and multipurpose hall in Tschlin
(Canton of Grisons; 1989–93)
Competition, first prize.
Completed project.

Iten residence in Chur
Braunsches Gut
Completed project.

Estate of holiday residences in Laax
(Canton of Grisons)
Competition, second prize.
Revision, second prize.

Lake shore planning in Flüelen
(Canton of Uri)
Competition, second prize.

School extension in Malans
(Canton of Grisons; 1989–90)
Competition, third prize.
Revision, second prize.

1990
PTT and GKB community centre in Sent
(Canton of Grisons)
Competition, purchased design.
Revision, first prize.

Höhere Technische Lehranstalt
(College of Technology) in Chur
Competition.

Development of "Oberer Quader"
site in Chur
Ideas competition, fifth prize.

Houses for the Cantonal Pension fund
in Schiers (Canton of Grisons)
Competition, fourth prize.

Industrial unit with special purification plant for the ARA in Chur
Completed project. In collaboration with the Cantonal Building Department and the Environmental Protection Department.

Renovation and restoration of the Marienkirche and cemetery in Lenz
(Canton of Grisons; 1990–93)
Completed project. Collaborated with the Cantonal Department for the Preservation of Monuments.

"Im Sunniga" residential estate
in Chur-Masans (1990–95)
Kirchgasse 68/70
Completed project.

1991
School for Wood Technology in Biel
(Canton of Berne)
Competition, second prize.

Renovation of Meerhafen residence
in Chur (1991–92)
Hegisplatz 4
Completed project. In collaboration with the Cantonal Department for the Preservation of Monuments.

"In den Lachen" residential estate in Chur (1991–)
Competition, Variant 1, first prize.
Competition, Variant 2, first prize.
District plan.

1992
School and community centre in Duvin
(Canton of Grisons)
Competition.

School and community centre in Molinis
(Canton of Grisons)
Competition.

Design for "Regierungsplatz"
(Government square) in Chur
Competition. In collaboration with
Valerio Olgiati, Chur,
and Maya Vonmoos, Zurich.

Community centre with PTT and Volg
in Sufers (Canton of Grisons)
Competition.

School and kindergarten in Malix
(Canton of Grisons; 1992–94)
Dorfstrasse
Completed project.

Werner residence in Trin
(Canton of Grisons; 1992–94)
Tignuppa
Completed project.

1993
Technical college in Bulle
(Canton of Fribourg)
Competition, third prize.

School and multipurpose hall in Fanas
(Canton of Grisons)
Competition, fourth prize.

Design and consultancy for Au bridge in Landquart (Canton of Grisons; 1993–94)
By-pass road to Prättigau.
Completed project. In collaboration with Cantonal Civil Engineering Inspectorate.

Hirsbrunner residence in Scharans
(Canton of Grisons; 1993–94)
Palidetta
Completed project.

School and community centre
with "Kursaal" in Flims
(Canton of Grisons; 1993–approx. 97)
Competition, first prize.

1994
Conversion and extension of Balzer studio and apartment in Haldenstein
(Canton of Grisons)
Oberplätzli 9
Completed project.

Casino, extension of Hotel Kulm, Badrutt's Palace and Parking Serletta
in St. Moritz (Canton of Grisons)
Competition, sixth prize.

School and multipurpose hall in Vella
(Canton of Grisons)
Competition, first prize.

School and multipurpose hall in Thusis
(Canton of Grisons)
Competition, second prize.

Health and golf centre in Alvaneu
(Canton of Grisons)
Competition, second prize.

Schulhaus und Mehrzweckhalle in Alvaschein 1988–1991

Aufgrund der knappen Platzverhältnisse im Dorfkern mußte der Neubau am Dorfrand, unterhalb eines steilen Abhanges, errichtet werden. Die Aufteilung in zwei Volumen – Schulhaus und Mehrzweckhalle – sollte deutlich in Erscheinung treten. Diese Rahmenbedingungen sind mit viel Gespür architektonisch thematisiert: Ein hoher, viergeschossiger Baukörper für die einzelnen Klassenzimmer ist von einer großen, gegen Süden und das Tal hin offenen Terrasse flankiert. Um diese ebene Fläche in der bewegten Topographie räumlich zu fassen, ist die eingeschossige Mehrzweckhalle in der gleichen Geometrie nach hinten versetzt. Ein transparenter Glaskubus, der eigentliche Eingang zum Schulhaus und zur Mehrzweckhalle, verbindet die beiden Trakte. Die ungleichen Volumen zeichnen sich aus durch unterschiedliche Materialien, Holz für die Mehrzweckhalle und Stein für das Schulhaus.

School and Multipurpose Hall in Alvaschein 1988–1991

Because of scarcity of space in the village centre, the new building had to be erected at the edge of the village, at the foot of a steep slope. The division into two blocks – the school and the multipurpose hall – was to be made clearly visible. These contextual conditions were very sensitively translated into architectural terms: a tall, four-storey building for the classrooms is flanked by a large terrace open on the side facing south towards the valley. To incorporate this flat area spatially into the variegated terrain, the single-storey multipurpose hall is placed symmetrically behind the school, and it shares the same geometry. A transparent glass cube, the entrance to the school and hall, links both wings of the structure. The unequal volumes are distinguished by the use of different materials, wood for the multipurpose hall and stone for the school.

Hintere Ansicht der gesamten Anlage bestehend aus Schulhaus und Mehrzweckhalle
View of whole complex from the rear showing school building and multipurpose hall

Innenraum der aus Holz gefertigten Mehrzweckhalle mit verschieden hohen Fenstern
Interior of wooden multipurpose hall with various height windows

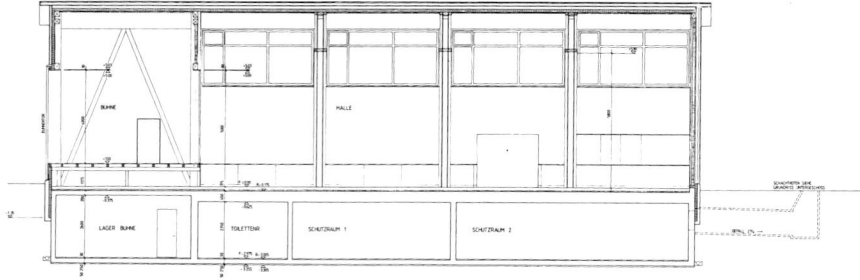

Längsschnitt durch die Mehrzweckhalle
Longitudinal section through the multipurpose hall

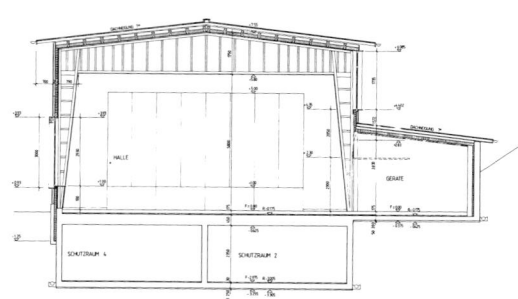

Querschnitt durch die Mehrzweckhalle und den rückseitigen Anbau
Cross section through the multipurpose hall and rear extension

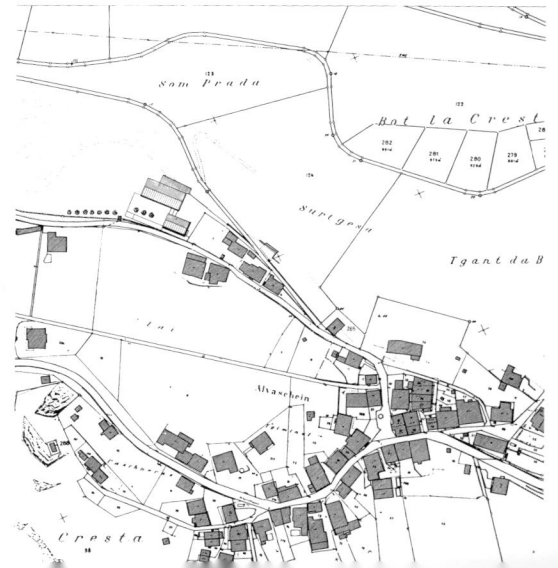

Situation / Situation

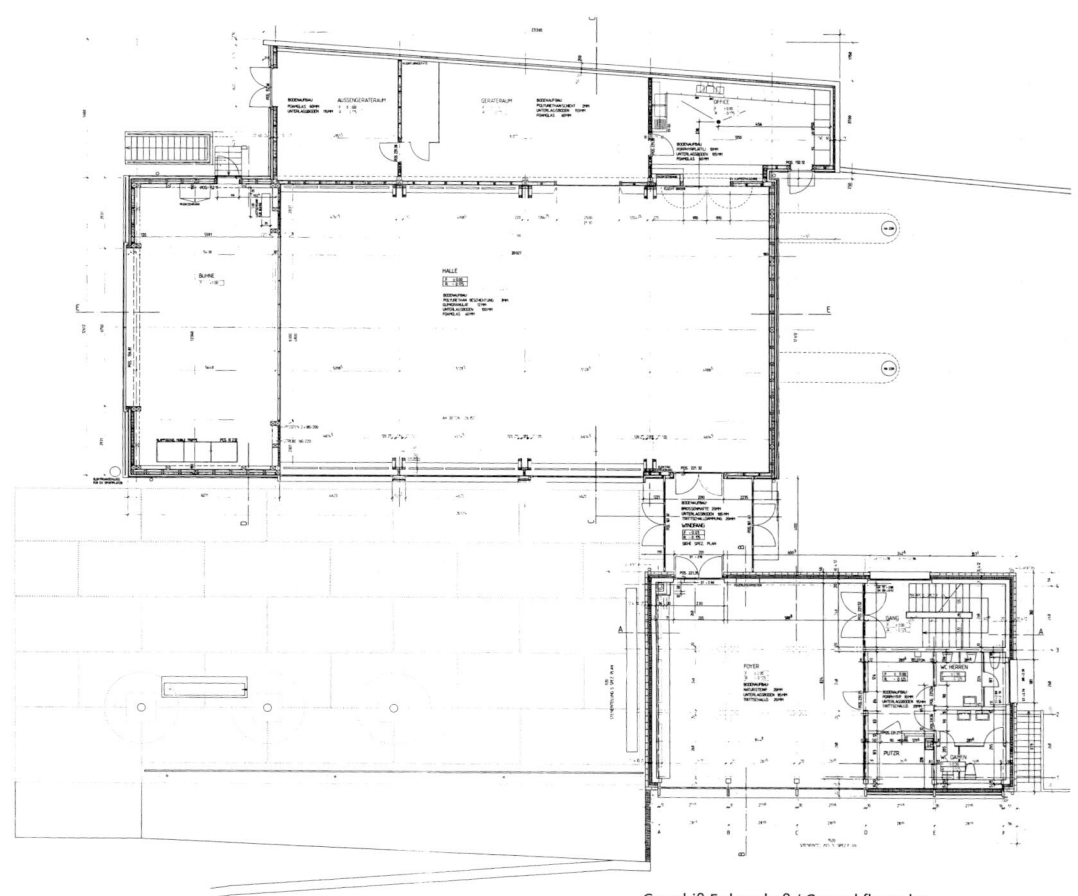

Grundriß Erdgeschoß / Ground floor plan

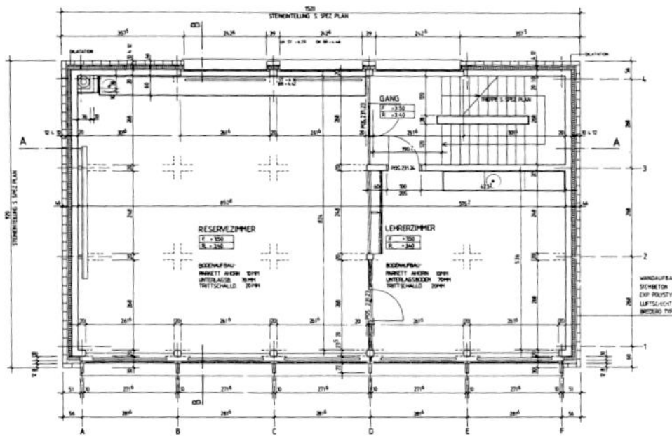

Grundriß erstes Obergeschoß / First floor plan

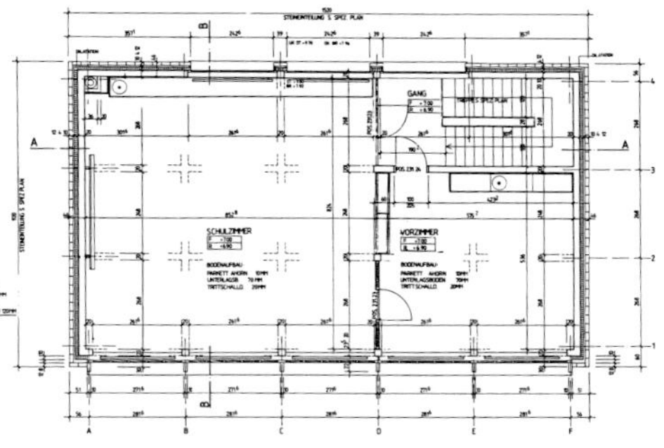

Grundriß zweites Obergeschoß / Second floor plan

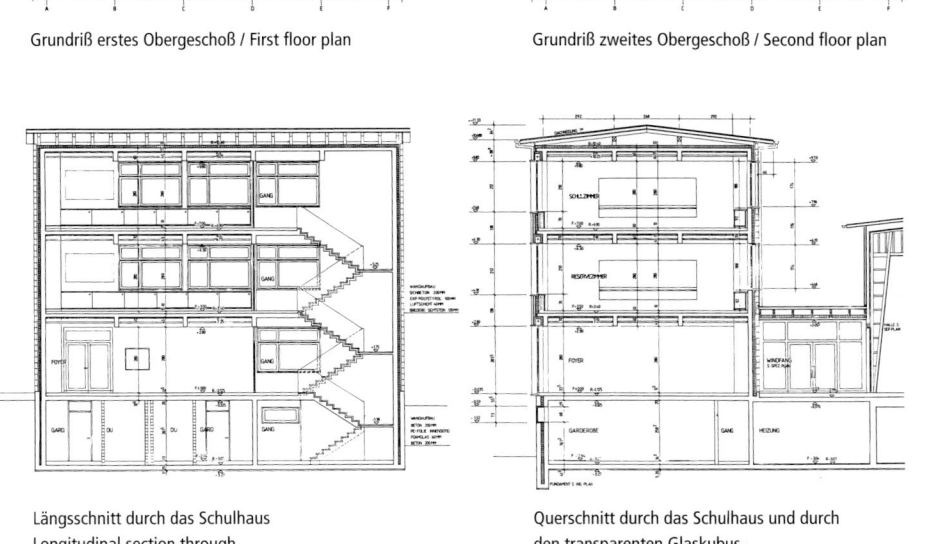

Längsschnitt durch das Schulhaus
Longitudinal section through
the school building

Querschnitt durch das Schulhaus und durch
den transparenten Glaskubus
Cross section through the school building
and transparent glass cube

Schulhaus und Mehrzweckhalle in Tschlin 1989–1993

Das Konzept des Entwurfs bestimmten weniger städtebauliche und architektonische Kriterien, als vielmehr das Thema des Lichtes, die einzigartige Stimmung im Unterengadin. Mitten in der dicht gewachsenen Dorfstruktur plazierten die Architekten das neue Volumen behutsam auf ein Plateau, senkrecht zur gegebenen Topographie, dicht neben die bestehende Schulanlage, damit die Aussicht über das weite Tal erhalten bleibt. Der leicht auskragende, massive, rotlasierte Betontrog scheint völlig entmaterialisiert, gleichsam schwebend. Der Baukörper ist geschlossen und nur von hochliegenden Bändern belichtet. Einzig die große Öffnung in der Stirnwand macht die Lage über dem Inntal auch im Innern erlebbar. Das blatt- oder hautartige Blechdach sucht eine Beziehung zum ländlichen Kontext.

School and Multipurpose Hall in Tschlin 1989–1993

The design concept was influenced less by architectural or planning criteria than by the theme of light, the unique atmosphere of the Lower Engadine. In the midst of the densely built-up village centre, the architects placed the new building cautiously on a plateau, perpendicularly to the prevailing topography, close beside the existing school site, so that the view over the broad valley was preserved. The slightly projecting, weighty, red-scumbled concrete box seems totally de-materialised, as if suspended in the air. The structure is closed, lightened only by high-placed window strips. Only the large opening in the façade allows the buildings's situation overlooking the Inn valley to be experienced from within. The shallow-angled saddleback roof is intended to relate the building to its rural context.

Ansicht des aus Beton gebauten Baukörpers, der zu schweben scheint
Elevation of the concrete building, which seems to be suspended in the air

Innenraum der aus Holz gefertigten Mehrzweckhalle mit ihren symmetrisch angeordneten Fenstern
Interior of the wooden multipurpose hall with symmetrically placed windows

Situation / Situation

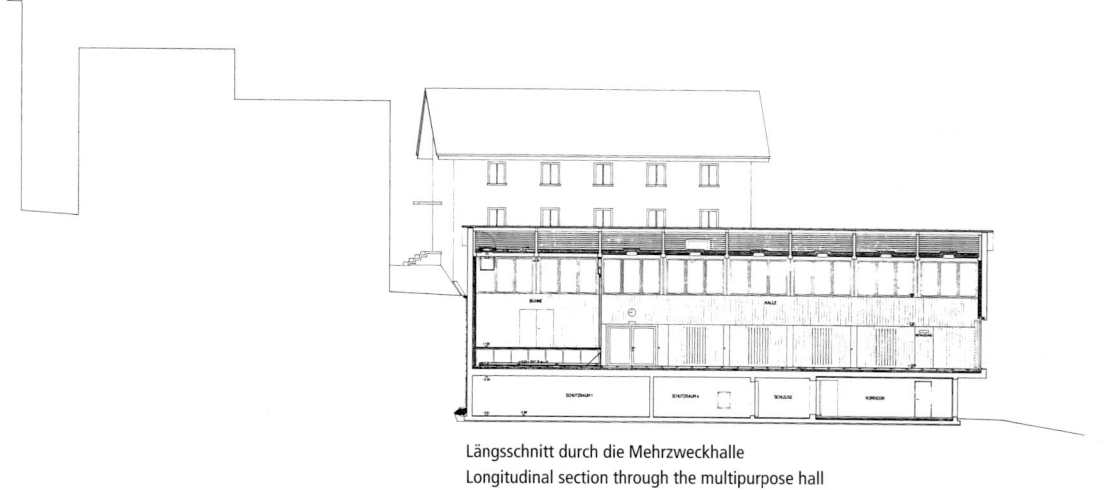

Längsschnitt durch die Mehrzweckhalle
Longitudinal section through the multipurpose hall

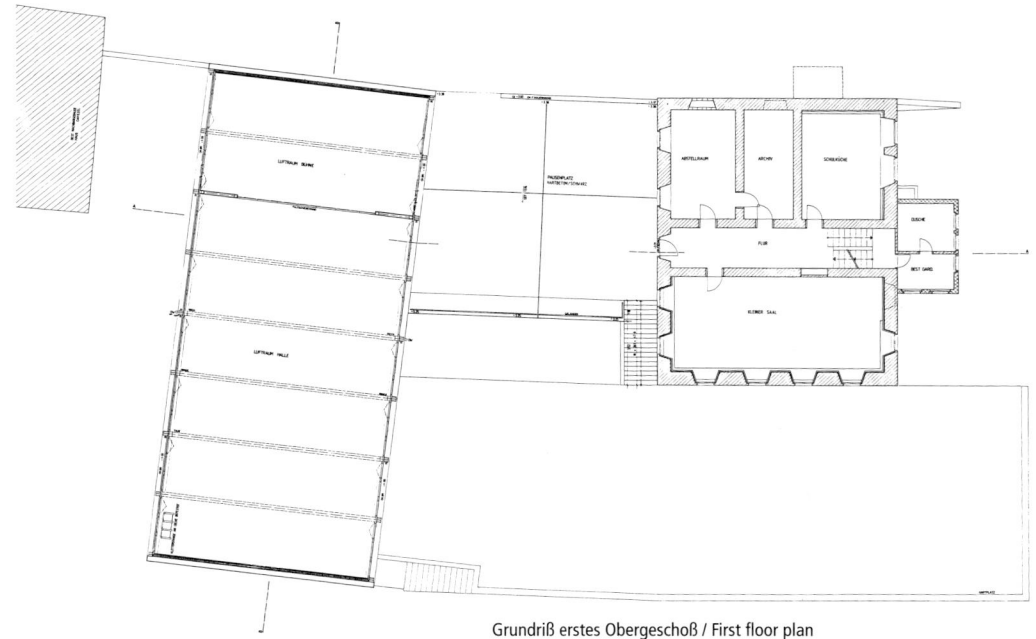

Grundriß erstes Obergeschoß / First floor plan

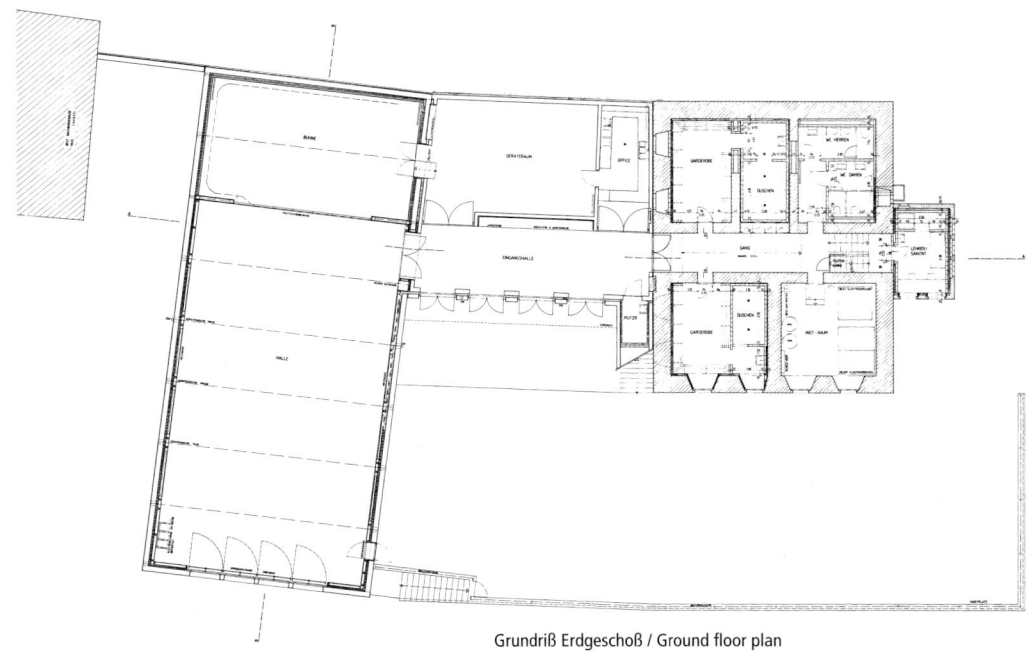

Grundriß Erdgeschoß / Ground floor plan

Wohnsiedlung «Im Sunniga» in Chur-Masans
The "Im Sunniga" Residential Estate in Chur-Masans
1990–1995

Die kleine Wohnsiedlung war ursprünglich Ausgangspunkt eines größeren Quartierplans. Die Bauten bilden eine locker zueinander in Beziehung stehende, wenngleich präzise Gruppe von drei Volumen, welche auf einem Schuttkegel wie Felsblöcke verstreut liegen. Als Zwischenräume entstehen ein Hof und einzelne Gebäudeterrassen. In den zwei identischen Baukörpern befinden sich je drei Duplex-Wohnungen, im unabhängigen Kubus zwei Geschoßwohnungen. Die Geschoßwohnungen sind durch einen offenen Laubengang erschlossen. Alle drei Baukörper sind aus Beton mit Aluminium- und Holzfenstern gebaut, was der gesamten Anlage ein einheitliches Erscheinungsbild gibt.

The small estate was originally the starting point for a larger district plan. The buildings form a loosely-related but precise group of three blocks scattered over a conical moraine slope like rocky outcrops. The spaces between them form a courtyard and terraces of the individual buildings. Each of the two identical buildings contains three maisonette apartments, while the cube has two apartments on separate storeys. Access to these apartments is by an outside walkway. All three buildings are built of concrete with aluminium and wooden window frames, giving the whole complex a unified appearance.

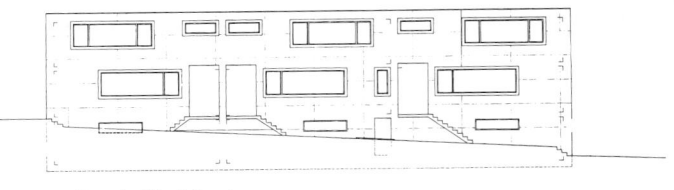

Nordfassade / North façade

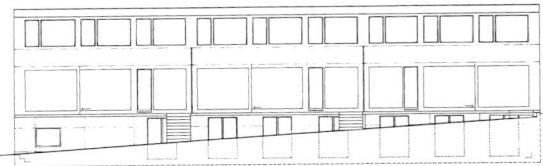

Südfassade / South façade

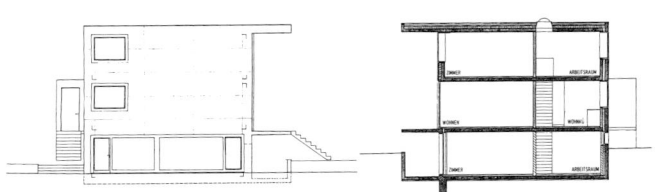

Westfassade / West façade

Querschnitt durch eine Duplex-Wohnung
Cross section through a maisonette apartment

Ansicht der beiden quer zum Hang gestellten Volumen mit je drei Wohnungen
Elevation of the two volumes at an angle to the slope; each volume contains three apartments

Collageartige Fensteranordnung der geschlosseneren Eingangsseite
Collage-like arrangement of windows along the semi-closed entrance side

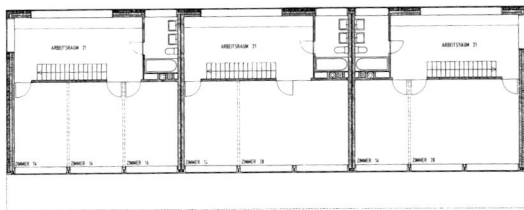

Grundriß erstes Obergeschoß / First floor plan

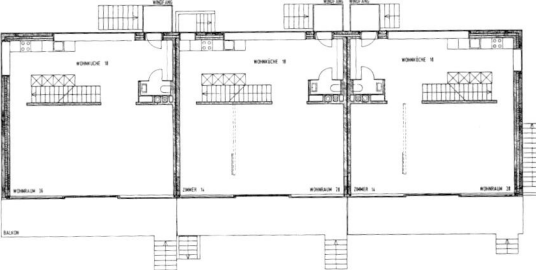

Grundriß Erdgeschoß / Ground floor plan

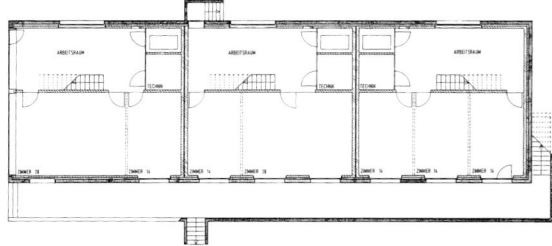

Grundriß Untergeschoß / Ground plan of basement level

Schweizerische Holzfachschule in Biel 1991

Der Neubau gliedert sich als Erweiterung einer bestehenden Anlage aus den 50er Jahren in einen dreigeschossigen, vollständig in Holz konstruierten Klassentrakt und in eine flache, ausgedehnte Werkhalle. Der Blick aus den inneren Pausenräumen in die weite Werkhalle stellt auf räumliche Weise die didaktische Verbindung zwischen Unterricht und Anwendung her. Die Klassentrakte sind unterzugsfrei nach dem Stützen-Platten-Prinzip aufgebaut, das heißt die quer vorgespannten Geschoßdecken aus Schichtholzplatten liegen nur auf einer Anzahl von Stützen auf. Da die Außenwände keine Tragfunktion haben, lassen sich großflächige, vorgehängte Fassadenverglasungen vornehmen. Der architektonische Ausdruck löst sich ab vom herkömmlichen Bild der Holzarchitektur.

School for Wood Technology in Biel 1991

The new building, an extension of an existing structure from the 1950s, is divided into a three-storey classroom wing constructed entirely of timber, and a long, wide, workshop building. The view from the recreation rooms into the large workshop area gives spatial expression to the pedagogical link between teaching and practice. The classroom zones are built without joists on the column-to-slab principle, i.e. the free spans of the laminated timber floor decks rest only on a number of columns. As the exterior walls have no structural function, large areas of curtain glazing are possible on the façades. The architectural idiom represents a departure form the traditional appearance of timber-frame buildings.

Modell des Wettbewerbes mit den angrenzenden Bauten aus den 50er Jahren
Competition model showing neighbouring 1950s buildings

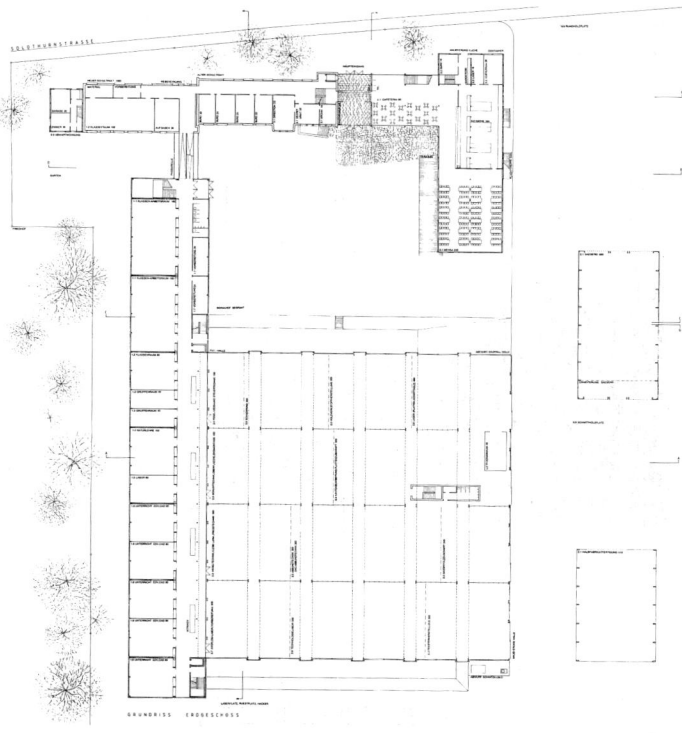

Grundriß Erdgeschoß / Ground floor plan

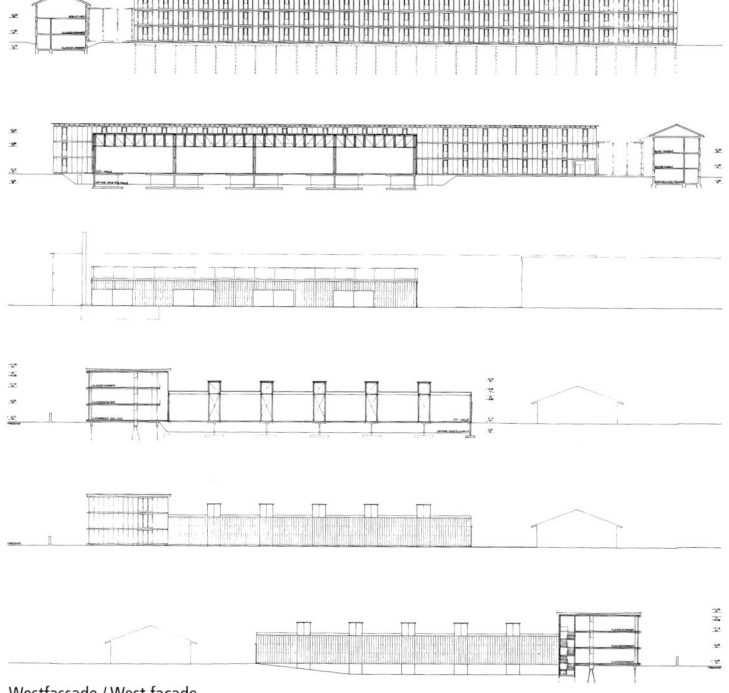

Westfassade / West façade

Längsschnitt durch die Werkhalle
Longitudinal section through the workshop building

Ostfassade der Werkhalle
East façade of the workshop building

Querschnitt durch den Klassentrakt und durch die Werkhalle
Cross section through the classroom buildings and workshop building

Südfassade / South façade

Nordfassade / North façade

Schulhaus und Kindergarten in Malix 1992–1994

Neben der bestehenden Mehrzweckhalle, die vor zehn Jahren von Peter Zumthor gebaut wurde, steht der neue dreigeschossige Bau. Als volumetrisch gleichwertiger Baukörper verbindet er sich mit dem bestehenden zur Gesamtschulanlage. Die Verschiebung zum Hang läßt einen offenen Platz entstehen. Das neue Volumen ist von drei Seiten vom Erdreich umschlossen. Die Lichtführung ist in doppeltem Sinne zum bestimmenden Thema der transparenten Schule gemacht: als Einblick vom inneren, zweigeschossigen Pausenraum in die Klassenzimmer und von außen in die Schule. Er erzeugt Tiefenschärfen, die den Raum in der Wahrnehmung bald auflösen, bald undurchdringbar erscheinen lassen.

School and Kindergarten in Malix 1992–1994

The new, three-storey building stands beside the existing multipurpose hall, built ten years ago by Peter Zumthor. As a structure of equivalent volume it combines with the existing part to form a single school complex. Its displacement towards the slope gives rise to an open space. The new block is thus surrounded by soil on three sides. The management of light in the interior is a key element in this transparent school, both in terms of the view from the inner, two-storey recreation room into the classrooms, and the view from outside into the school. This gives rise to focal depths that sometimes dissolve the perception of space and sometimes make it seem impenetrable.

Die vollständig aus Glas gebaute und damit transparente Fassade des Schulhauses von der Straße her gesehen
The completely glazed, transparent façade of the school building viewed from the street

Seitliche Ansicht mit der bestehenden Mehrzweckhalle im Hintergrund
Side elevation with existing multipurpose hall in the background

Innenansicht des zweigeschossigen Pausenraumes
Interior elevation of the two-storey recreation room

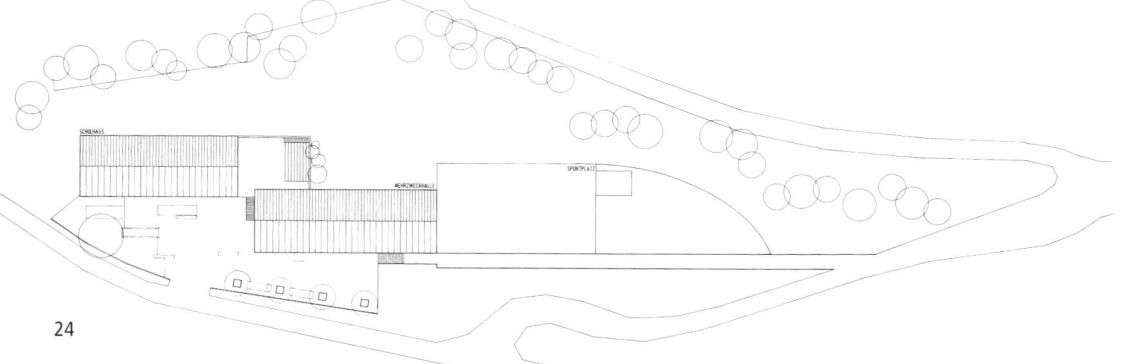

Situation des neuen Schulhauses mit der bestehenden Mehrzweckhalle, durch deren Verschiebung ein offener Platz entsteht
Situation of the new school building with existing multipurpose hall displaced to create an open area

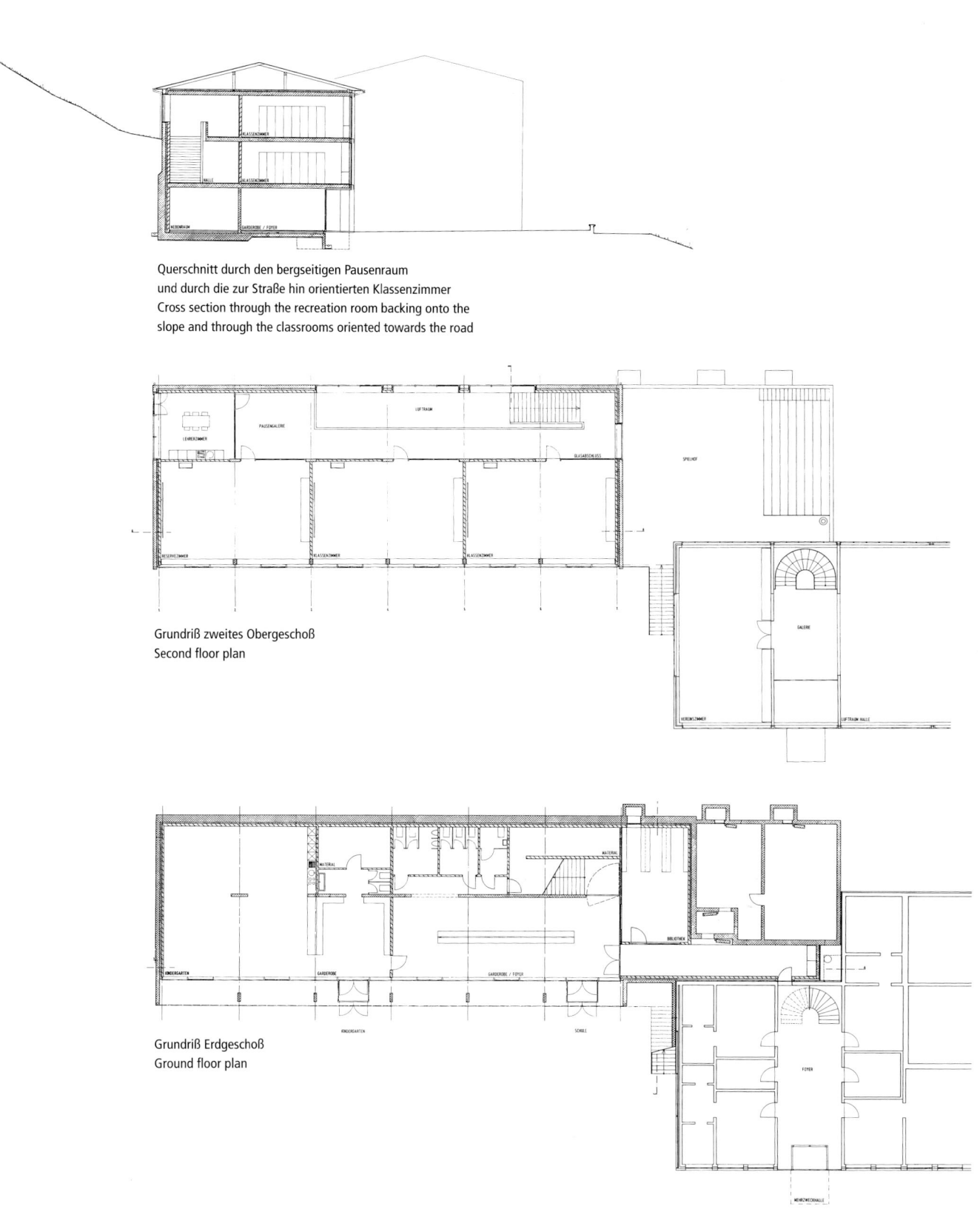

Querschnitt durch den bergseitigen Pausenraum
und durch die zur Straße hin orientierten Klassenzimmer
Cross section through the recreation room backing onto the
slope and through the classrooms oriented towards the road

Grundriß zweites Obergeschoß
Second floor plan

Grundriß Erdgeschoß
Ground floor plan

Wohnhaus Werner in Trin
1992–1994

Dieses kleine Wohnhaus, über dem Dorf Trin gelegen, ist als Refugium für das Alter gebaut. Der Baukörper aus glattgeschaltem, dünnwandigem Sichtbeton, mit einer äußeren Haut aus schwarzem Eternitschiefer gefertigt, erscheint von außen als undurchdringlicher Monolith. Von der inneren, höhlenartigen Eingangshalle aufsteigend, weitet sich das kleinkammrige Raumgefüge halbgeschossig fortschreitend und kulminiert im Wohnraum. Dieser Bereich ist von einem einfachen, auf drei Wandscheiben aufgelegten Betonfaltwerk überspannt. Als Raum der Kontemplation dient er einerseits dem stillen Genuß konkreter Kunst, andererseits werden gezielte Ausschnitte aus der Landschaft fragmentarisch wiederaufgenommen und durch entsprechende Lasuren auf den Wänden abgebildet.

Werner Residence in Trin
1992–1994

This small house, situated above the village of Trin, is built as a refuge for old age. The structure, built of smooth-skinned, thin-walled, fair-faced concrete with an outer skin of black asbestos cement slate, looks from outside like an impenetrable monolith. From the inner, cave-like entrance hall a sequence of small room rises in half-storey steps to culminate in the living room. This space is covered by a simple folded-concrete structure resting on three wall slabs. As a space for contemplation, it can be used on the one hand for the quiet enjoyment of concrete art, while on the other selected fragments from the landscape are reproduced in scumbled images on the walls.

Oberster Raum mit kontemplativem Charakter
Uppermost area, more contemplative in character

Ansicht der mit schwarzem Eternitschiefer verkleideten Fassade
Elevation of the façade clad with black Eternit slate

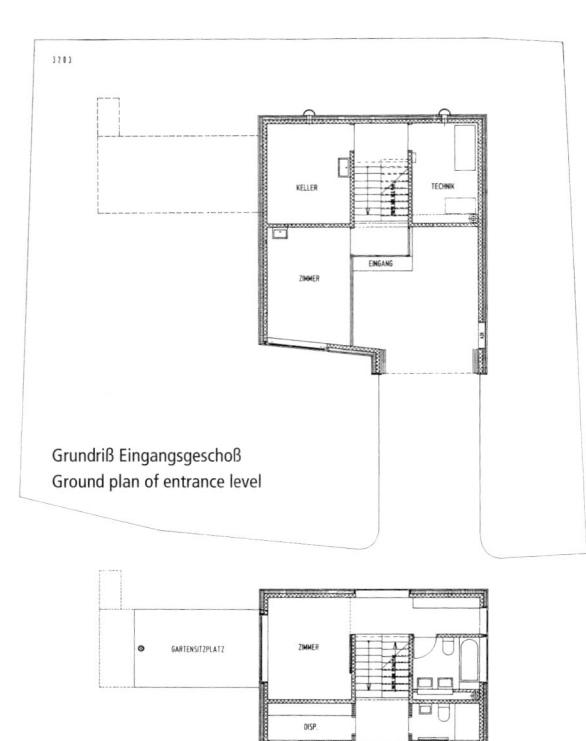

Grundriß Eingangsgeschoß
Ground plan of entrance level

Grundriß Zimmergeschoß
Ground plan of floor with rooms

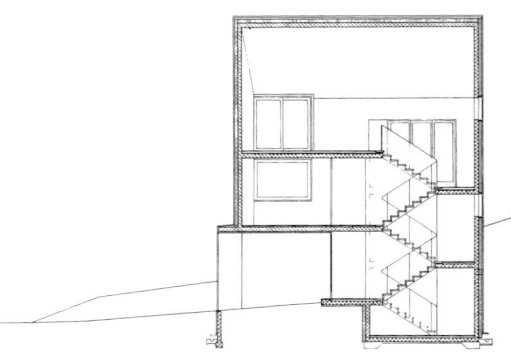

Längsschnitt durch die drei verschiedenen Geschosse
Longitudinal section through the three different floors

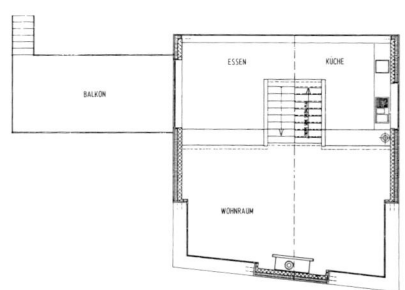

Grundriß Wohngeschoß
Ground plan of residential floor

Wohnhaus Hirsbrunner in Scharans 1993–1994

An schöner Aussichtslage inmitten der Siedlungserweiterung des Dorfes Scharans drückt sich der Neubau an das nahe Nachbarshaus, um so den einzigartigen Ausblick einzufangen. Das Wohnhaus ist ein Holzrahmenbau. Im Grundriß bilden drei längsgerichtete Tragwände zwei lange Räume, in denen raumteilend Naßzellen, Treppe und Küche als unabhängige Elemente plaziert sind. Jedes Geschoß ist als aufeinandergelegte Schicht konstruiert. Die Schnittstelle zwischen geschlossener und offener Holzrahmenwand sowie total verglaster Stirnwand im Süden und Norden, ohne entsprechende Queraussteifung, bezeichnet den Systemwechsel zur traditionellen Riegelwand.

Hirsbrunner Residence in Scharans 1993–1994

Located with a fine prospect within the residential estate extending from the village of Scharans, the new building huddles against the neighbouring house in order to have access to the unique view. The house is a timer-framed structure. In plan three longitudinal load-bearing walls form two long rooms, in which bathrooms, staircase and kitchen are placed as independent elements. The floors are constructed as superimposed layers. The interface between open and closed timber-framed walls and with the completely glazed south and north façades without cross bracing, marks the departure of this system from the traditional framed wall.

Ansicht des Holzrahmenbaus
Elevation of the wood-framed building

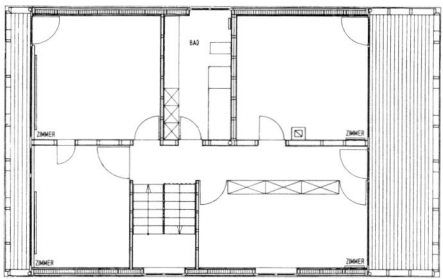

Grundriß Dachgeschoß / Ground plan of attic floor

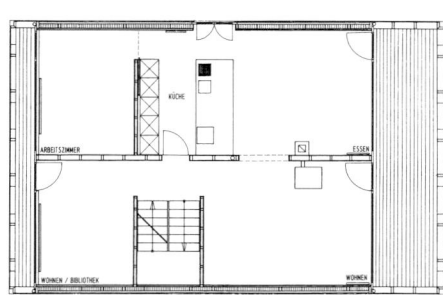

Grundriß Obergeschoß / Ground plan of upper floor

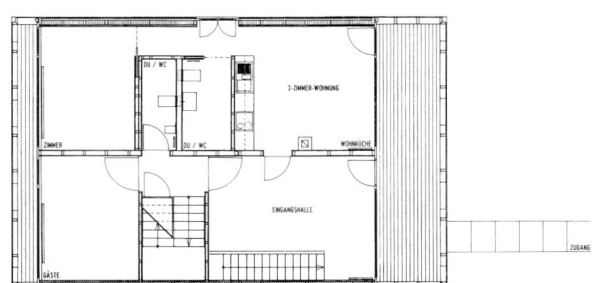

Grundriß Eingangsgeschoß / Ground plan of entrance level

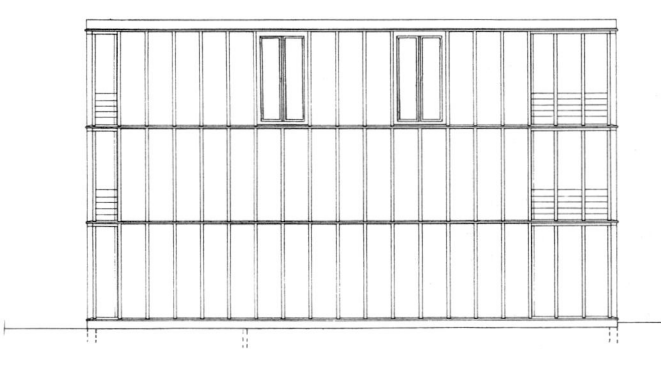

Westfassade / West façade

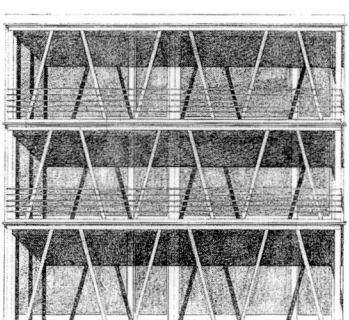

Nord- und Südfassade / North and south façade

Ueli Brauen · Doris Waelchli, Lausanne

Thematisierte Kontextualität

Mit großer Sensibilität haben Ueli Brauen und Doris Waelchli bisher Wettbewerbsprojekte, verschiedene Umbauten und einen Neubau entworfen. Ihre Arbeiten sind charakterisiert durch die intensive Auseinandersetzung mit dem Ort und dem Kontext im erweiterten Sinn. Der Entwurfsprozeß der beiden wickelt sich stets in der gleichen Reihenfolge ab, unabhängig davon, ob es sich um groß- oder kleinräumige Konzeptionen handelt: Analysieren und Entwerfen finden parallel und kontinuierlich statt, wobei an einem bestimmten Punkt ein Konzept als Synthese sämtlicher Gegebenheiten zur Leitidee des Projektes wird. Beim Wettbewerb für ein Sportzentrum in Yverdon-les-Bains war es beispielsweise die besonders flache Topographie – die Horizontalität –, die das Thema des Entwurfes bestimmte. Ihr Schaffen kann mit einem Zitat Luigi Snozzis charakterisiert werden: «Es gibt nichts zu erfinden, alles ist wieder zu finden.» Einen weiteren Schwerpunkt legen sie auf die Wahl der Materialien und deren Anwendung. Die formale architektonische Haltung der beiden Architekten basiert auf Einfachheit und Ehrlichkeit sowie auf Zweckmäßigkeit und Zurückhaltung.

Context as Design Theme

Ueli Brauen and Doris Waelchli have, to date, designed competition projects, various conversions and one new building, with great sensitivity. Their works are characterised by their in-depth study of place and context in the widest sense. Their design process always follows the same sequence, regardless of whether they are dealing with a large or small scale project: analysis and design are carried forward continuously in parallel; then, at a certain point, a concept emerges as the guiding idea of the project, synthesising all the relevant factors. For example, in the competition for a sports centre in Yverdon-les-Bains it was the especially flat topography – the horizontality – that determined the theme of the design. Their work can be characterised by a quotation from Luigi Snozzi: "Nothing has to be invented, everything has to be rediscovered." Another main concern of theirs is the choice and use of materials. The two architects' formal approach is based on simplicity and integrity, as well as on functionality and restraint.

Biographie

Ueli Brauen

1954
Geboren in Aarberg.

1970–73
Lehre als Tiefbauzeichner.

1973–76
Ingenieurstudium an der HTL in Burgdorf.

1976–78
Zahlreiche Studienreisen: Griechenland, Ägypten, Lybien, Tunesien, Algerien, Marokko, Italien.

1979–82
Mitarbeiter des Landwirtschaftsministeriums in Oman.

1982–88
Architekturstudium an der ETH-Lausanne.

1985–86
Mitarbeit im Büro Mario Botta in Lugano.

1988
Diplom bei Professor Mario Botta an der ETH-Lausanne.

1988–90
Eigenes Büro in Lausanne.

1988–90
Assistent bei Professor Alain Tschumi an der ETH-Lausanne.

Seit 1990
Dozent an der HTL in Freiburg.

Seit 1990
Gemeinsames Büro mit Doris Waelchli in Lausanne.

Doris Waelchli

1963
Geboren in Huttwil.

1982–88
Architekturstudium an der ETH-Lausanne.

1985–86
Praktikum im Büro Clémençon, Herren und Roost in Bern und Herzog & de Meuron in Basel.

1988
Diplom bei Professor Luigi Snozzi an der ETH-Lausanne.

1988–89
Mitarbeit im Büro José Luis Mateo in Barcelona.

1989
Aufenhalt an der Cité Internationale des Arts in Paris (Stipendium des Kantons Bern).

1989–90
Mitarbeit im Büro Marques & Zurkirchen in Luzern.

1990–91
Assistentin bei Gastprofessorin Inès Lamunière an der ETH-Lausanne.

1991–93
Assistentin bei Professorin Inès Lamunière an der ETH-Zürich.

1993–95
Assistentin bei Gastprofessor José Luis Mateo an der ETH-Zürich.

Seit 1990
Gemeinsames Büro mit Ueli Brauen in Lausanne.

Auszeichnungen

1992
Distinction Vaudoise d'Architecture.

1993
Eidgenössisches Kunststipendium.

1994
Eidgenössisches Kunststipendium.

Ausgewähltes Werkverzeichnis

1989
Erweiterung Hotel Angleterre in Lausanne-Ouchy
Wettbewerb, erster Preis.

Studentenheim, Turnhalle und Sportanlagen in Lausanne
Wettbewerb, Ankauf.

Ausstellungsbeitrag: «Paris – Architecture et Utopie», Paris
Projekt für das Quartier Tolbiac.

1990
Kirchgemeindezentrum Vuillermet in Lausanne
Wettbewerb, erster Preis.

Gestaltung Autobahntrassee der N9 am Gerundensee in Siders (Kanton Wallis)
Ideenwettbewerb, erster Preis.

Sportzentrum St. Leonhard in Freiburg
Ideenwettbewerb, Ankauf.

Wohnhaus Suter in Montblesson (Kanton Waadt; 1990–92)
Route du Jorat 42c
Ausgeführtes Projekt.

1991
Wohnhaus für Zöllner in Villeneuve (Kanton Waadt)
Studienauftrag.

Katholisches Begegnungszentrum in Morges (Kanton Waadt)
Studienauftrag.

Sportzentrum «Aux Iles» in Yverdon-les-Bains (Kanton Waadt)
Wettbewerb, erster Preis.

1992
Erweiterung Firmensitz der Uhrenfabrik Corum in La Chaux-de-Fonds
Wettbewerb, dritter Preis.

Firmensitz der Schweizerischen Bankgesellschaft in Delémont
Wettbewerb, fünfter Preis.

Regionaler Sitz der Waadtländer Kantonalbank in Lutry (Kanton Waadt)
Studienauftrag.

Umbau Wohnhaus Krompholz in St–Sulpice (Kanton Waadt; 1992–93)
Chemin des Chantres 42
Ausgeführtes Projekt.

1993
Umbau Wohnhaus Perrin in Epalinges (Kanton Waadt)
Chemin des Planches 12
Ausgeführtes Projekt.

Wohnüberbauung für die Lonza in Visp (Kanton Wallis)
Wettbewerb, vierter Preis.

Katholische Kirche mit Kirchgemeindehaus in Lausanne-Bellevaux
Studienauftrag.

1994
Umbau Ferienwohnung Fayet in Noville (Kanton Waadt)
Les Grangettes
Ausgeführtes Projekt.

Garderobengebäude und Außensportanlagen in Yverdon (Kanton Waadt)
Vorprojekt.

Fußgängerbrücke in Ecublens (Kanton Waadt)
Vorprojekt.

Kaufhaus Türmli in Altdorf
Wettbewerb, dritter Preis.

Erweiterung Berufsschule in Yverdon-les-Bains (Kanton Waadt)
Wettbewerb, erster Preis.

Biography

Ueli Brauen

1954
Born in Aarberg

1970–73
Trained as civil engineering draughtsman

1973–76
Studied engineering at the HTL
(College of Technology) in Burgdorf

1976–78
Numerous study trips: Greece, Egypt,
Libya, Tunisia, Algeria, Morocco, Italy

1979–82
Worked at Ministry of Agriculture
in Oman

1982–88
Studied architecture at the ETH Lausanne

1985–86
Worked at the Mario Botta architectural
office in Lugano

1988
Graduated with diploma under
Prof. Mario Botta at the ETH Lausanne

1988–90
Own architectural office in Lausanne

1988–90
Assistant to Prof. Alain Tschumi
at the ETH Lausanne

Since 1990
Lecturer at the HTL in Fribourg

Since 1990
Joint architectural office
with Doris Waelchli in Lausanne

Doris Waelchli

1963
Born in Huttwil

1982–88
Studied architecture at the ETH Lausanne

1985–86
Practical training at the Clémençon,
Herren and Roost architectural office
in Berne and Herzog & de Meuron
in Basle.

1988
Graduated with diploma under
Prof. Luigi Snozzi at the ETH Lausanne

1988–89
Worked at the José Luis Mateo
architectural office in Barcelona

1989
Stayed at the Cité Internationale des Arts
in Paris
(scholarship from Canton of Berne)

1989–90
Worked at Marques & Zurkirchen
architectural office in Lucerne

1990–91
Assistant to Visiting Professor
Inès Lamunière at the ETH Lausanne

1991–93
Assistant to Professor Inès
Lamunière at the ETH Zurich

1993–95
Assistant to Professor José Luis Mateo
at the ETH Zurich

Since 1990
Joint architectural office with Ueli Brauen
in Lausanne.

Awards
1992
Distinction Vaudoise d'Architecture

1993
Swiss state art scholarship

1994
Swiss state art scholarship

Selected list of Work

1989
Extension to Hotel Angleterre
in Lausanne-Ouchy
Competition, first prize.

Student hostel, gymnasium and sports
facilities in Lausanne
Competition, purchased design.

Exhibition entry: "Paris – Architecture
et Utopie", Paris
Project for the Tolbiac quarter.

1990
Parish centre at Vuillermet in Lausanne
Competition, first prize.

Design for N9 motorway development
on the Gerundensee in Siders
(Canton of Valais)
Ideas competition, first prize.

Sports centre at St. Leonhard in Fribourg
Ideas competition, purchased design.

Suter residence in Montblesson
(Canton of Vaud; 1990–92)
Route du Jorat 42c
Completed project.

1991
Residence for customs staff in Villeneuve
(Canton of Vaud)
Study commission.

Catholic meeting house in Morges
(Canton of Vaud)
Study commission.

Sports centre "Aux Iles" in Yverdon-les-
Bains (Canton of Vaud)
Competition, first prize.

1992
Extension of head office of
Usine Horlogère Corum
in La Chaux-de-Fonds
Competition, third prize.

Head office of Schweizerische
Bankgesellschaft in Delémont
Competition, fifth prize.

Regional headquarters of Waadtländer
Kantonalbank in Lutry (Canton of Vaud)
Study commission.

Conversion of Krompholz residence
in St-Sulpice (Canton of Vaud; 1992–93)
Chemin des Chantres 42
Completed project.

1993
Conversion of Perrin residence
in Epalinges (Canton of Vaud)
Chemin des Planches 12
Completed project.

Residential development for Lonza
in Visp (Canton of Valais)
Competition, fourth prize.

Catholic church with parish hall
in Lausanne-Bellevaux
Study commission.

1994
Conversion of Fayet holiday residence
in Noville (Canton of Vaud)
Les Grangettes
Completed project.

Changing rooms building and outdoor
sports facilities in Yverdon
(Canton of Vaud)
Preliminary project.

Pedestrian bridge in Ecublens
(Canton of Vaud)
Preliminary project.

Türmli department store in Altdorf
(Canton of Uri)
Competition, third prize.

Extension of the training school
in Yverdon-les-Bains (Canton of Vaud)
Competition, first prize.

Wohnhaus Suter in Montblesson
1990–1992

Die Parzelle, ein sanfter Südhang, liegt am Ende des Dorfes und ist auf drei Seiten von Feldern und Wald umgeben. Auf dem kleinen Grundstück galt es ein Volumen zu projektieren, das das bestehende angrenzende Ferienhaus, ein kleines Chalet, nicht beeinträchtigt. Die gesetzlich geforderten minimalen Grenzabstände bestimmten die Dimensionen des neuen Gebäudes. Im Innern sind die Nebenräume und die Verkehrszone gegen Nordosten auf ein Minimum beschränkt, so daß sich großzügige Räume auf die unberührte Landschaft hin öffnen. Auf raffinierte Weise können die Schiebeläden als vorgelagerte, aus Holz gefertigte Sonnenschutzelemente geöffnet und geschlossen werden. Sie lassen Innen- und Außenraum ineinander übergehen.

Suter Residence in Montblesson
1990–1992

The building plot, a gentle south slope, lies at the end of the village and is surrounded on three sides by fields and woodland. The task was to design for the small site a structure that would not be detrimental to the existing nearby holiday home, a small chalet. The minimum legal clearances from the boundary determined the dimensions of the new building. Inside, the north-east facing ancillary areas and corridors are reduced to a minimum, so that spacious rooms open on to untouched landscape. Sophisticated means are provided for opening and closing the sliding blinds and the projecting wooden sun screens. They allow interior and exterior space to interpenetrate.

Ansicht des Wohnhauses mit völlig geschlossenen Schiebeläden
Elevation of the house with sliding blinds fully closed

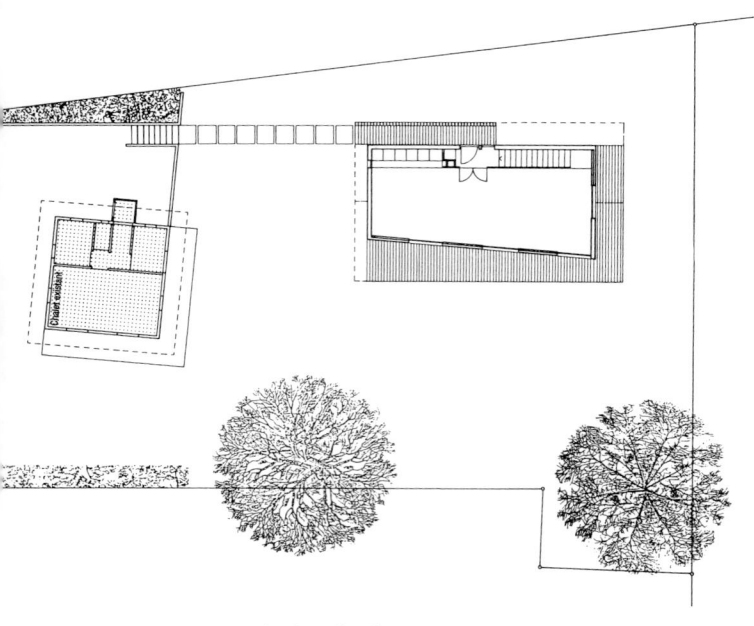

Situation / Situation

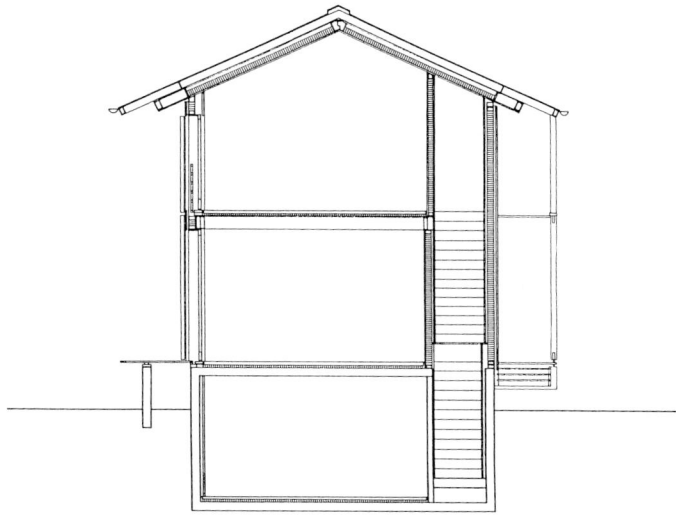

Querschnitt durch das Wohnhaus und die seitliche Erschließung
Cross section through the residence and side areas

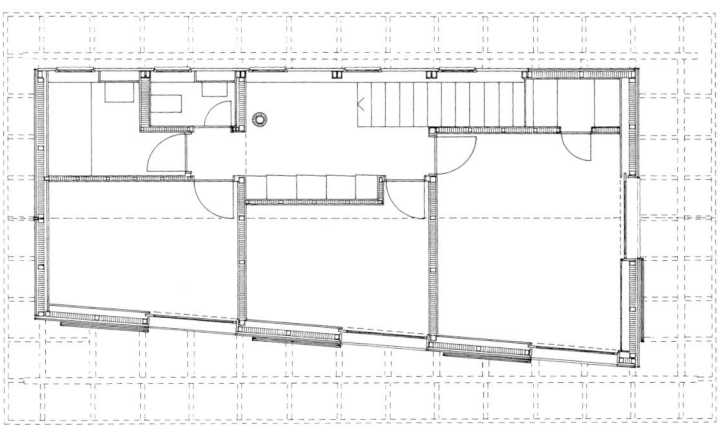

Grundriß Obergeschoß / Ground plan of upper floor

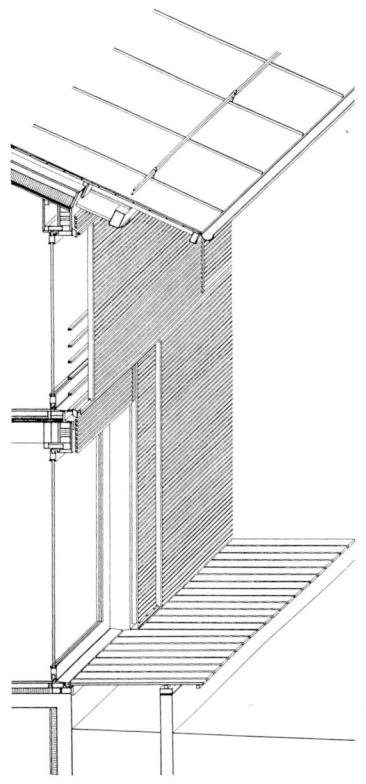

Fassadenkonstruktion mit den Schiebeläden aus Holz
Façade construction with sliding wooden blinds

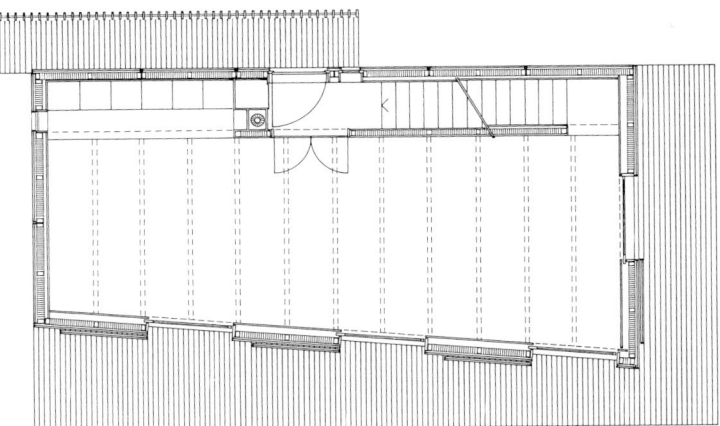

Grundriß Erdgeschoß / Ground floor plan

Kirchgemeindezentrum Vuillermet in Lausanne 1990

Die Schwierigkeit dieser Aufgabe war der Umgang mit der historischen Bausubstanz – besonders der Kathedrale und ihrem ehemaligen Kreuzgang – in unmittelbarer Nähe. Der Entwurf von Ueli Brauen setzt sich durch seinen zeitgenössischen Ausdruck deutlich von der Umgebung ab, interpretiert jedoch die ursprüngliche Klosteranlage neu: Auf den alten Fundamenten des Kreuzganges baut er sein einziges Volumen auf, das durch einen innenliegenden, begrünten privaten Hof charakterisiert ist. Die Anlage fällt durch die kompakte und gutorganisierte Anordnung der Funktionen auf.

Parish Centre Vuillermet in Lausanne 1990

The difficulty of this commission lay in dealing with the historic fabric – especially the cathedral and its former cloister in the immediate vicinity. Ueli Brauen's design introduces a distinct contemporary note into its surroundings, yet at the same time constitutes a re-interpretation of the original monastery site. On the old foundations of the cloister he erected his single structure, characterised by a grassed private inner courtyard. The complex is striking for its compact and well-organized arrangement of functions.

Modell der Wettbewerbseingabe innerhalb der historischen Bausubstanz
Model of competition entry: inside the historic building substance

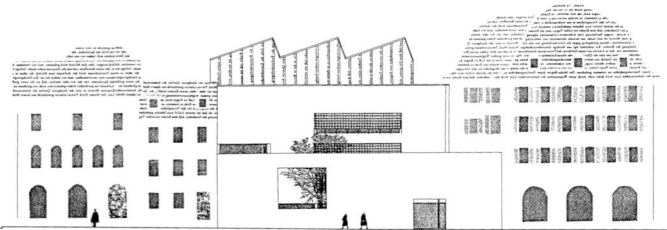

Südfassade von der Straße aus gesehen / South façade viewed from the street

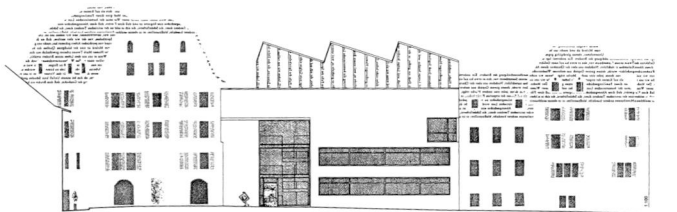

Nordfassade / North façade

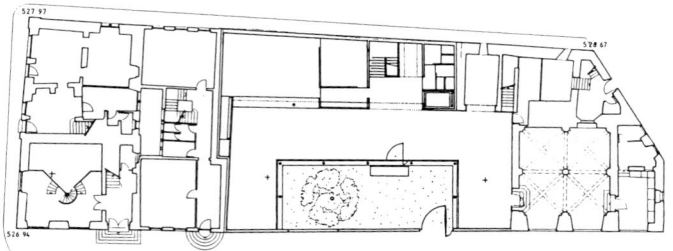

Grundriß Erdgeschoß / Ground floor plan

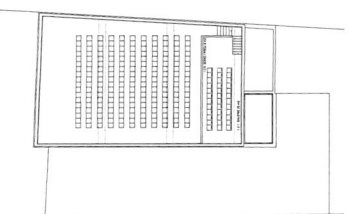

Grundriß fünftes Obergeschoß / Fifth floor plan

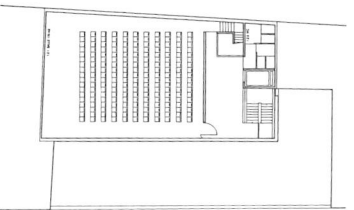

Grundriß viertes Obergeschoß / Fourth floor plan

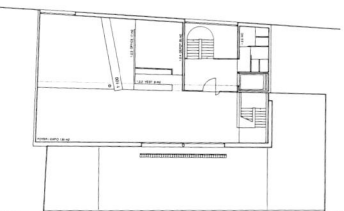

Grundriß drittes Obergeschoß / Third floor plan

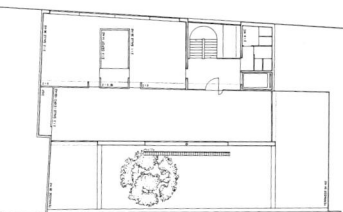

Grundriß zweites Obergeschoß / Second floor plan

Sportzentrum «Aux Iles» in Yverdon-les-Bains 1991

Die Topographie, eine meliorierte, ehemalige Moorebene, war bestimmend für das Konzept des Entwurfs. Diese Qualität des Ortes – die Horizontalität – sollte mit Respekt erhalten werden und im Gebäude sogar verstärkt zum Ausdruck kommen. Deshalb ist das Volumen möglichst niedrig und transparent gehalten. Horizontale Lamellen verstärken die Entwurfsidee. Die gestalteten Außenräume stehen kohärent und auf besonders ökonomische Art und Weise mit den innenliegenden in Beziehung. Die vorgeschlagene Konstruktion unterstreicht den einfachen und zweckmässigen Charakter.

"Aux Iles" Sports Centre at Yverdon-les-Bains 1991

The topography, ameliorated former moorland, determined the design concept. The quality of the place – its horizontality – was to be respected and even given heightened expression in the building. The structure was therefore kept as low and transparent as possible. Horizontal louvres reinforce the design idea. The design of the outer spaces is related in a coherent and especially economical way with the interior. The proposed construction type emphasises the simple and functional character of the building.

Modell der Wettbewerbseingabe mit der nahen Umgebung
Model of competition entry with surrounding area

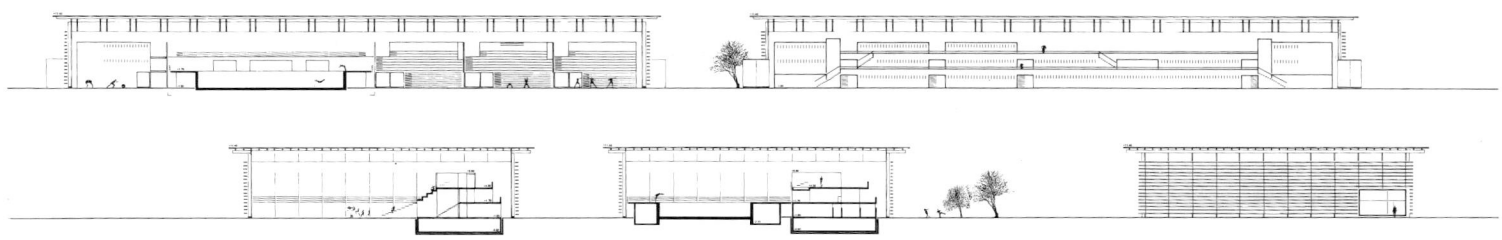

Längsschnitt durch die Turnhallen und durch die Erschließung.
Querschnitt durch die Tribüne und durch die Schwimmhalle. Nordfassade
Longitudinal section through the gymnasiums and transition areas.
Cross section through the stage and the swimming pool building. North façade

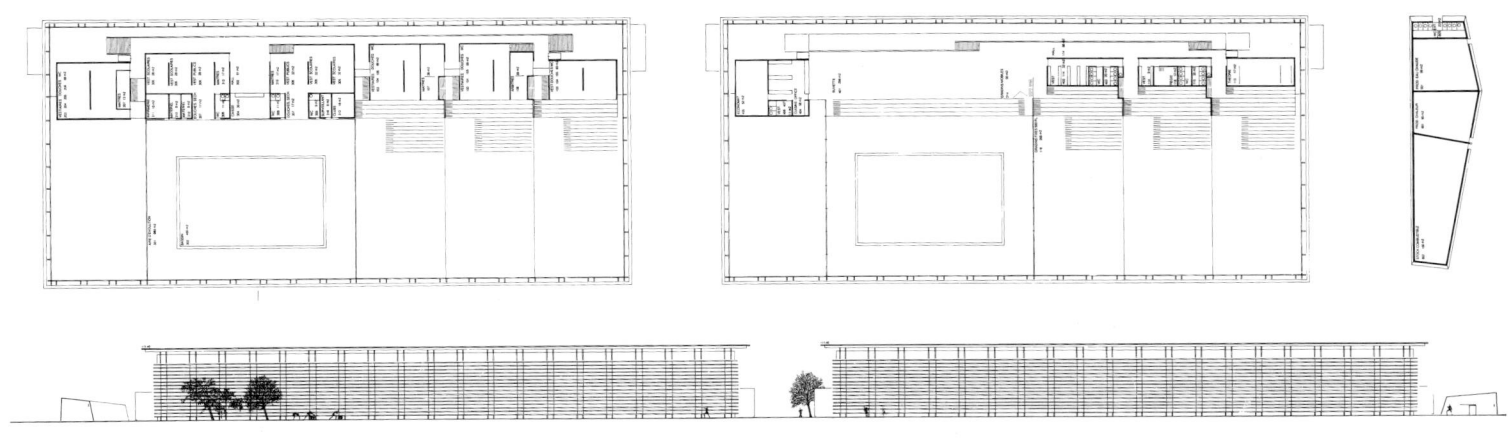

Grundriß erstes Obergeschoß und zweites Obergeschoß. Ostfassade. Westfassade. Südfassade
Ground plan of first floor and second floor. East façade. West façade. South façade

Umbau Wohnhaus Krompholz in St-Sulpice 1992–1993

Das Wohnhaus, anfangs dieses Jahrhunderts erbaut, befand sich ursprünglich inmitten der Stadt Lausanne. Nach rund dreißig Jahren mußte es der städtischen Bebauung weichen, so daß es Stück für Stück demontiert und, wegen der neuen Erschließungssituation, mit gewissen Änderungen in St-Sulpice wiederaufgebaut wurde. Der Eingriff der Architekten besteht einerseits darin, die Ankommenden an neuen Stütz- und Begrenzungsmauern entlang zum ursprünglichen Eingang zu führen und andererseits, das Innere des Hauses entsprechend den Ansprüchen des Bauherrn umzubauen. So wurde das Dachgeschoß geöffnet, um das vom See an der Decke reflektierte Licht in die zentrale Halle zu führen.

Conversion of Krompholz Residence in St-Sulpice 1992–1993

The house, built at the beginning of this century, originally stood in the centre of Lausanne. After about thirty years it had to give way to city development plans, and was dismantled piece by piece and reassembled in St-Sulpice, with some changes due to the specifics of its new location. The architects' contribution involves on the one hand guiding people arriving at the house to the original entrance along new supporting and boundary walls and, on the other, converting the interior of the house to meet the requirements of the owner. For example, the attic storey was opened to bring light reflected from the lake into the central hall.

Großzügiger Wohnraum mit Cheminée / Extensive living area with fireplace

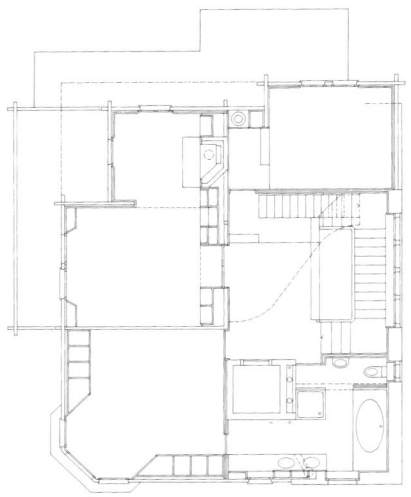

Grundriß Obergeschoß / Ground plan of upper floor

Querschnitt durch das Wohnhaus
Cross section through the residence

Grundriß Erdgeschoß
mit den neuen Stütz- und Begrenzungsmauern
Ground floor plan with new supporting and boundary walls

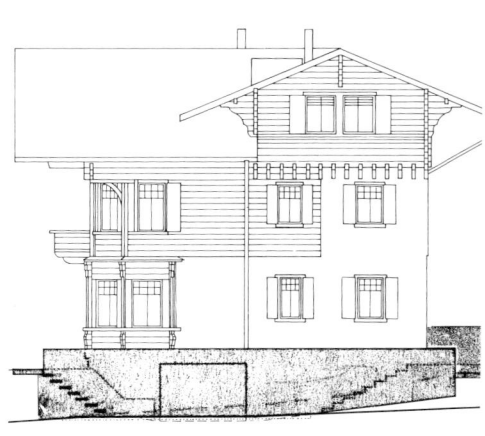

Ostfassade / East façade

Umbau Ferienwohnung Fayet in Noville 1994

Der Wirtschaftsteil des bestehenden Bauernhauses am Genfersee, ein Holzständerbau, soll den speziellen familiären Verhältnissen entsprechend partiell in eine Ferienwohnung umgebaut werden. Die Architekten erstellen im ersten Obergeschoß ein L-förmiges Volumen, dessen drei Raumzonen durch Schiebeelemente voneinander getrennt werden können. Am Tag bleiben die Schiebetüren offen, um die Räume großzügig erscheinen zu lassen sowie um von den unterschiedlichen Lichtverhältnissen zu profitieren. In der Nacht werden die Elemente geschlossen, so daß traditionelle Zimmer entstehen, die von der im Zentrum liegenden Küche erschlossen werden. Obwohl die finanziellen Mittel beschränkt waren und mit einfachen Materialien gearbeitet wurde, entstand durch die räumliche Gestaltung und die besondere Farbgebung eine einzigartige Atmosphäre.

Conversion of Fayet Holiday Residence in Noville 1994

Part of the working section of the existing, post-and-beam construction farmhouse on Lake Geneva, was to be converted into a holiday residence meeting the special requirements of the family. On the first storey the architects produced an L-shaped space, where its three room-zones can be separated by sliding partitions. During the day the partitions remain open, to make the room seem spacious and to take advantage of the varying lighting conditions. At night the partitions are closed, giving rise to traditional rooms with access from the kitchen at the centre. Although financial means were limited and simple materials were used, the management of space and the special colour scheme have produced a unique atmosphere.

Lichtstimmung durch das große frontale Fenster, das mit Lamellen besonders artikuliert ist
Unique atmosphere created by light entering the large front window; louvres add a special note

Blick vom Hauptraum in Richtung Küche
View from the main room towards the kitchen

Grundriß erstes Obergeschoß / First floor plan

Südostfassade / Southeast façade

Raffaele Cavadini · Michele Arnaboldi, Locarno

Geheimnisvolle Orte

Die beiden im Tessin geborenen und aufgewachsenen Architekten praktizieren eine für sie optimale Bürogemeinschaft: Sie arbeiten teilweise zusammen, führen jedoch unabhängig voneinander, in unmittelbarer Nähe, ein eigenes Büro. Größere Aufgaben und städtebauliche Wettbewerbe werden gemeinsam angegangen, während kleinere, objekthafte Entwürfe selbständig ausgeführt werden. Diese spannende Form der Kollaboration wahrt die Individualität und den Entwicklungsspielraum des einzelnen, beinhaltet aber gleichzeitig das Lösen der anfallenden Konflikte, die stets entstehen, wenn zwei Menschen intensiv miteinander arbeiten. Beiden gemeinsam ist in ihrer Architektur das Respektieren, Analysieren und Interpretieren der gegebenen Situation, eine Fähigkeit, die sie von Luigi Snozzi, bei dem sie während einiger Jahre arbeiteten, gelernt haben. Ein besonderes Anliegen ist ihnen auch der sinnvolle Umgang mit den Materialien. Als bevorzugten Baustoff nennen sie den Beton, am liebsten roh, da er die größten Freiheiten erlaubt und dem kulturellen Ort (Tessin) adäquat ist. Über allem jedoch steht das «Material» Licht, durch dessen raffinierte Anwendung Cavadini und Arnaboldi einzigartige Raumstimmungen entstehen lassen, eingedenk der Aussage Louis Kahns: «Material lebt durch Licht. [...] Auch die Atmosphäre lebt durch das Licht. Alles, was ist, lebt vom Licht.» Von großer Bedeutung sind ihnen ferner die Gestaltung der Außenräume im Sinne Snozzis: «Architektur ist Leere. Es liegt an dir, sie zu definieren.». Mittels präziser Akzente versuchen sie räumliche Qualitäten zu steigern und lassen so geheimnisvolle Orte entstehen.

Mysterious Places

The two architects, who were born and grew up in Ticino, operate what is for them an ideal joint architectural partnership: they sometimes work together, but each has their own independent architectural office close by. They work together on major commissions and town planning competitions, while smaller designs for individual buildings are executed separately. This exciting form of collaboration preserves individuality and scope for individual development, but at the same time provides the solution to the conflicts which always arise when two people work intensively together. What both have in common in their architecture is a respect for the given situation, which is analysed and interpreted – an ability they acquired through Luigi Snozzi, with whom they worked for a number of years. A special concern of theirs is appropriate use of materials. They name concrete as their preferred medium, especially exposed concrete, since it allows the greatest freedom and suits the cultural environment (Ticino). The "material" they place above all else, however, is light; through its sophisticated use Cavadini and Arnaboldi produce unique spatial moods, mindful of the words of Louis Kahn: "Material comes to life through light. [...] The atmosphere, too, lives through light. Everything that exists lives from light." They also attach great importance to the treatment of outdoor spaces in keeping with Snozzi's dictum: "Architecture is emptiness. It's up to you to define it." By precise placement of accents they strive to heighten spatial qualities, allowing mysterious places to come into being.

Biographie

Raffaele Cavadini

1954 Geboren in Mendrisio.

1973–74 Architekturstudium an der ETH-Zürich.

1974 Mitarbeit im Büro Ivano Gianola in Mendrisio.

1975–80 Architekturstudium an der Universität Venedig.

1980 Promotion bei Professor Vittorio Gregotti in Venedig.

1981 Mitarbeit im Büro Aurelio Galfetti in Bellinzona.

1981–82 Assistent bei Dozent Ivano Gianola an der Universität Genf.

1982–83 Assistent bei Professor Ernst Studer an der ETH-Zürich.

1982–85 Mitarbeit im Büro Luigi Snozzi in Locarno.

1986 Gastprofessor an der SCI-ARC in Vico Morcote, Tessin.

1986–89 Diplomassistent bei Professor Luigi Snozzi an der ETH-Lausanne.

1987–88 Gastprofessor an der ETH-Lausanne.

Seit 1985 Eigenes Büro in Locarno.

Seit 1986 Partielle Arbeitsgemeinschaft mit Michele Arnaboldi.

Michele Arnaboldi

1953 Geboren in Ascona.

1972–79 Architekturstudium an der ETH-Zürich.

1979 Diplom bei Professor Dolf Schnebli an der ETH-Zürich.

1979–85 Mitarbeit im Büro Luigi Snozzi in Locarno.

1982–85 Assistent bei Professor Dolf Schnebli an der ETH-Zürich.

1986–92 Diplomassistent bei Professor Dolf Schnebli an der ETH-Zürich.

1994–95 Gastprofessor an der Washington University in St. Louis, USA.

Seit 1985 Eigenes Büro in Locarno.

Seit 1986 Partielle Arbeitsgemeinschaft mit Raffaele Cavadini.

Ausgewähltes Werkverzeichnis

Raffaele Cavadini

1987 Hotel Garni Nessi in Locarno (1987–89) Via Varenna 79 Ausgeführtes Projekt.

1988 Wohnhaus Cavadini in Brissago (Kanton Tessin) In Cella Ausgeführtes Projekt.

1990 Wohnhaus Kalt in Locarno-Monti (Kanton Tessin; 1990–91) · Via del Tiglio Ausgeführtes Projekt.

Wohnungen Vairora in Gordola (Kanton Tessin; 1990–91) Gaggiola Ausgeführtes Projekt.

1991 Mehrzweckhalle und Gemeindehaus in Iragna (Kanton Tessin) Wettbewerb, erster Preis.

Wohnhaus Calzascia-Vairora in Gerra Piano (Kanton Tessin; 1991–92) Ausgeführtes Projekt.

Wohnhaus Juri in Ambri (Kanton Tessin; 1991–92) Ausgeführtes Projekt.

1992 Wohnhaus Svanascini in Tremona (Kanton Tessin; 1992–93) Ausgeführtes Projekt.

1993 Kapelle in Iragna (Kanton Tessin; 1993–94) Wettbewerb, erster Preis. Ausgeführtes Projekt.

Wohnhäuser Pasinelli/Bianchi/Cavadini in Minusio (Kanton Tessin; 1993–94) Via Navegna Ausgeführtes Projekt.

1994 Gestaltung Platz in Giubiasco (Kanton Tessin) Ausgeführes Projekt.

Michele Arnaboldi

1986 Erweiterung Wohnhaus Ortelli in Mendrisio (Kanton Tessin) Ausgeführtes Projekt.

Aufstockung Weinkeller Chiodi in Ascona (Kanton Tessin) Via Delta 24 Ausgeführtes Projekt.

Renovierung Mulino di Basso in Ascona (Kanton Tessin; 1986–87) Via Muraccio 3 Ausgeführtes Projekt.

1988 Wohnhaus Campiglio in Locarno-Monti (Kanton Tessin; 1988–89) Ausgeführtes Projekt.

1989 Wohnhaus Righetti in Arcegno (Kanton Tessin; 1989–91) Ausgeführtes Projekt.

Wohnungen Quattrini in Minusio (Kanton Tessin; 1989–91) Via Borenco 16 Ausgeführtes Projekt.

Kommunale Wohnungen in Ascona (Kanton Tessin; 1989–92) Via architetto Pisoni 10–12 Ausgeführtes Projekt.

1990 Wohnungen Cocconi-Lieber in Solduno (Kanton Tessin; 1990–92) Via Arbivecchio Ausgeführtes Projekt.

1991 Quartierplanung für Wohnungen in Locarno (Kanton Tessin; 1991–92) Vorprojekt.

1993 Fünf Wohnhäuser in Arcegno (Kanton Tessin; 1993–96 Projekt.

Gemeinsame Arbeiten

1986 Zusammen mit Luigi Snozzi an der Triennale von Milano: «Le città immaginate», (1986–87).

1987 Quartierplanung in Caslano (Kanton Tessin; 1987–94) Wettbewerb, erster Preis. Masterplan.

1988 Schulhaus und Renovation Verwaltungsgebäude in Cureglia (Kanton Tessin) Wettbewerb, erster Preis.

Verwaltungszentrum in Locarno (Kanton Tessin) Wettbewerb, zweiter Preis.

Gestaltung Place de Rome in Martigny (Kanton Wallis) Ideenwettbewerb, zweiter Preis.

1989 Verwaltungsgebäude in Monthey (Kanton Wallis) Wettbewerb.

Bahnhof in Locarno (Kanton Tessin) Vorprojekt.

Rathaus in Magliaso (Kanton Tessin) Wettbewerb, erster Preis.

Rathaus und Kindergarten in Cavigliano (Kanton Tessin) Wettbewerb, zweiter Preis.

Gestaltung Piazza Grande in Locarno (Kanton Tessin) Wettbewerb, vierter Preis.

Planung Areal Orti Pianello in Cureglia (Kanton Tessin; 1989–92) Ausgeführtes Projekt.

1990 Pfarrhaus und Kindergarten in Avegno (Kanton Tessin) Wettbewerb, dritter Preis.

Erweiterung ETH-Hönggerberg in Zürich Wettbewerb.

1991 Temporärer Holzpavillon anläßlich der 700-Jahr-Feier in Neuenburg Ausgeführtes Projekt.

Überbauung Areal «Frauenhof» in Altstätten (Kanton St. Gallen) Wettbewerb.

Hotel und Sportzentrum in Airolo (Kanton Tessin) Wettbewerb, zweiter Preis.

1992 Seminar: Planung und Gestaltung der Magadino-Ebene (Kanton Tessin) Projekt.

Kommunales Verwaltungsgebäude in Soazza (Kanton Graubünden) Wettbewerb, zweiter Preis.

Gestaltung Weltausstellung «Expo 2000» in Hannover (seit 1992) Wettbewerb, erster Preis, Masterplan 1:1000.

1993 Europan in Berlin Wettbewerb.

Wohn- und Verwaltungszentrum in Bellinzona Wettbewerb, Ankauf.

Gewerbe- und Dienstleistungsbetriebe in Gümligen (Kanton Bern) Wettbewerb.

1994 Kommunales Bürohaus in Poschiavo (Kanton Graubünden) Wettbewerb, Ankauf.

Raiffeisen-Bank in Intragna (Kanton Tessin) Wettbewerb, erster Preis.

Biography

Raffaele Cavadini
1954
Born in Mendrisio
1973–74
Studied architecture at the ETH Zurich
1974
Worked at the Ivano Gianola architectural office in Mendrisio
1975–80
Studied architecture at the University of Venice
1980
Doctorate under Professor Vittorio Gregotti in Venice
1981
Worked at the Aurelio Galfetti architectural office in Bellinzona
1981–82
Assistant to Ivano Gianola at the University of Geneva
1982–83
Assistant to Professor Ernst Studer at the ETH Zurich
1982–85
Worked at the Luigi Snozzi architectural office in Locarno
1986
Visiting Professor at the SCI-ARC in Vico Morcote, Ticino
1986–89
Diploma assistant to Prof. Luigi Snozzi at the ETH Lausanne
1987–88
Visiting Professor at the ETH Lausanne
Since 1985
Own architectural office in Locarno
Since 1986
Partial working partnership with Michele Arnaboldi.

Michele Arnaboldi
1953
Born in Ascona
1972–79
Studied architecture at the ETH Zurich
1979
Graduated with diploma under Prof. Dolf Schnebli at the ETH Zurich
1979–85
Worked the Luigi Snozzi architectural office in Locarno
1982–85
Assistant to Prof. Dolf Schnebli at the ETH Zurich
1986–92
Diploma assistant to Prof. Dolf Schnebli at the ETH Zurich
1994–95
Visiting Professor at Washington University, St. Louis, USA
Since 1985
Own architectural office in Locarno
Since 1986
Partial partnership with Raffaele Cavadini.

Selected list of Work

Raffaele Cavadini
1987
Hotel Garni in Locarno (1987–89) Via Varenna 79 Completed project.
1988
Cavadini residence in Brissago (Canton of Ticino) In Cella Completed project.
1990
Kalt residence in Locarno-Monti (Canton of Ticino; 1990–91) Via del Tiglio Completed project.
Vairora Apartments in Gordola (Canton of Ticino; 1990–91) Gaggiola Completed project.
1991
Multipurpose and parish hall apartments in Iragna (Canton of Ticino) Competition, first prize.
Calzascia-Vairora residence in Gerra Piano (Canton of Ticino; 1991–92) Completed project.
Juri residence in Ambri (Canton of Ticino; 1991–92) Completed project.
1992
Svanascini residence in Tremona (Canton of Ticino; 1992–93) Completed project.
1993
Chapel in Iragna (Canton of Ticino; 1993–94) Competition, first prize. Completed project.
Pasinelli/Bianchi/Cavadini residences in Minusio (Canton of Ticino; 1993–94) Via Navegna Completed project.
1994
Design of square in Giubiasco (Canton of Ticino) Completed project.

Michele Arnaboldi
1986
Extension of Ortelli residence in Mendrisio (Canton of Ticino) Completed project.
Upward extension of Weinkeller Chiodi in Ascona (Canton of Ticino) Via Delta 24 Completed project.
Renovation of Mulino di Basso in Ascona (Canton of Ticino; 1986–87) Via Muraccio 3 Completed project.
1988
Campiglio residence in Locarno-Monti (Canton of Ticino; 1988–89) Completed project.
1989
Righetti residence in Arcegno (Canton of Ticino; 1989–91) Completed project.
Quattrini apartments in Minusio (Canton of Ticino; 1989–91) Via Borenco 16 Completed project.
Local authority-owned apartments in Ascona (Canton of Ticino; 1989–92) Via architetto Pisoni 10–12 Completed project.
1990
Cocconi-Lieber apartments in Solduno (Canton of Ticino; 1990–92) Via Arbivecchio Completed project.
1991
District plan for apartments in Locarno (Canton of Ticino; 1991–92) Preliminary project.
1993
Five residences in Arcegno (Canton of Ticino; 1993–96) Project.

Joint projects
1986
With Luigi Snozzi at the Milan Triennale: "Le città immaginate", (1986–87).
1987
District plan in Caslano (Canton of Ticino; 1987–94) Competition, first prize. Master plan.
1988
School and renovation of administrative building in Cureglia (Canton of Ticino) Competition, first prize.
Administrative centre in Locarno (Canton of Ticino) Competition, second prize.
Design for Place de Rome in Martigny (Canton of Valais) Ideas competition, second prize.
1989
Administrative building in Monthey (Canton of Valais) Competition.
Station in Locarno (Canton of Ticino) Preliminary project.
Town hall in Magliaso (Canton of Ticino) Competition, first prize.
Town hall and kindergarten in Cavigliano (Canton of Ticino) Competition, second prize.
Design for Piazza Grande in Locarno (Canton of Ticino) Competition, fourth prize.
Plan for Orti Pianello site in Cureglia (Canton of Ticino; 1989–92) Completed project.
1990
Rectory and kindergarten in Avegno (Canton of Ticino) Competition, third prize.
Extension of ETH Hönggerberg in Zürich Competition.
1991
Temporary wood pavilion for 7th centenary celebrations in Neuchâtel Completed project.
Development of Frauenhof site in Altstätten (Canton of St.Gallen) Competition.
Hotel and sports centre in Airolo (Canton of Ticino) Competition, second prize.
1992
Seminar: Planning and development of the Magadino plain (Canton of Ticino) Project.
Local authority administrative building in Soazza (Canton of Grisons) Competition, second prize.
Design for "Expo 2000" World Fair in Hanover (since 1992) Competition, first prize. Master plan 1:1000.
1993
Europan in Berlin Competition.
Residential and administrative centre in Bellinzona Competition, purchased design.
Commercial premises in Gümligen (Canton of Berne) Competition.
1994
Communal office building in Poschiavo (Canton of Grisons) Competition, purchased design.
Raiffeisen Bank in Intragna (Canton of Ticino) Competition, first prize.

Wohnhaus Cavadini in Brissago 1988

An einem Steilhang, inmitten einer üppigen südländischen Vegetation mit direkter Sicht auf den Lago Maggiore, kann Raffaele Cavadini sein privates Wohnhaus, ohne Kompromisse eingehen zu müssen, realisieren. Er stellt den eingeschossigen, quaderförmigen Baukörper (15 m x 6.5 m), der mit einem flachen Dach abgeschlossen ist, auf vier dünne Stützen, so daß das Volumen zu schweben scheint. Der Eingang in den großzügigen Wohnraum erfolgt über eine seitliche Treppe und eine Terrasse. Küche und Badezimmer sind hangwärts angeordnet. Gegen Norden befinden sich zwei kleine Zimmer. Der Bau besticht durch seine auf ein Minimum reduzierte Formensprache und durch seine Materialisierung und Farbgebung.

Cavadini Residence in Brissago 1988

On a steep slope amid luxuriant Mediterranean vegetation with a direct view of Lake Maggiore, Raffaele Cavadini has been able to realise his private residence without having to make compromises. He has placed the single-storey block (15 m x 6.5 m), covered by a flat roof, on four slender columns, so that it seems to float. The entrance to the spacious living-room is reached by a side staircase and terrace. Kitchen and bathroom are situated facing the slope. Two small rooms face north. The building's charm lies in an idiom reduced to a minimum and in the use of materials and colour.

Wohnhaus, das durch seine bis auf ein Minimum reduzierte Architektursprache auffällt
House, notable for its architectural idiom reduced to a minimum

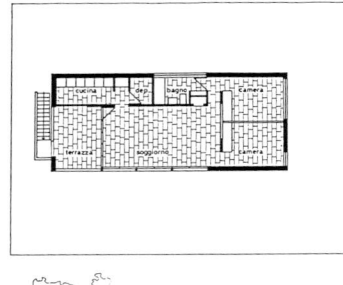

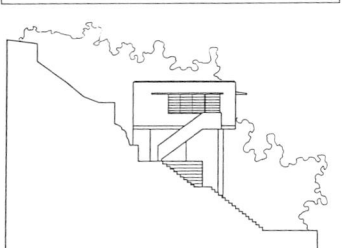

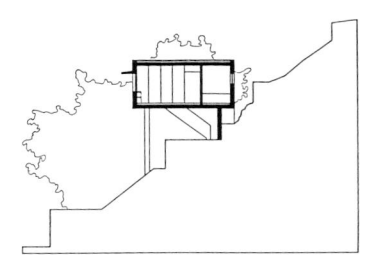

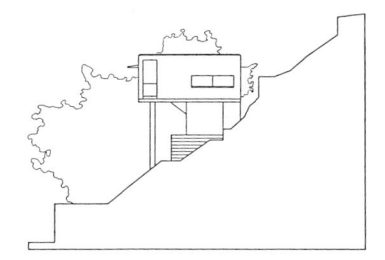

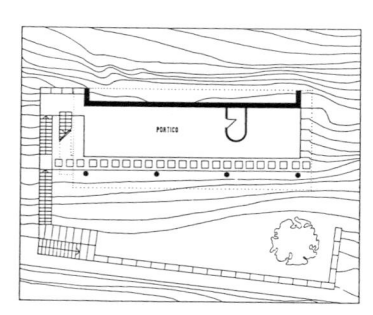

Situation inmitten der steil abfallenden Topographie
Situation surrounded by steep slopes

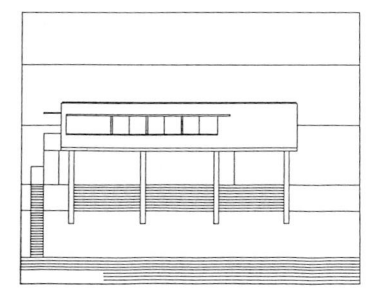

Grundriß Erdgeschoß / Ground floor plan

Südwestfassade / Southwest façade

Südostfassade / Southeast façade

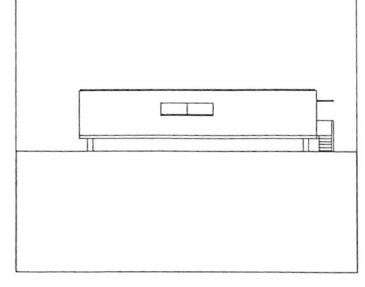

Querschnitt durch das auf Stützen stehende Wohnhaus
Cross section through the house supported on columns

Nordostfassade / Northeast façade

Nordwestfassade / Northwest façade

Wohnhaus Kalt in Locarno-Monti
1990–1991

Die Parzelle befindet sich auf einer leichten Anhöhe oberhalb von Locarno und ist umgeben von zahlreichen Wohnhäusern. Der Neubau von Raffaele Cavadini besteht aus zwei zusammengehörenden Volumen: aus dem aus Bruchstein gefertigten Sockel und dem daraufliegenden Baukörper, einer reinen, weißen Betonkonstruktion. Bemerkenswert sind die scharf ausgeschnittenen Öffnungen der Fenster und insbesondere des zentralen Hofes, der sich zum See und zum Himmel hin wendet. Um diesen Außenraum, das Herz der Konzeption, ordnen sich die Innenräume U-förmig an. Sie fallen durch ihre zweckmässige, funktionale Anordnung auf. Eine leichte und transparente Passerelle verbindet die beiden Flügel.

Kalt Residence in Locarno-Monti
1990–91

The building plot is on slightly raised ground above Locarno and is surrounded by numerous houses. Raffaele Cavadini's new building consists of two interrelated volumes: the socle, made of quarrystone and the building itself resting on it, a pure, white concrete structure. Noteworthy features are the sharply delineated window openings and the central courtyard, which faces the lake and sky. Around this outdoor space, which is the heart of the concept, the rooms form a U-shaped configuration. They catch the eye by their functional arrangement. A light, transparent footbridge connects the two wings.

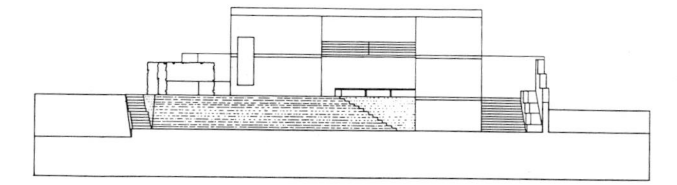

Südfassade / South façade

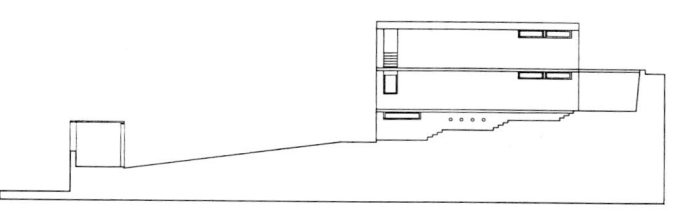

Westfassade / West façade

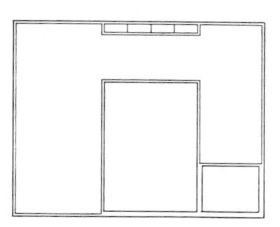

Dachaufsicht / Top view of roof

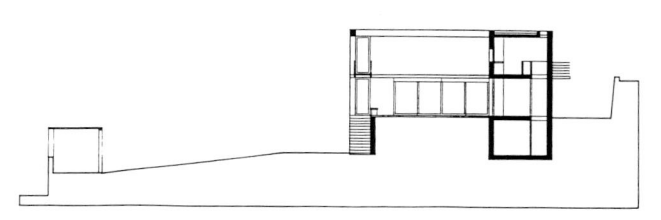

Querschnitt durch den zentralen Hof
Cross section through the central courtyard

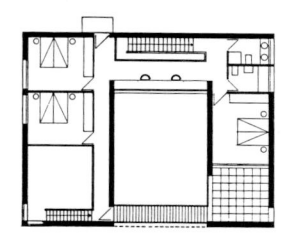

Grundriß erstes Obergeschoß
First floor plan

Ansicht des Sockels aus Bruchstein und des daraufliegenden Baukörpers aus Beton sowie des zentralen Hofs

Elevation of the quarrystone base and the concrete building volume above, and of central courtyard

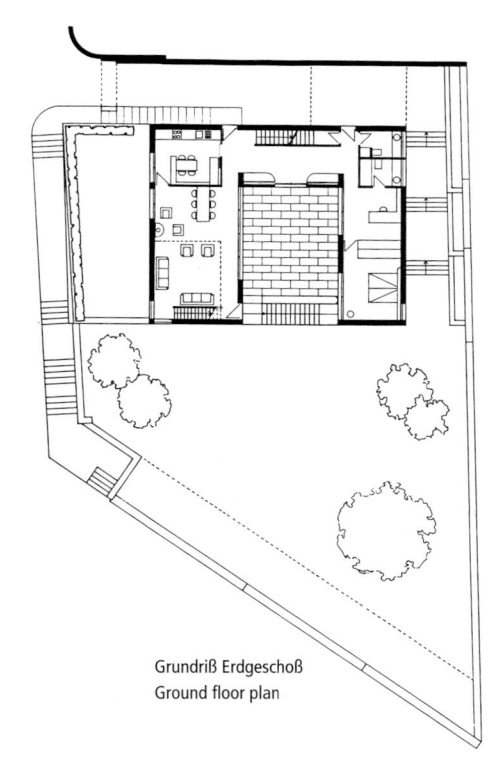

Grundriß Erdgeschoß
Ground floor plan

Wohnhaus Calzascia-Vairora in Gerra Piano 1991–1992

Die bemerkenswerte Lage der Parzelle inmitten von Weinbergen, mit Sicht auf den Lago Maggiore und die umliegenden Hügel, bestimmte maßgebend den Entwurf von Raffaele Cavadini. Das Projekt setzt sich aus zwei Gärten und zwei Volumen zusammen, die miteinander eine Einheit bilden: der längs zum Hang gestellte, zweigeschossige Baukörper sowie der senkrecht dazu plazierte gleichhohe Turm, der im Erdgeschoß offen ist und so einen einzigartigen Raum bildet. Der Eingang führt durch diesen Raum. Im Innern geleitet einen eine Treppe ins Obergeschoß weiter. Auffallend sind die zahlreichen, außerordentlich präzise gestalteten Innen- und Außenräume, die eine hohe Wohnqualität ermöglichen.

Calzascia-Vairora Residence in Gerra Piano 1991–1992

The unique situation of the building plot amid vineyards, with a view of Lake Maggiore and the surrounding hills, decisively influenced Raffaele Cavadini's design. The project comprises two gardens and two buildings forming a unity: the two-storey main structure, placed along the slope, and the tower, of the same height, at right angles to it. The tower is open on the ground floor, forming a unique space. The entrance leads through this area. Once inside, a staircase takes you to the first storey. A striking feature are the many, extremely precisely proportioned inner and outer spaces, which provide a high-quality living environment.

Das aus zwei Voumen bestehende Wohnhaus, das eine Einheit bildet / House consisting of two volumes forming one whole

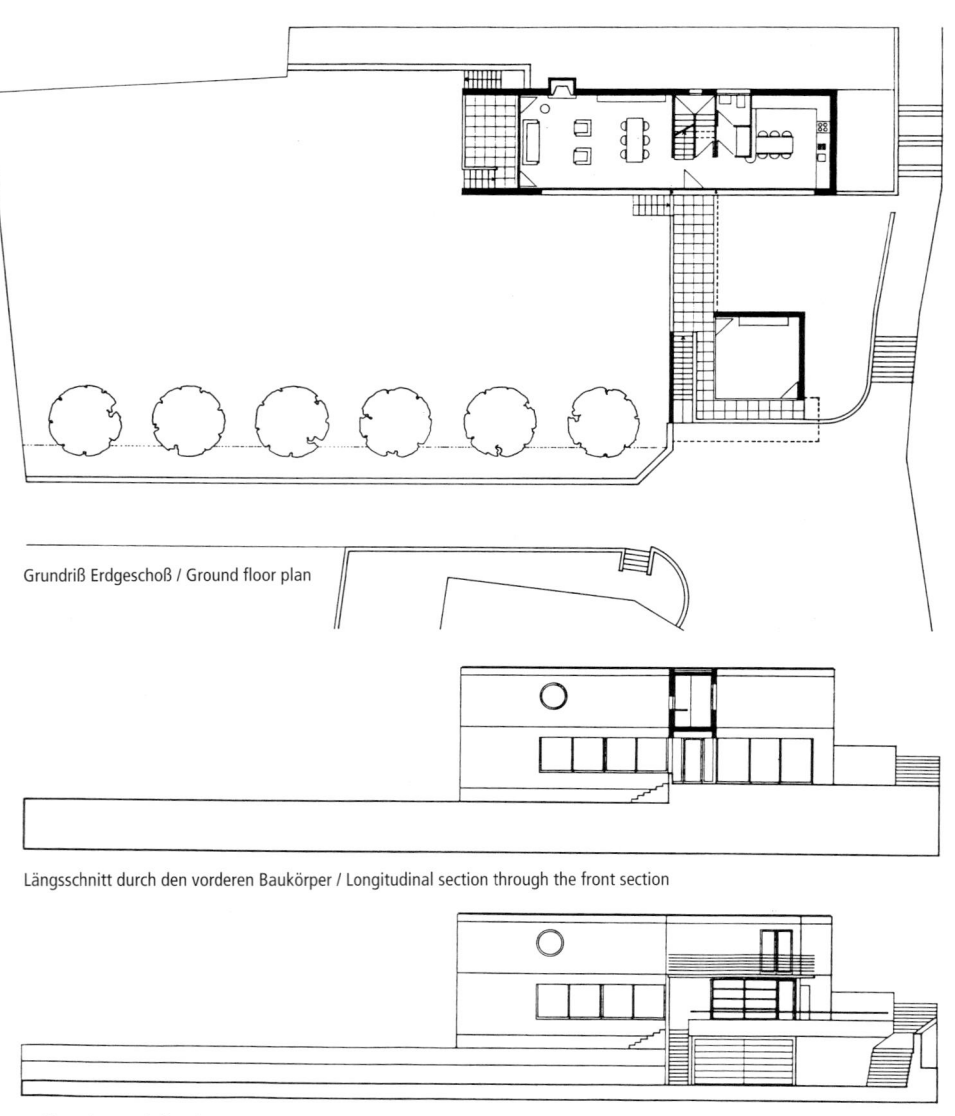

Grundriß Erdgeschoß / Ground floor plan

Längsschnitt durch den vorderen Baukörper / Longitudinal section through the front section

Südfassade / South façade

Kapelle in Iragna
1993–1994

Die Aufgabenstellung dieses Projektes von Raffaele Cavadini beinhaltete die Gestaltung einer kleinen Kapelle, die vor allem als Aufbahrungshalle zu dienen hat, sowie deren Außenräume. Von besonderer Bedeutung ist der Zugang in den Innenraum, der durch einen spiralförmig angelegten Weg artikuliert wird. Dieser dient der Vorbereitung und Sammlung. Die karge, rohe, auffallend schlichte Ausführung erzeugt im Innern eine stille, konzentrierte Atmosphäre. Charakteristisch ist die Materialisierung, außen Bruchstein und innen Beton, sowie die Lichtführung, die dem Raum die ihm gebührende Qualität verleiht.

Chapel in Iragna
1993–1994

Raffaele Cavadini's task in this project was to design a small chapel to be used primarily as a funeral parlour, and its surroundings. The approach to the interior, along a spiral path, is of especial importance. The path helps to prepare and compose the mind. The bare, stark, strikingly plain finish of the interior produces a tranquil, concentrated atmosphere. The use of materials – quarrystone outside and concrete inside – is characteristic, as is the unique treatment of light, which endows the space with a fitting quality.

Aufgang zur kleinen Kapelle aus Bruchstein, die aus demselben Material geschaffen ist wie die spiralförmige Mauer, die den Weg artikuliert
Quarrystone approach to small chapel; the same material is used for the spiral wall giving definition to the path

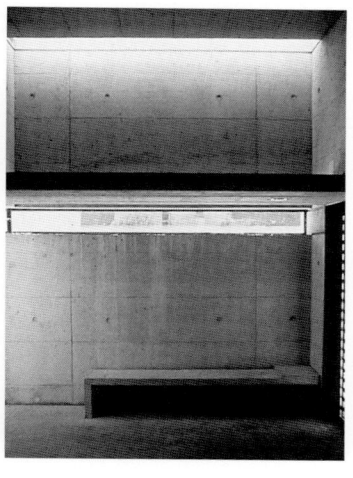

Mystische Stimmung im Innenraum
Mystical mood in the interior

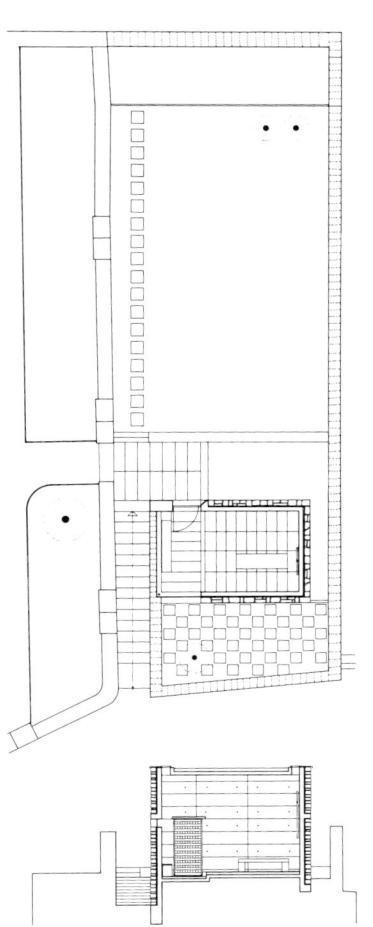

Grundriss Erdgeschoß / Ground floor plan

Längsschnitt durch die Kapelle
Longitudinal section through the chapel

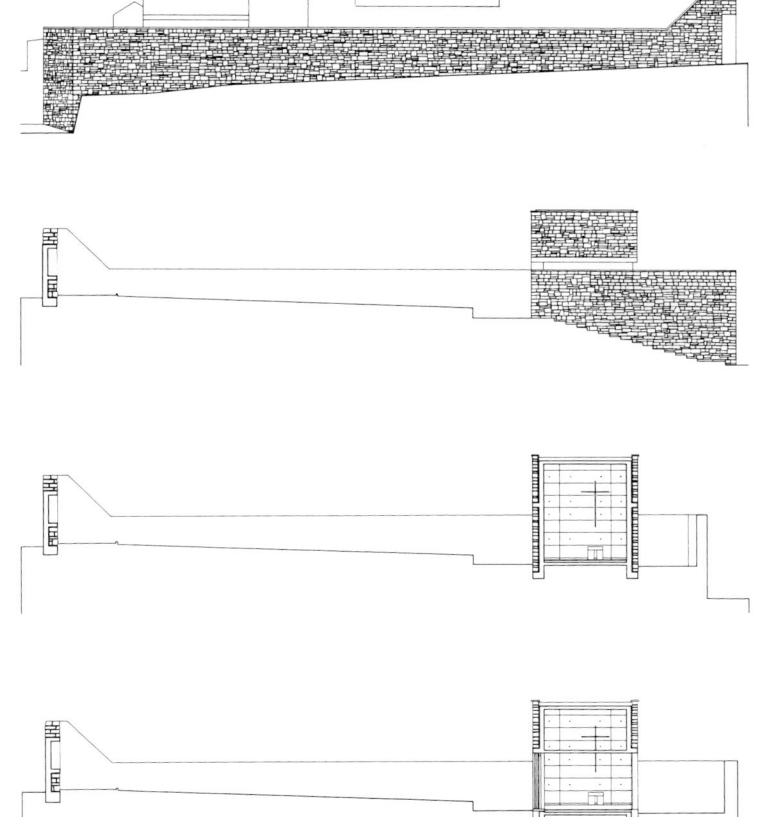

Nordfassade / North façade

Südfassade / South façade

Querschnitt durch die vordere Partie des Innenraumes
Cross section through the front section of the interior

Querschnitt durch die hintere Partie des Innenraumes
Cross section through the back section of the interior

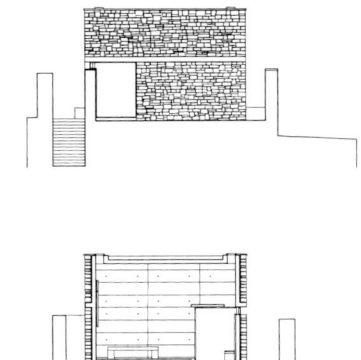

Fassade Bruchsteinmauer / Quarrystone façade

Westfassade / West façade

Längsschnitt durch den kleinen Vorgarten mit Ansicht der Ostfassade
Longitudinal section through the small front garden with elevation of east façade

Längsschnitt durch die Kapelle
Longitudinal section through the chapel

Wohnhäuser Pasinelli/Bianchi/Cavadini in Minusio
1993–1994

Mit minimalen Eingriffen erreichte Raffaele Cavadini bei diesen drei zusammengebauten Wohnhäusern, die sich unmittelbar an einem kleinen Bach befinden, ein Maximum an Wohnqualität. Umgeben von Grünraum befinden sie sich unweit des Stadtzentrums. Nebst den nötigen Wohnräumen besitzen alle drei L-förmigen Einheiten eine großzügige Terrasse und einen individuellen Garten. Auffallend ist die Positionierung der Öffnungen, da sie präzise Landschaften rahmen und eine klare Beziehung zum Innenraum haben. Die Fenster, als formale und funktionale Einheit, sind ein wesentlicher Bestandteil der Raumstruktur.

Pasinelli/Bianchi/Cavadini Residences in Minusio
1993–1994

In these three adjoining houses situated directly beside a small stream, Raffaele Cavadini has attained maximum quality with minimum means. Though surrounded by greenery, the houses are not far from to the town centre. Apart from the necessary living rooms, each of the three L-shaped units has a large terrace and an individual garden. The placing of the openings is a striking feature, as they frame clearly-defined landscapes and have a clear relation to the interior. The windows, as a formal and functional unit, are an essential component of the spatial structure.

Ansicht der südwestlichen Gartenfassade der drei zusammengebauten Wohnhäuser
Elevation of southwest garden façade of the three linked houses

Großzügiges Fenster im Wohnzimmer, das den Ausblick zum individuellen Garten freigibt
Large lounge window, giving view of private garden

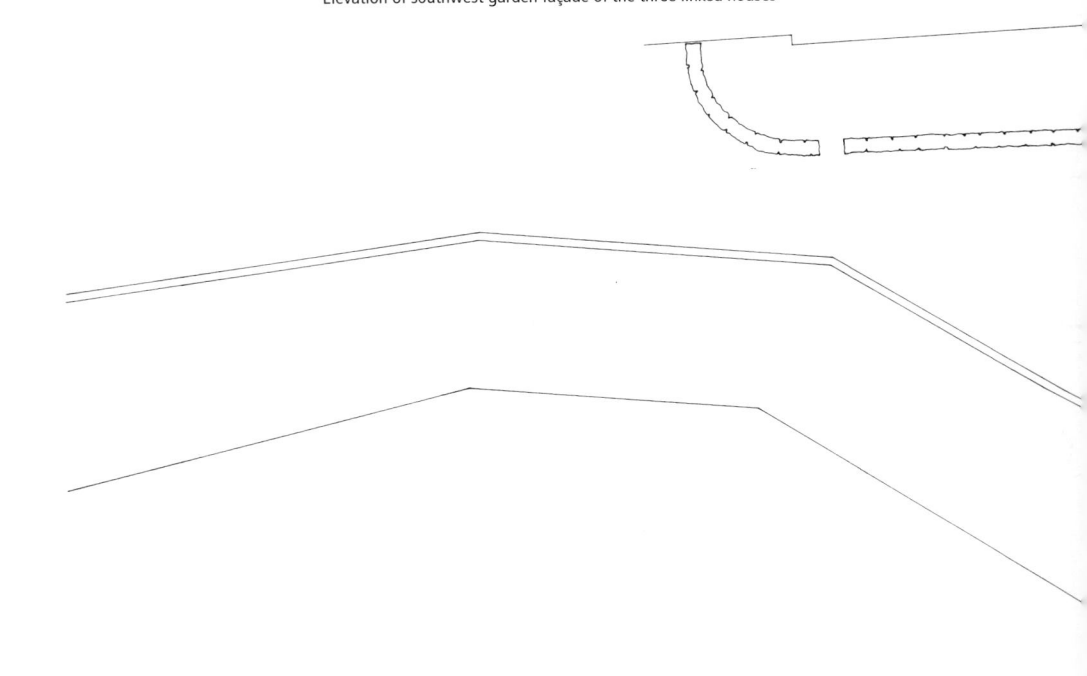

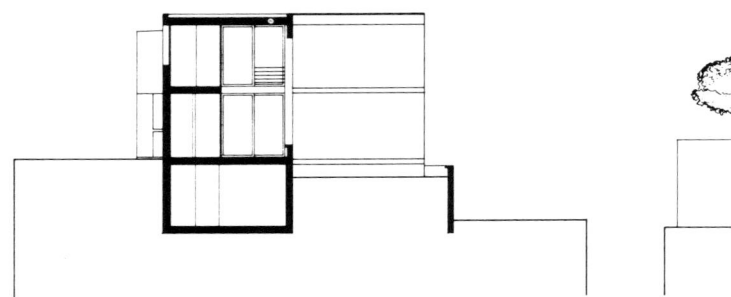

Südostfassade / Southeast façade

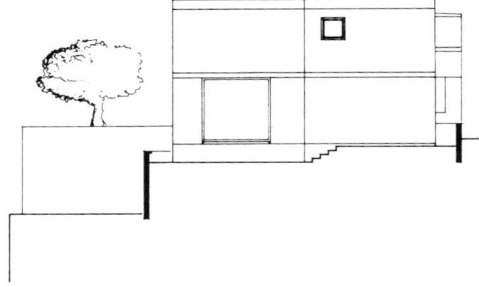

Querschnitt durch den individuellen Garten
Cross section through the private garden

PIANO TERRENO

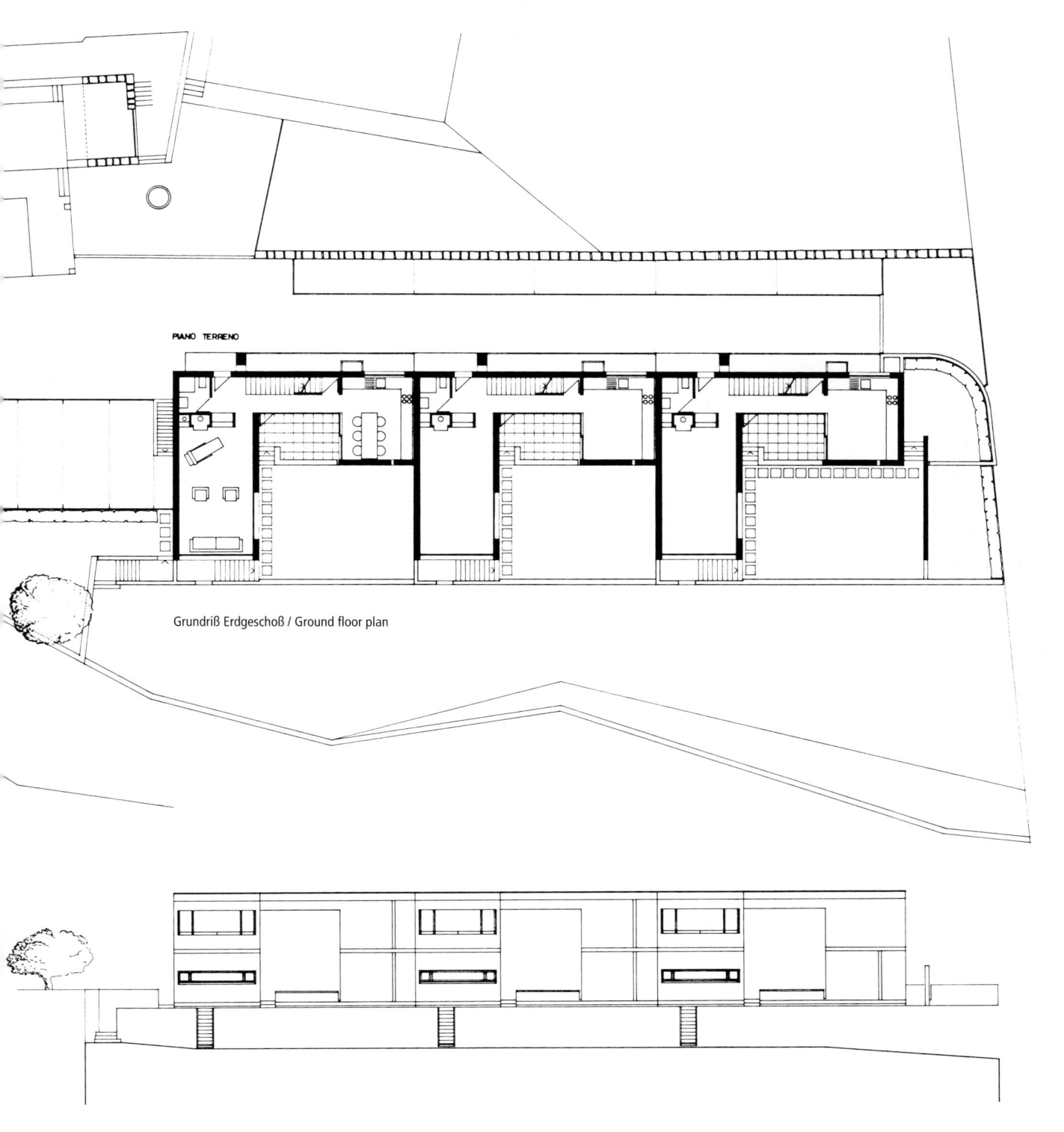

Grundriß Erdgeschoß / Ground floor plan

Südwestfassade / Southwest façade

Wohnhaus Righetti in Arcegno
1989–1991

Dieses Wohnhaus von Michele Arnaboldi fällt durch die sensible Einfügung in die terrassierte Topographie und durch die konstruktive Ausführung mit Vorspannbeton (die gebräuchliche Konstruktionsweise im Brückenbau) auf. Das senkrecht zum Hang und damit quer auf der Parzelle stehende, mit direkter Sicht auf die Magadino-Ebene orientierte Volumen weist zwei unabhängige Wohnungen auf. Die formale Gestaltung des Baukörpers ist deshalb bemerkenswert, weil mittels konstruktiver Innovationen architektonische Intentionen verwirklicht sind, so etwa die starke Transparenz der Fenster, die dank des Vorspannbetons stützenfrei ausgeführt werden konnten.

Righetti Residence in Arcegno
1989–1991

This residence by Michele Arnaboldi attracts the eye through its sensitive incorporation into a terraced landscape, and through its constructional use of prestressed concrete (the usual method for bridge building). The building, at right-angles to the slope and thus transverse to the plot, with a direct view of the Magadino plain, contains two separate apartments. The formal treatment of the building is noteworthy in that structural innovations are used to achieve architectonic ends, such as the extreme transparency of the windows, constructed without columns thanks to the prestressed concrete.

Ansicht der Südfassade mit den zwei aufeinanderliegenden, unabhängigen Wohnungen
Elevation of south façade with two separate apartments on different levels

Wohnzimmer, das durch die Fensterfront und das Oberlicht eine besondere Atmosphäre bekommt
Lounge. Window wall and skylight create a special atmosphere

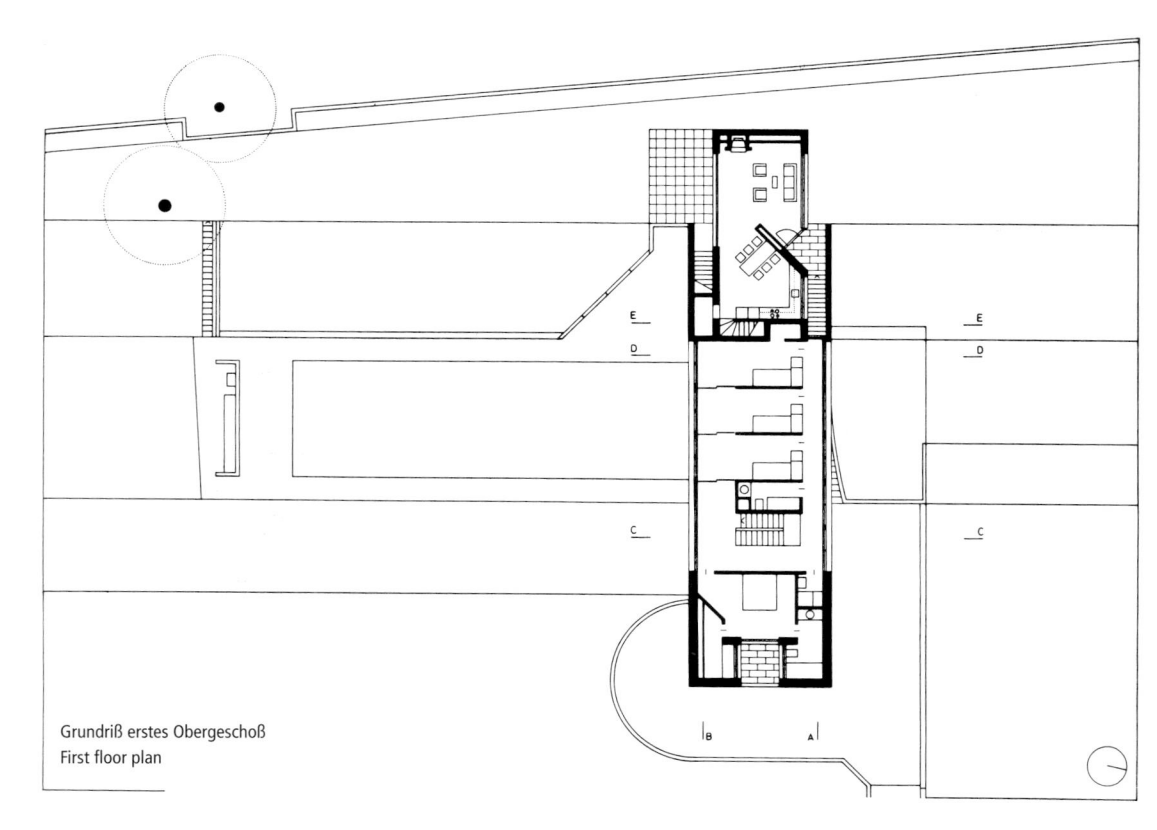

Grundriß erstes Obergeschoß
First floor plan

Nordfassade / North façade

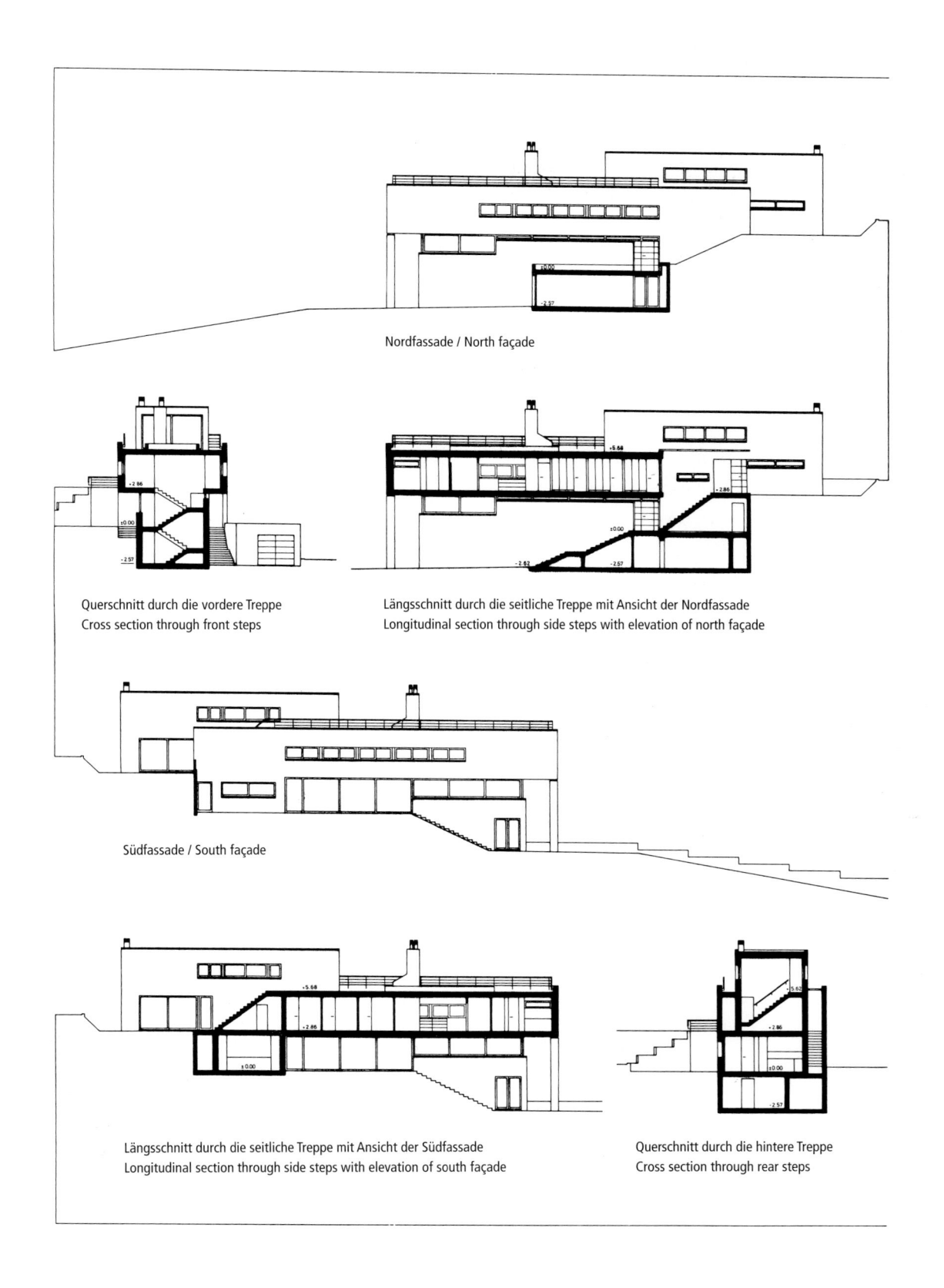

Querschnitt durch die vordere Treppe
Cross section through front steps

Längsschnitt durch die seitliche Treppe mit Ansicht der Nordfassade
Longitudinal section through side steps with elevation of north façade

Südfassade / South façade

Längsschnitt durch die seitliche Treppe mit Ansicht der Südfassade
Longitudinal section through side steps with elevation of south façade

Querschnitt durch die hintere Treppe
Cross section through rear steps

Wohnungen Quattrini in Minusio
1989–1991

Dieser sechsgeschossige Komplex mit zehn Wohnungen von Michele Arnaboldi befindet sich inmitten der städtischen Agglomeration. Das quaderförmige Volumen, mit einer geometrisch anders gestalteten, weit auskragenden Terrasse, nimmt deutlich Bezug auf die Umgebung, insbesondere auf die einmalige Sicht auf den See. Auffallend ist die durch das Treppenhaus stark perforierte Eingangsfassade, die dem Komplex eine lebendige Struktur verleiht. Bemerkenswert sind die klar gegliederten, zweckmäßigen Grundrisse, die zusammen mit dem rohen Sichtbeton und dem sorgfältigen Handwerk eine eigene Faszination erzeugen.

Quattrini Apartments in Minusio
1989–1991

This six-storey complex with ten apartments by Michele Arnaboldi is located in the midst of the built-up area of the town. The rectangular block, with a large projecting terrace of a different geometrical shape, is clearly related to its surroundings, especially to the exceptional view of the lake. The entrance façade, strongly perforated by the stairwell, is a striking feature which gives the complex a vibrant texture. The clearly structured, functional floor plans are also noteworthy; together with the rough exposed concrete and the careful craftsmanship, they produce a special fascination.

Ansicht der stark perforierten Ostfassade mit dem Eingang und der Nordfassade mit den weit auskragenden Terrassen
Elevation of distinctive, punctuated east façade with entrance and north façade with projecting terraces

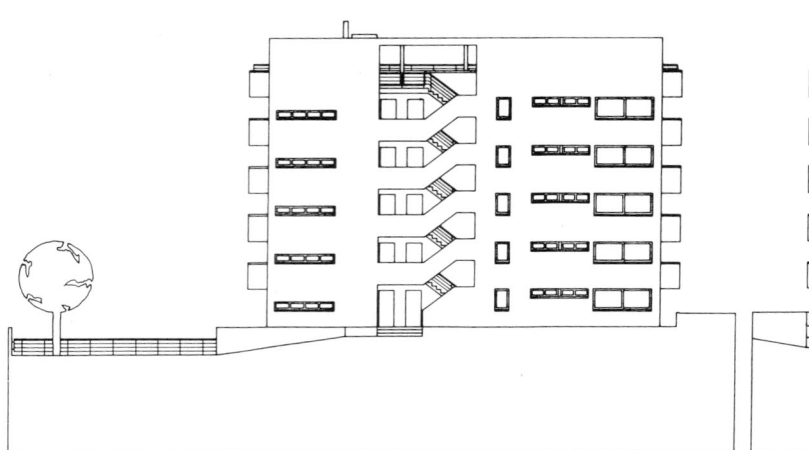

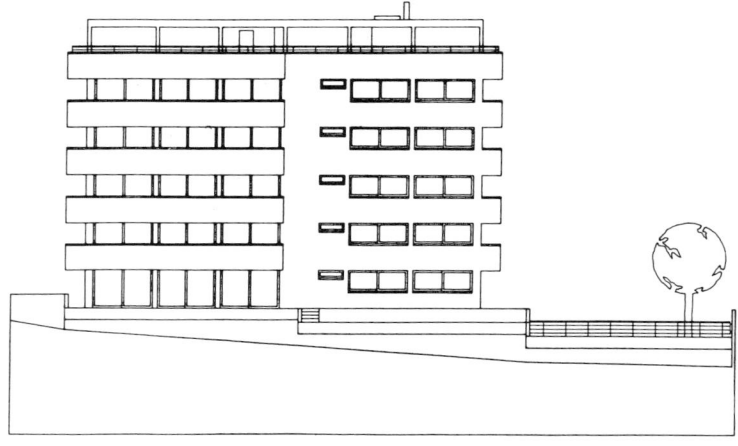

Ostfassade / East façade

Westfassade / West façade

Grundriß Kellergeschoß
Ground plan of basement level

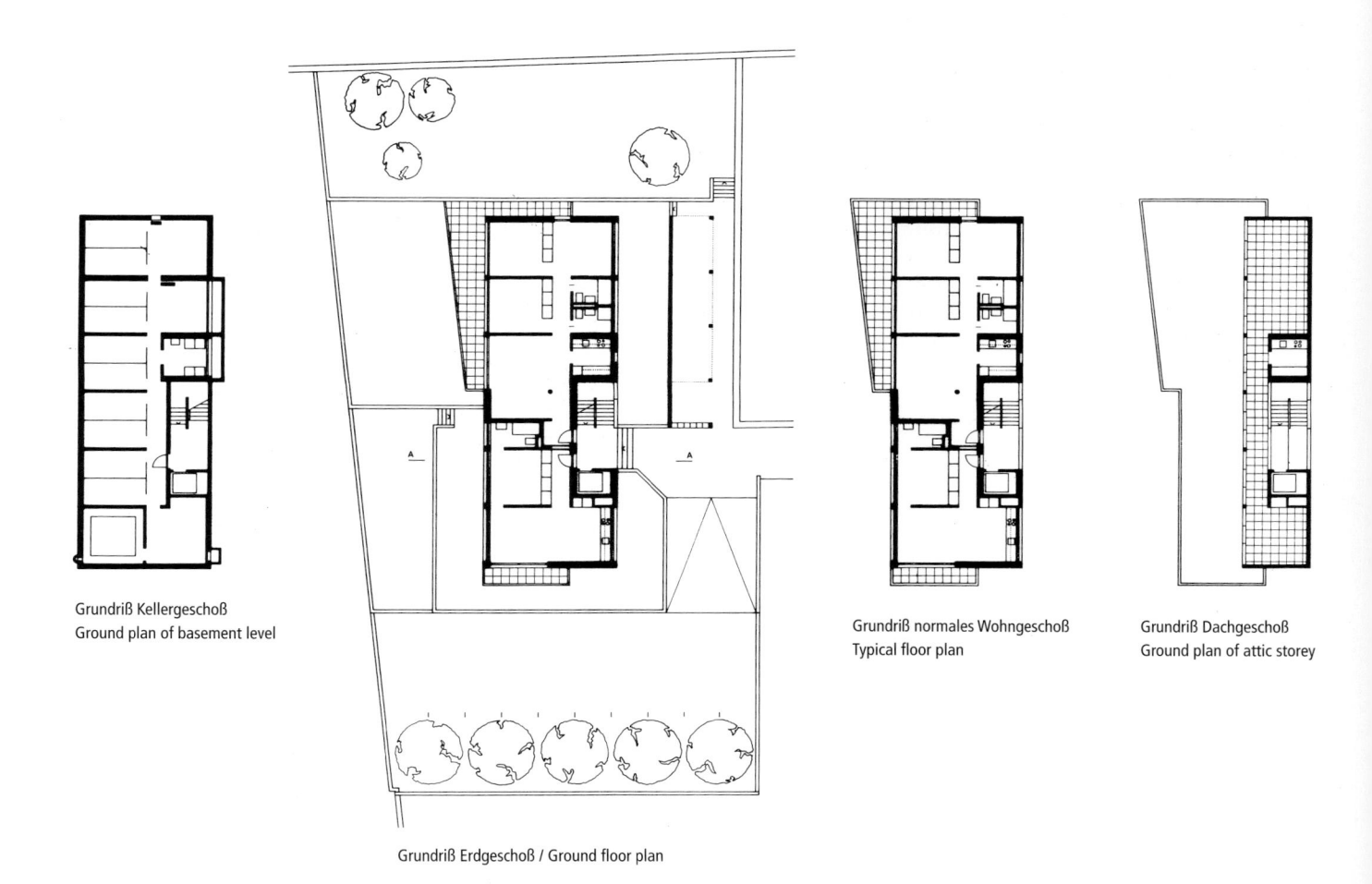

Grundriß Erdgeschoß / Ground floor plan

Grundriß normales Wohngeschoß
Typical floor plan

Grundriß Dachgeschoß
Ground plan of attic storey

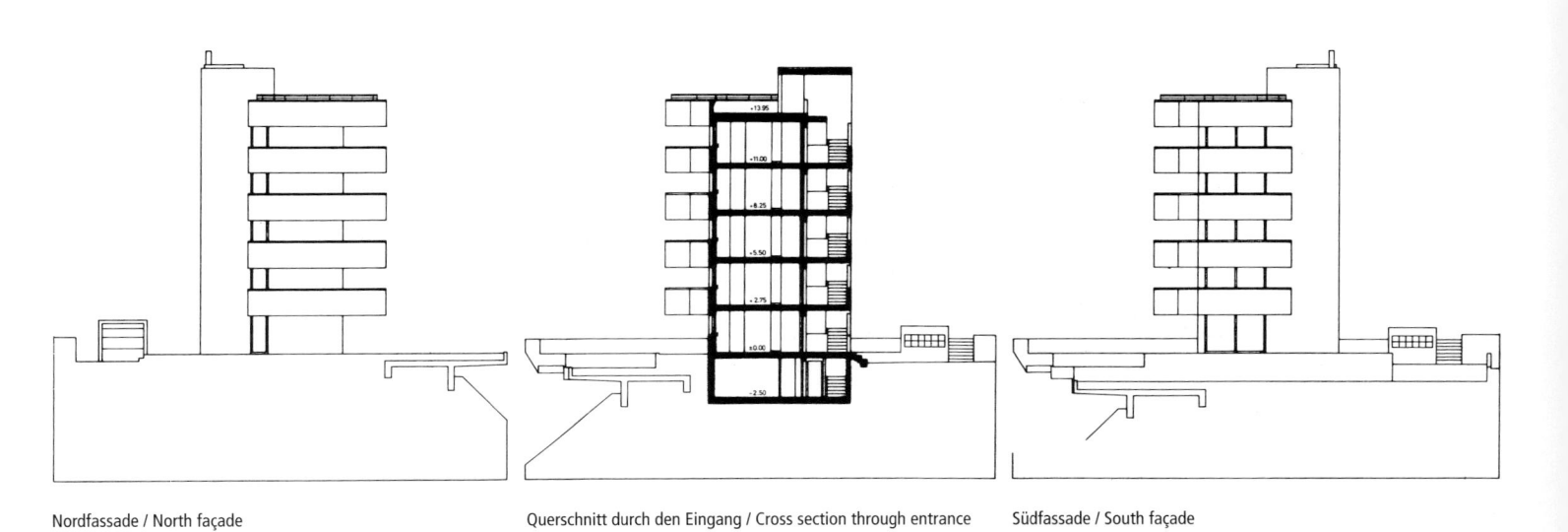

Nordfassade / North façade

Querschnitt durch den Eingang / Cross section through entrance

Südfassade / South façade

**Kommunale Wohnungen in Ascona
1989–1992**

Der mit der Schmalseite zur Straße gerichtete dreigeschossige Bau von Michele Arnaboldi setzt sich aus zwei spiegelbildlichen Gebäudeteilen zusammen, die in der Mitte einen gemeinsamen öffentlichen Hof bilden. Zu Fuß erfolgt der Eingang durch eine zentrale, gedeckte, aber außenliegende Treppe. Mit dem Auto gelangt der Bewohner, die Bewohnerin direkt ins Untergeschoß, von wo die Erschließung nach oben führt. Die verschiedenen Passagen und Plätze innerhalb des Gebäudes dienen, nebst der Erschließung, vor allem der Kommunikation. Die unterschiedlich großen Wohnungen sind mit einfachen, oftmals roh belassenen, zweckmässigen Materialien ausgeführt.

**Local Authority-Owned Apartments in Ascona
1989–1992**

Michele Arnaboldi's three-storey building, the short side of which faces the road, is made up of two parts, each forming a mirror image of the other, with a common public courtyard between them. Access on foot is by a central, covered but external staircase. By car the resident drives directly into the basement, from which there is access to the building above. The various corridors and lobbies inside the building are intended especially to aid communication, as well as access. The apartments, of different sizes, are executed in functional materials, often left exposed.

Ansicht der dreigeschossigen Wohnanlage von der Straße
Elevation of the three-storey residential complex viewed from the street

Zentrale gedeckte, außenliegende Treppe, die aus rohen Materialien gefertigt ist
Central, covered, external staircase, of exposed construction materials

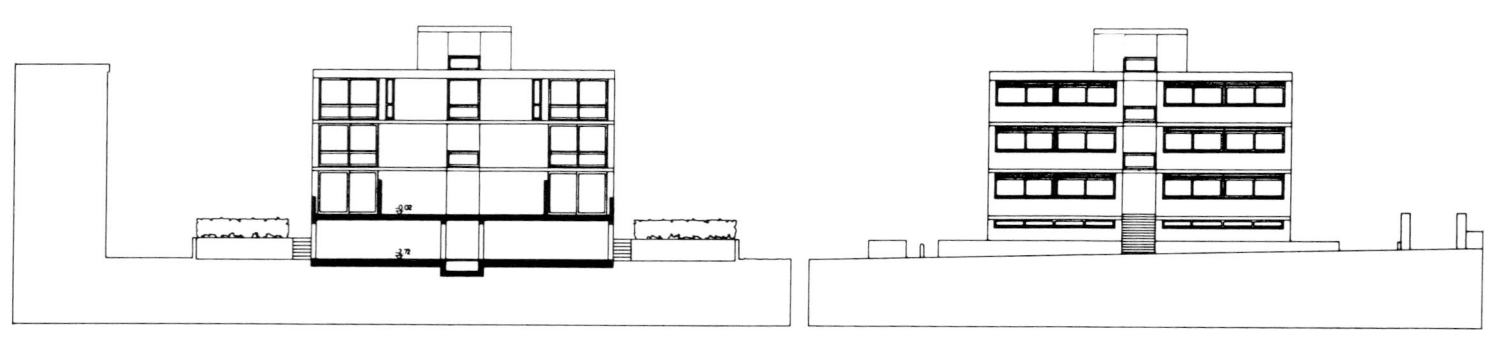

Querschnitt durch den gemeinsamen Hof mit unterirdischer Garage
Cross section through the shared courtyard with basement parking

Ostfassade / East façade

Grundriß Erdgeschoß / Ground floor plan

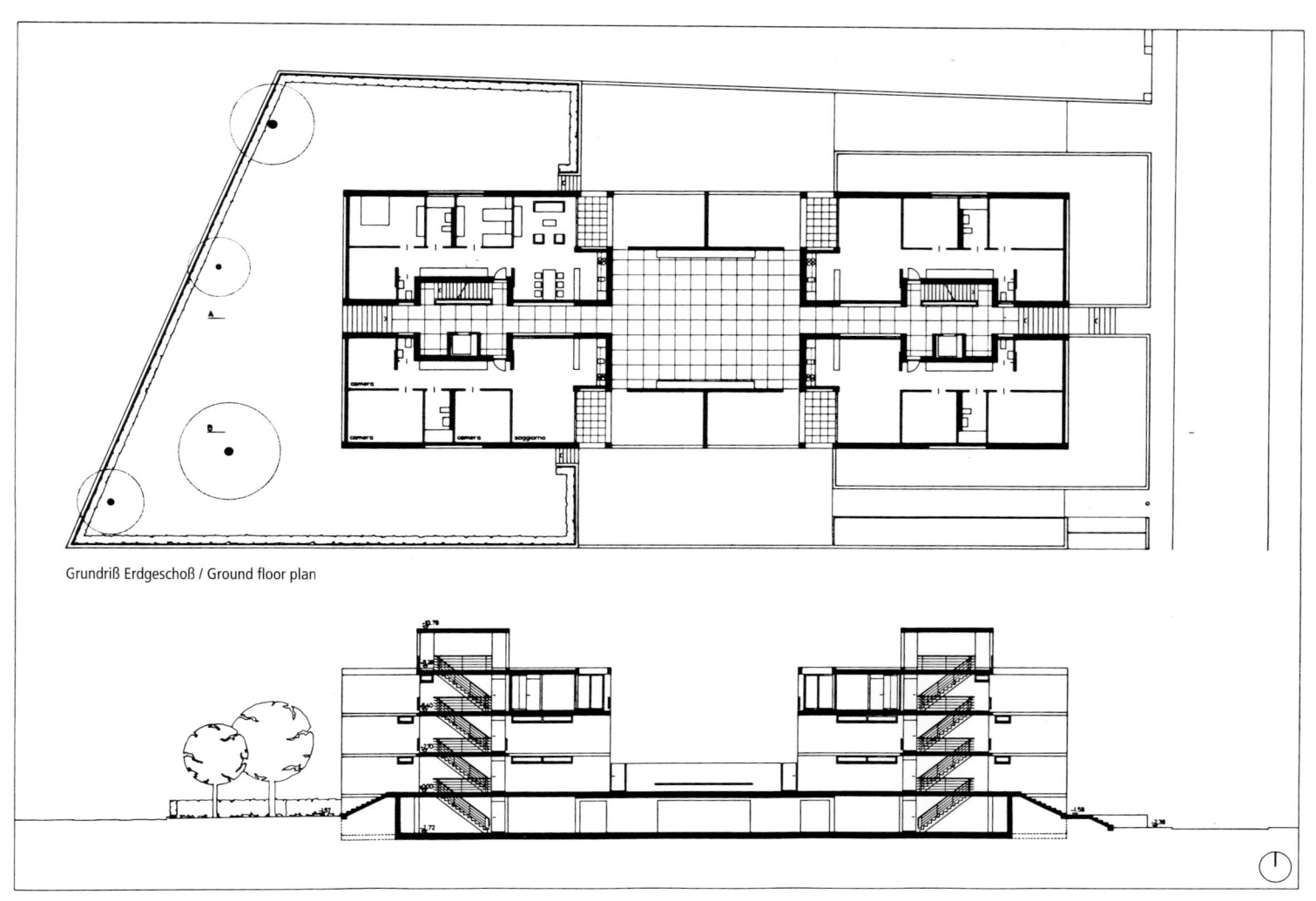

Längsschnitt durch die Treppe / Longitudinal section through stairs

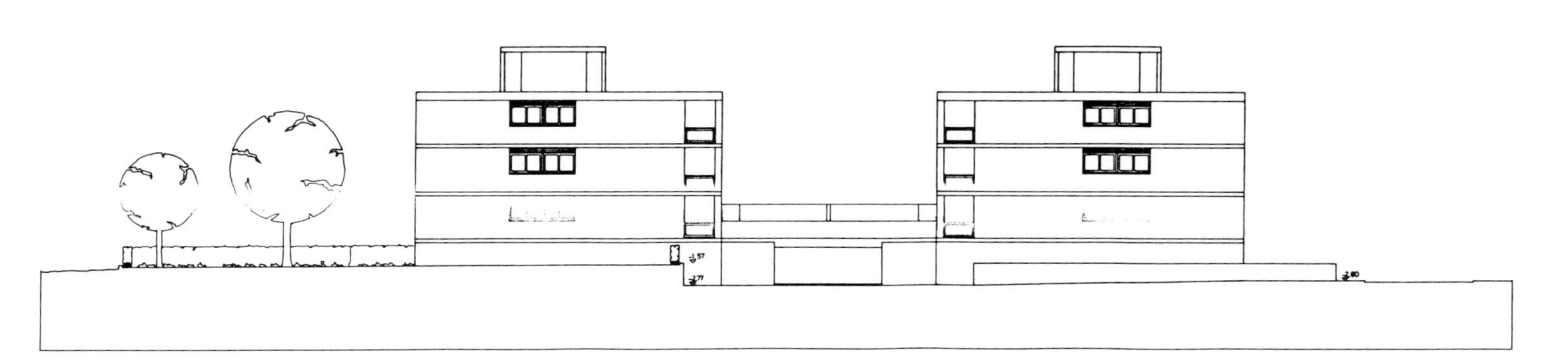

Südfassade / South façade

Gestaltung Weltausstellung «Expo 2000» in Hannover seit 1992

Die Aufgabe bestand darin, auf dem 200 Hektaren großen Gelände ein stadt- und landschaftsplanerisches Konzept für den gesamten Messebereich zu entwickeln, in das auch ein Weltausstellungsgelände als Zwischennutzung eingefügt werden kann. Das Programm umfaßte ferner die Projektierung von 20000 Wohnungen, eines Museums, eines Hotelzentrums sowie eines Stadions. Zwei gegebene örtliche Charakteristika bestimmen das Wettbewerbsprojekt: einerseits das existierende Messegelände, andererseits der nahegelegene Kronberg. Das Entwurfskonzept versucht bestehende, noch intakte Infrastrukturen zu erhalten, gleichzeitig aber neue qualitative Innen- und Außenräume zu schaffen. Besondere Bedeutung schenken die Architekten der Reduzierung des privaten Verkehrs. Die Prägnanz des Entwurfes beruht auf der Zusammenfassung aller Funktionsbereiche in drei geometrische Großformen. Nachdem Cavadini und Arnaboldi diesen Wettbewerb mit dem ersten Preis gewannen, wurden sie mit der Ausarbeitung eines Masterplanes beauftragt.

Design for the "Expo 2000" World Fair in Hanover Since 1992

The commission involved developing a town planning and landscaping concept for the whole exhibition site of 200 hectares, which was also to incorporate a World Fair ground as a temporary use. The programme also included the outline design for 20,000 apartments, a museum, a hotel centre and a stadium. Two given local characteristics determine the competition project: first, the existing exhibition ground, and second the nearby Kronberg. The design concept attempts to preserve existing infrastructures which are still intact, while at the same time creating qualitatively new indoor and outdoor spaces. The architects attach special importance to reducing private traffic. The design attains its incisiveness by bringing together all functional areas in three overriding geometrical forms. Having been awarded first prize in the competition, Cavadini and Arnaboldi were commissioned to elaborate a master plan.

Modell des Wettbewerbes / Competition model

Situation / Situation

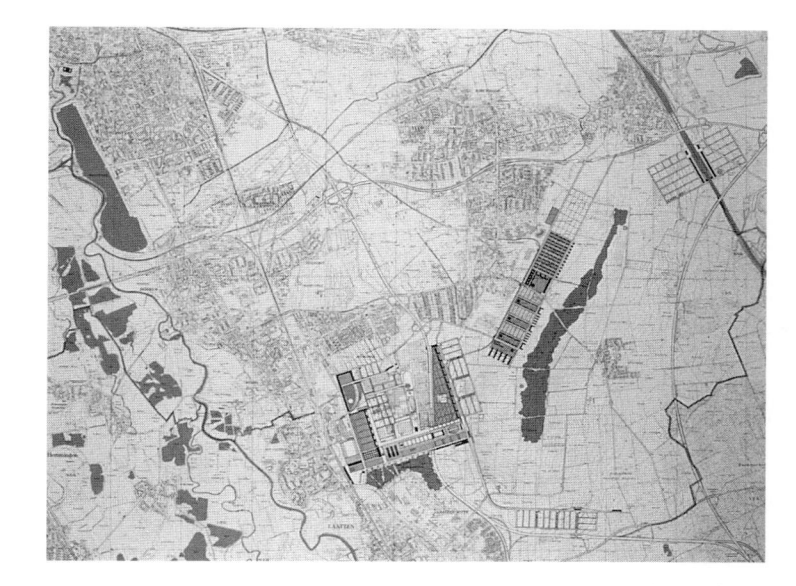

Situation / Situation

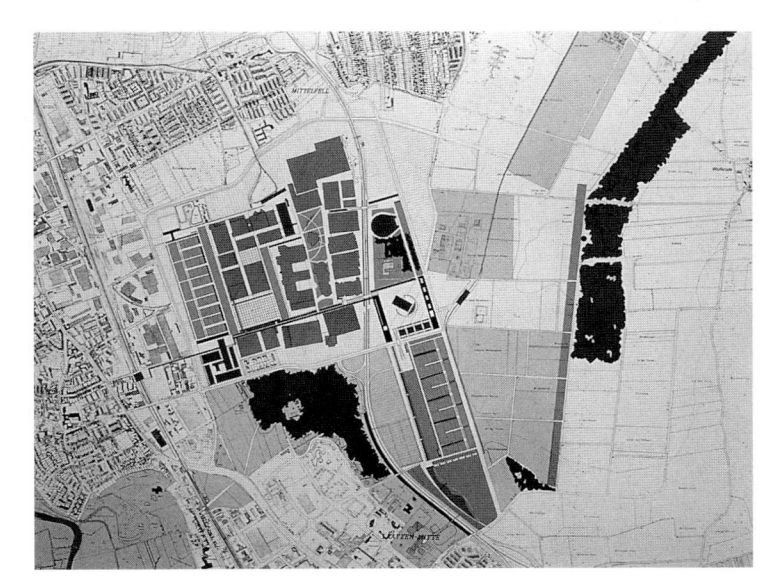

Masterplan / Masterplan

55

Jean-Pierre Dürig · Philippe Rämi, Zürich

Große Strukturen

Das architektonische Schaffen Jean-Pierre Dürigs und Philippe Rämis zeichnet sich durch eine auffallend große Anzahl Wettbewerbsprojekte im In- und Ausland aus. Unter den zahlreichen Arbeiten, an denen die beiden Architekten im Zeitraum von rund fünf Jahren teilnahmen und oftmals auch mit Preisen ausgezeichnet wurden, ist derzeit ein Projekt in Ausführung. Es handelt sich dabei um ein Bürohaus am Stölzlpark in Salzburg, das mit dem Thema weiterbauen an der Stadt umschrieben werden kann. Manchmal sind es ganz persönliche Eindrücke, Stimmungen, die ein Projekt bestimmen und ein Thema liefern. So war beispielsweise der individuelle Charakter der Röntgenstraße ausschlaggebend für den Entwurf des Röntgenareals in Zürich. Den Entwürfen oftmals gemeinsam sind die ordnenden, großen Strukturen, die den Projekten eine selbstverständliche Großzügigkeit verleihen. Innerhalb dieser scheinbar beliebig erweiterbaren Anlagen sind urbanistische und ortstypische Elemente – wie beispielsweise Höfe, Plätze, Passagen oder Wege – eingefügt, die den Maßstab zur umliegenden Situation herstellen. Die bewußte Offenheit, die für diese Arbeiten charakteristisch ist, beinhaltet die Chance zum sukzessiven Verfeinern, adäquaten Anpassen und beispielsweise zum Bestimmen der Funktion im letzten Augenblick.

Large-Scale Structures

The architectural output of Jean-Pierre Dürig and Philippe Rämi is distinguished by a strikingly large number of competition entries in and outside Switzerland. Among the many projects the two architects have been involved in over a period of about five years, often being awarded prizes, one is currently being executed. It is an office block beside the Stölzlpark in Salzburg, the theme of which can be summed up as "adding to the city's fabric". Sometimes it is quite personal impressions or moods that decide a project and provide its theme. For example, the unique character of the Röntgenstrasse was decisive for the design of the Röntgen site in Zurich. What the designs often have in common are their large-scale organizing structures, which endow projects with an unassuming generosity of proportions. Within these complexes, that seem capable of enlargement at will, planning features and elements typical of the locality – such as courtyards, squares, passages or footpaths – are inserted, providing a measure for the surrounding milieu. The deliberate openness which characterises these works gives an opportunity for successive refinement, for appropriate adaptation and, in some cases, for deciding a function at the last moment.

Biographie

Jean-Pierre Dürig

1958
Geboren in Winterthur.

1979–85
Architekturstudium an der ETH-Zürich.

1985
Diplom bei Professor Franz Oswald an der ETH-Zürich.

1982–87
Mitarbeit im Büro Ernst Gisel in Zürich.

1987
Eigenes Büro in Zürich.

Seit 1990
Gemeinsames Büro mit Philippe Rämi in Zürich.

Philippe Rämi

1955
Geboren in Zollikon.

1971–75
Lehre als Hochbauzeichner.

1976–78
Lehre als Möbelschreiner bei Freba in Weisslingen.

1971–80
Mitarbeit im Büro Claude Paillard in Zürich.

1981–90
Mitarbeit im Büro Ernst Gisel in Zürich.

Seit 1990
Gemeinsames Büro mit Jean-Pierre Dürig in Zürich.

Ausgewähltes Werkverzeichnis

1985
Wohnüberbauung in Zürich-Selnau
Wettbewerb.

1986
Kulturzentrum Gessnerallee in Zürich
Wettbewerb.

Fernmeldegebäude in Zürich-Binz
Wettbewerb, zweiter Preis.

1987
Wohnüberbauung Zweierstraße in Zürich
Wettbewerb.

Städtebaulicher Beitrag in La Chaux-de-Fonds (Kanton Neuenburg)
Ideenwettbewerb.

Sidi-Areal in Winterthur
Wettbewerb.

1988
Postbetriebsgebäude in St. Gallen
(1988–93)
Wettbewerb, erster Preis. Bauprojekt.

1989
Erweiterung Museum in Schaffhausen
Wettbewerb.

Gestaltung Bahnhofgebiet in Baden
(Kanton Aargau)
Wettbewerb.

Gestaltung Bahnhofgebiet in Brig
(Kanton Wallis)
Wettbewerb.

Gestaltung Seeufer in Flüelen
(Kanton Uri)
Wettbewerb.

Kongreß- und Kulturzentrum
in Luzern (1989–90)
Zweistufiger Wettbewerb. Einladung zur zweiten Stufe.

1990
Dorfplatzhaus in Horgen (Kanton Zürich)
Wettbewerb.

Umbau Mehrfamilienhaus in Zürich
Vorprojekt.

Röntgenareal in Zürich
Wettbewerb, erster Ankauf.

Wohnsiedlung in Zürich-Affoltern
Wettbewerb.

Gemeindezentrum und Wohnüberbauung in Winkel (Kanton Zürich)
Wettbewerb.

Malatelier in Zürich-Oerlikon
Magdalenenstraße 9
Ausgeführtes Projekt.

1991
Volkart-Areal in Winterthur
Wettbewerb.

Europan in Alcalà de Henares (Spanien)
Wettbewerb.

Erweiterung Technikum in Rapperswil
(Kanton St. Gallen)
Wettbewerb, zweiter Preis.

Altersheim in Fällanden (Kanton Zürich)
Wettbewerb. Erster Ankauf.

Försterschule und Pflegeheim in Lyss
(Kanton Bern)
Ideenwettbewerb, erster Ankauf.

Wohnsiedlung in Zürich-Eichrain
Wettbewerb.

Umnutzung Industrieareal in Zürich-Oerlikon
Ideenwettbewerb, vierter Preis.

Gestaltung Bahnhofgebiet in Frauenfeld
(Kanton Thurgau; 1991–92)
Wettbewerb, erster Preis. Vorprojekt.

Wohnsiedlung Färbereiareal in Zofingen
(Kanton Aargau; 1991–93)
Wettbewerb, erster Preis. Vorprojekt.

Bürohaus am Stölzlpark in Salzburg
(1991–95)
Wettbewerb, erster Preis.
Ausgeführtes Projekt.

1992
SBB-Station in Zürich-Seebach
Studie.

SBB-Station in Zürich-Affoltern
Studie.

Gestaltung Bundesplatz in Bern
Wettbewerb.

Wohnsiedlung in Zollikon
(Kanton Zürich)
Wettbewerb.

Städtebaulicher Beitrag für Karlsruhe
Internationaler Ideenwettbewerb.

Zentrumsüberbauung Zollikerberg
(Kanton Zürich)
Wettbewerb, erster Ankauf.

Gestaltung Bahnhofgebiet in Dübendorf
(Kanton Zürich; 1992–93)
Testplanung.

Universität in Nikosia (Zypern; 1992–93)
Internationaler zweistufiger Ideenwettbewerb, erster Preis.

1993
Europan in Madrid
Wettbewerb.

Regierungsviertel in Berlin
Internationaler Ideenwettbewerb.

Gewerbe- und Dienstleistungsbetriebe
in Gümligen (Kanton Bern)
Wettbewerb, Ankauf.

Berufsschulhaus Schützenareal in Zürich
Wettbewerb, dritter Preis.

1994
Gestaltung Innenstadt in Brig
(Kanton Wallis)
Wettbewerb.

Wohnüberbauung in Biel-Madretsch
(Kanton Bern)
Studienauftrag.

Wiederaufbau der Souks in Beirut
Internationaler Ideenwettbewerb,
lobende Erwähnung.

Oper in Cardiff
Wettbewerb.

Umbau Wohnhaus Mittelbergsteig
in Zürich
Konzeptstudie.

Umnutzung Industriegebiet Alpi
in Salzburg (1994–unbestimmt)
Vorprojekt.

Ladenumbau in Zürich (1994–95)
Haldenbachstraße 2
Ausgeführtes Projekt.

Biography

Jean-Pierre Dürig

1958
Born in Winterthur

1979–85
Studied architecture at the ETH Zurich

1985
Graduated with diploma under
Prof. Franz Oswald at the ETH Zurich

1982–87
Worked at the Ernst Gisel architectural
office in Zurich

1987
Own architectural office in Zurich

Since 1990
Joint architectural office
with Philippe Rämi in Zurich.

Philippe Rämi

1955
Born in Zollikon

1971–75
Trained as architectural draughtsman

1976–78
Trained as cabinet maker
at Freba in Weisslingen

1971–80
Worked at the Claude Paillard
architectural office in Zurich

1981–90
Worked at the Ernst Gisel
architectural office in Zurich

Since 1990
Joint architectural office
with Jean-Pierre Dürig in Zurich.

Selected list of Work

1985
Residential development in Zurich-Selnau
Competition.

1986
Gessnerallee cultural centre in Zurich
Competition.
Telecommunications building
in Zurich-Binz
Competition, second prize.

1987
Residential development on
Zweierstrasse in Zurich
Competition.
Town planning contribution
in La Chaux-de-Fonds
(Canton of Neuchâtel)
Ideas competition.
Sidi site in Winterthur
Competition.

1988
Post office building St. Gallen (1988–93)
Competition, first prize. Final project.

1989
Museum extension in Schaffhausen
Competition.
Design of station district in Baden
(Canton of Aargau)
Competition.
Design of station district in Brig
(Canton of Valais)
Competition.
Lake shore planning in Flüelen
(Canton of Uri)
Competition.
Congress and cultural centre
in Lucerne (1989–90)
Two-stage competition. Invitation
to second stage.

1990
House on village square in Horgen
(Canton of Zurich)
Competition.
Conversion of multiple dwelling in Zurich
Preliminary project.
Röntgen site in Zurich
Competition, first purchased design.
Residential estate in Zurich-Affoltern
Competition.
Parish centre and residential
development in Winkel
(Canton of Zurich)
Competition.
Painter's studio in Zurich-Oerlikon
Magdalenenstrasse 9
Completed project.

1991
Volkart site in Winterthur
Competition.
Europan in Alcalà de Henares (Spain)
Competition.
Extension to College of Technology
in Rapperswil (Canton of St. Gallen)
Competition, second prize.
Old people's home in Fällanden
(Canton of Zurich)
Competition, first purchased design.
Forestry school and nursing home
in Lyss (Canton of Berne)
Ideas competition,
first purchased design.
Residential estate in Zurich-Eichrain
Competition.
Redevelopment of industrial site
in Zurich-Oerlikon
Ideas competition, fourth prize.
Design for station district in Frauenfeld
(Canton of Thurgau; 1991–92)
Competition, first prize.
Preliminary project.
Residential estate on dye-works site
in Zofingen (Canton of Aargau; 1991–93)
Competition, first prize.
Preliminary project.
Office building by Stölzlpark
in Salzburg (1991–95)
Competition, first prize.
Completed project.

1992
SBB station in Zurich-Seebach
Study.
SBB Station in Zurich-Affoltern
Study.
Design for Bundesplatz in Berne
Competition.
Residential estate in Zollikon
(Canton of Zurich)
Competition.
Town planning proposal for Karlsruhe
International ideas competition.
Development of centre of Zollikerberg
(Canton of Zurich)
Competition, first purchased design.
Design for station district in Dübendorf
(Canton of Zurich; 1992–93)
Test plan.
University in Nicosia (Cyprus; 1992–93)
International two-stage ideas
competition, first prize.

1993
Europan in Madrid
Competition.
Government quarter in Berlin
International ideas competition.
Commercial premises in Gümligen
(Canton of Berne)
Competition, purchased design.
Vocational school on Schützen site
in Zurich
Competition, third prize.

1994
Design for town centre of Brig
(Canton of Valais)
Competition.
Residential development
in Biel-Madretsch (Canton of Berne)
Study commission.
Rebuilding of souks in Beirut
International ideas competition,
honourable mention.
Opera house in Cardiff
Competition.
Conversion of residence at
Mittelbergsteig in Zurich
Concept study.
Redevelopment of industrial area
at Alpi in Salzburg (1994–)
Preliminary project.
Shop conversion in Zurich (1994–95)
Haldenbachstrasse 2
Completed project.

Röntgenareal in Zürich 1990

Die Röntgenstraße, eine der schönsten Straßen Zürichs, strahlt durch ihren sanften Bogen, ihre Dimension sowie durch den Rhythmus der Häuser und Kreuzungen eine für diese Stadt einzigartige Großzügigkeit aus. Diesen Charakter versuchten die Architekten in ihrem Projekt wiederzugeben: eine kammartige, auf der orthogonalen Geometrie aufbauende Bebauung mit inneren Höfen ist ergänzt durch ein langes, schmales Volumen mit einem vorgelagerten Garten. Die an der Straße beziehungsweise an den Geleisen liegenden Baukörper sind öffentlichen Funktionen, Läden, Büros, Restaurant, vorbehalten, während die eher innenliegenden, geschützen Räume dem Wohnen dienen. Auffallend ist die strenge, konsequente, klare und nüchterne Architektursprache.

Röntgen Site in Zurich 1990

Through its gentle curve, its dimensions and the rhythm of its buildings and intersections, the Röntgenstrasse, one of the finest streets in Zurich, gives a feeling of spaciousness unique in the city. The architects have tried to reproduce this character in their project. A comb-like development with interposed courtyards, based on a right-angle concept, is supplemented by a long, narrow building with a garden at the front. The buildings adjacent to the street or the tracks are set aside for public functions, shops, offices, a restaurant, while the more internal and protected spaces are used for residential purposes. The severe, clear, sober and logical idiom is a striking feature.

Modell der Wettbewerbseingabe, deren vorgeschlagene Bebauung auf der orthogonalen Geometrie aufbaut
Competition model for a development based on orthogonal geometry

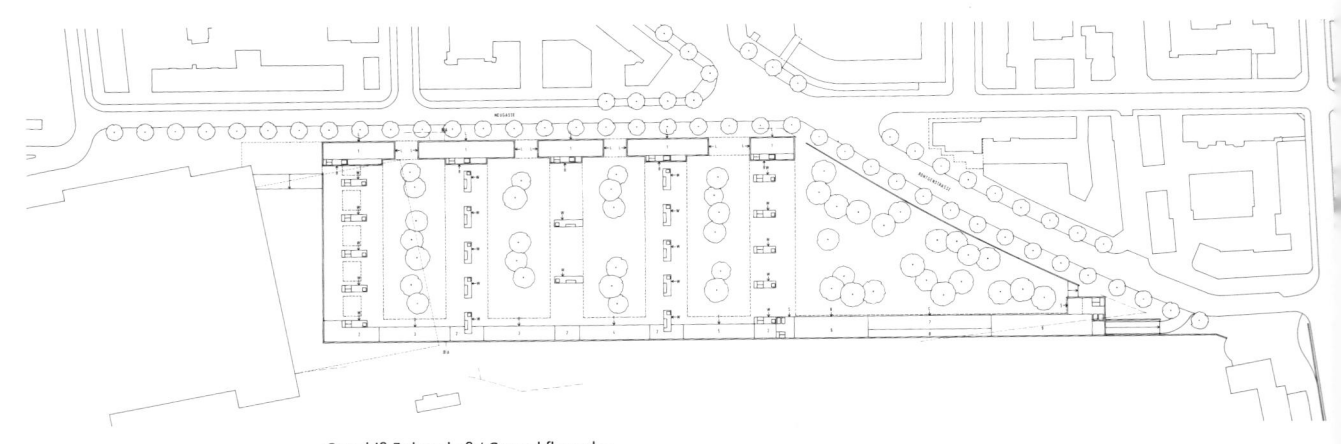

Grundriß Erdgeschoß / Ground floor plan

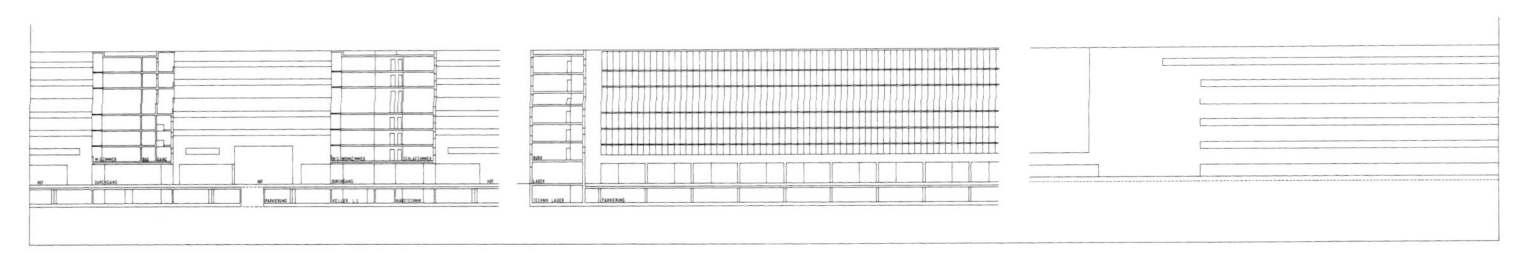

Längsschnitt durch die kammartig angeordneten Trakte
Longitudinal section through comb-like development

Querschnitt durch den längsgerichteten Baukörper
Cross section through the longitudinal building volume

Nordfassade / North façade

Wohnsiedlung in Zürich-Eichrain 1991

Die komplexe Problematik der gegebenen Situation – der Lärm der Autobahn, die Neigung des Geländes, die Form des Grundstückes und die Besonnung – finden ihren Ausdruck in zwei einbündigen, durch Laubengänge erschlossenen, geknickten und dem Hangverlauf entsprechend schrägen Baukörpern, die sich zur freien Landschaft hin öffnen. Ein im Grundriß dreieckförmiges Volumen, das Werkstätten enthält, verbindet die beiden Bauten. Um die Sicht möglichst zu gewährleisten ist das hintere Volumen sechsgeschossig, während das vordere drei Geschosse aufweist.

Residential Estate in Zurich-Eichrain 1991

The complex problems posed by the given situation – noise from the motorway, the sloping site, the shape of the plot and the direction of the sunlight – find expression in two angled, interlinked, linear blocks, with access by walkways, arranged diagonally to accommodate the slope, and opening towards the countryside. A building with a triangular floor plan, containing workshops, links the two blocks. To give the best possible view the rear block has six storeys while the front one has three.

Modell der Wettbewerbseingabe mit der umliegenden Situation
Competition model with surroundings

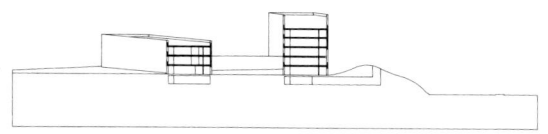

Querschnitt durch die beiden längsgerichteten Volumen
Cross section through both longitudinal volumes

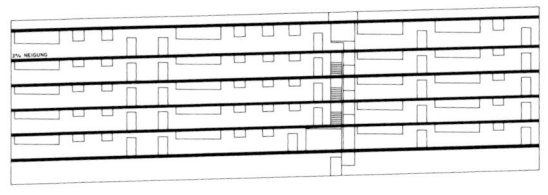

Längsschnitt durch den hinteren, sechsgeschossigen Baukörper
Longitudinal section through the six-storey volume at the rear

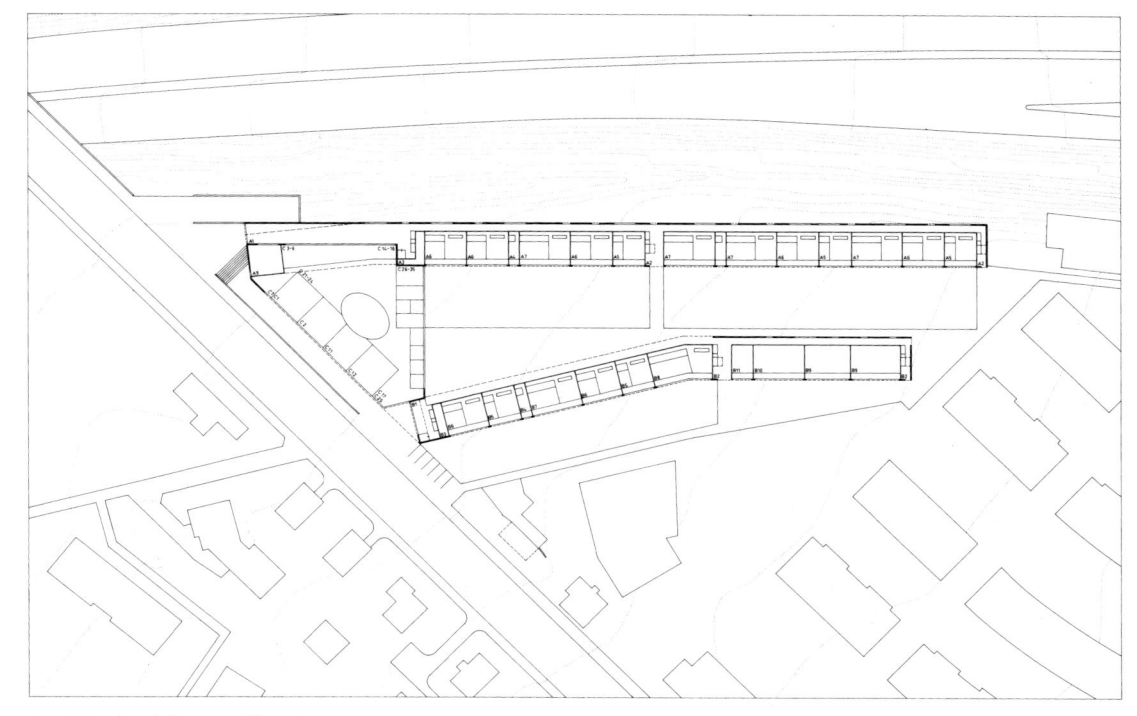

Grundriß Erdgeschoß / Ground floor plan

Umnutzung Industrieareal in Zürich-Oerlikon 1991

Vor rund 100 Jahren wurde Zürich zum ersten Mal erweitert, Seefeld, Wiedikon, Aussersihl und das Industrieareal sind klassische Stadterweiterungen. Dieses Bebauungsmuster wurde in großzügigeren Dimensionen – im Sinne der Röntgenstraße – für das neue Projekt übernommen: die Höfe werden zu Gärten, die Straßen zu Alleen. Die bestehenden Industriebauten werden integriert. Die Baufluchten, Bauhöhen und Gebäudetiefen werden bestimmt, die Grundstücke parzelliert und die öffentlichen Nutzungen festgelegt. Vom Maßstab her hebt sich die vorgeschlagene Umnutzung deutlich von ihrer Umgebung ab und bringt damit zum Ausdruck, daß es sich um eine erneute Erweiterung, um eine zeitgemäße Entwicklung handelt.

Redevelopment of Industrial Site in Zurich-Oerlikon 1991

Zurich was enlarged for the first time about 100 years ago; Seefeld, Wiedikon, Aussersihl and the industrial site are typical urban expansion zones. This development pattern was taken over on a large scale – in the same way as for the Röntgenstrasse – for the new project: the courtyards become gardens, the streets avenues. The existing industrial buildings have been integrated. The building lines, the heights and depths of buildings have been defined, the plots parcelled out and the public utilities decided. In terms of scale the proposed redevelopment is set off sharply from its surroundings, thereby expressing the fact that this is a new extension and a development in keeping with the times.

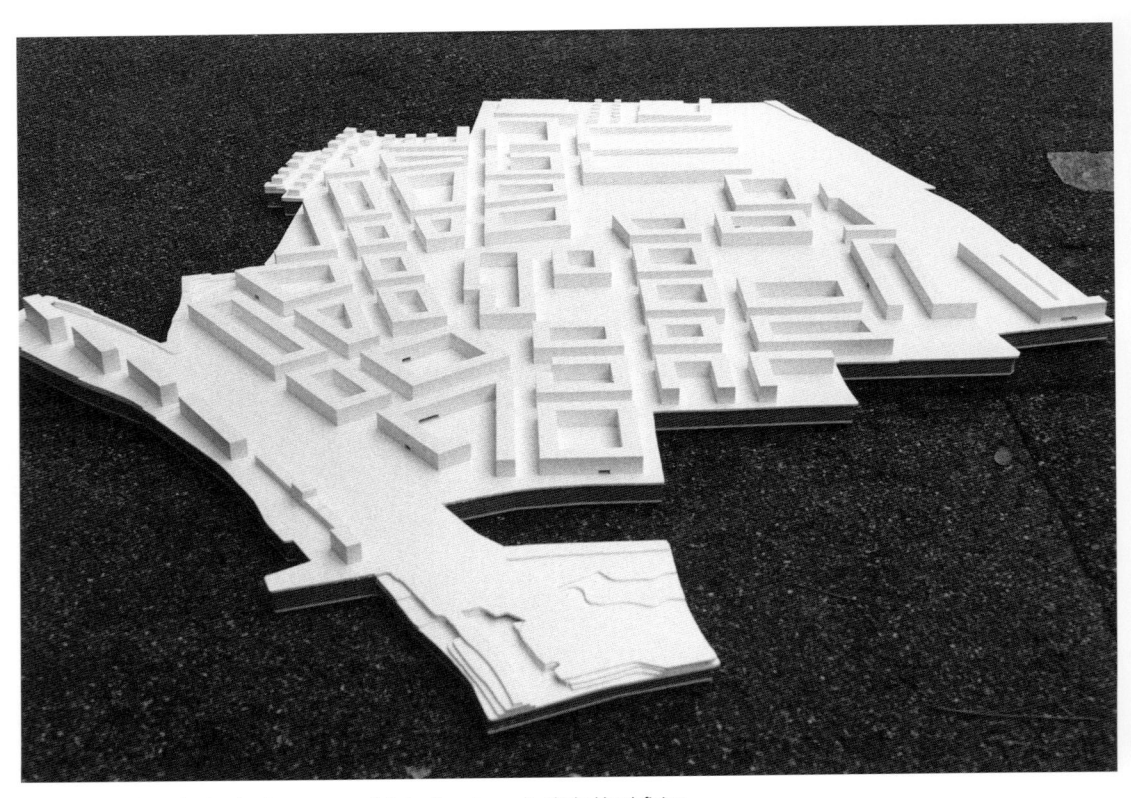

Modell der Wettbewerbseingabe, deren neue, großzügige Umnutzung die Blöcke klar definiert
Competition model showing clear remodelling of the blocks

Verschiedene perspektivische Ansichten innerhalb der vorgeschlagenen Struktur
Various perspective elevations inside the proposed structure

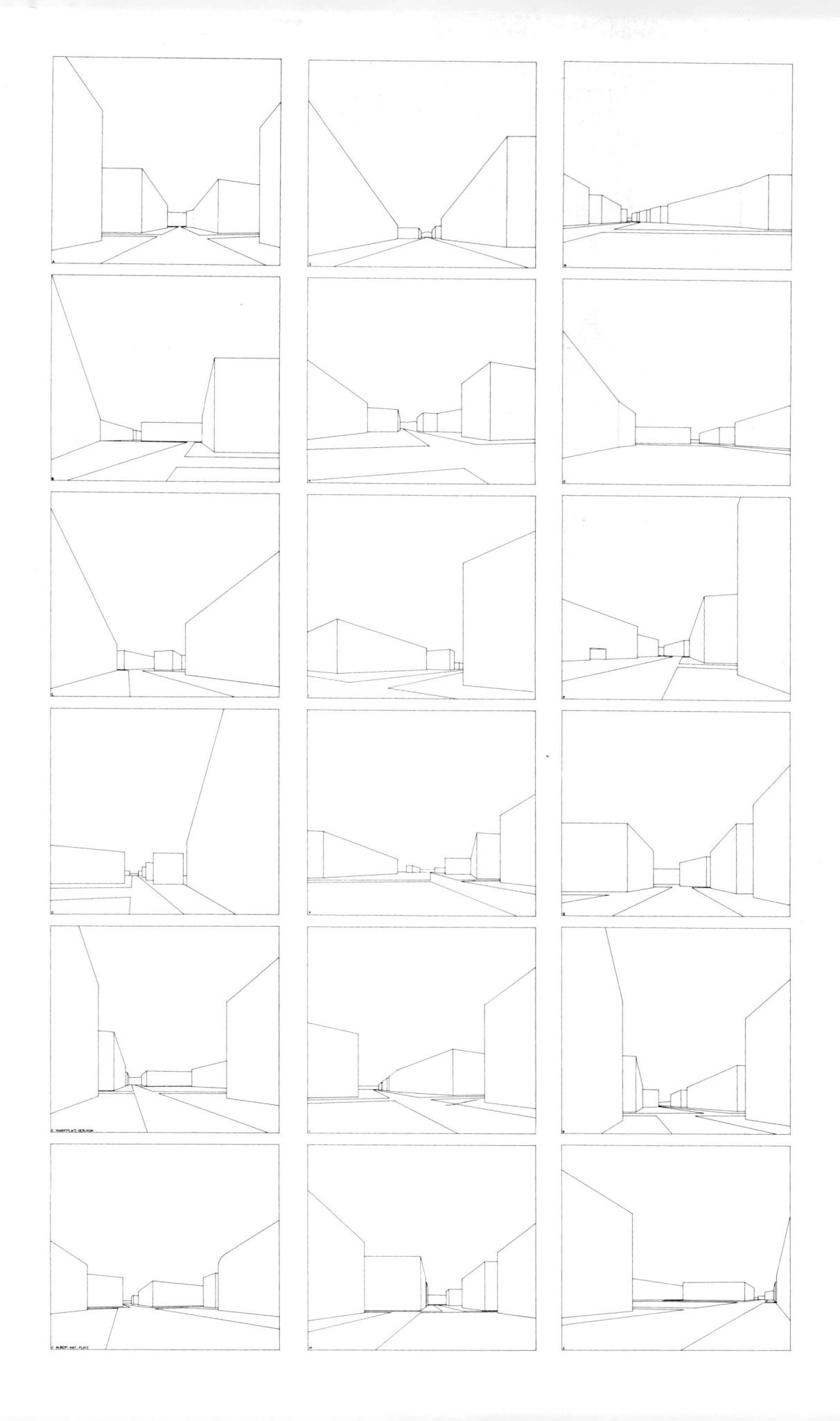

Berufsschulhaus Schützenareal in Zürich 1993

Der Gesamtcharakter der wunderbaren Schulhäuser aus der Zeit nach der Jahrhundertwende in Zürich, wie beispielsweise das Schulhaus an der Ämtlerstraße in Wiedikon, an der Ligusterstraße in Oerlikon, an der Zeppelinstraße auf dem Milchbuck oder an der Limmatstraße im Industriequartier, war prägend für den Entwurf des Berufsschulhauses Schützenareal. In einer freien kompositorischen Anordnung faßten die Architekten Eingang, Halle, Treppe, Turnhallen, Aula, Schulzimmer und Nebennutzungen zu einer Einheit zusammen. Um den Straßenraum zu betonen, ist das Hauptvolumen direkt an die Straße plaziert. Rückwärtig ist die Halle als Annex weitergeführt. Sie ist von der Aula und verschiedenen Ausstellungsräumen flankiert. Bemerkenswert ist die einfache Gliederung der gesamten Anlage.

Vocational School on the Schützen Site in Zurich 1993

The general character of the wonderful, turn-of-the-century school buildings in Zurich, such as the schools on Ämtlerstrasse in Wiedikon, on Ligusterstrasse in Oerlikon, on Zeppelinstrasse at Milchbuck or on Limmatstrasse in the industrial district, decisively shaped the design for the vocational training school on the Schützen site. In a freely composed arrangement the architects have brought together the entrance, vestibule, staircase, gymnasia, hall, classrooms and ancillary functions in a single unit. To emphasise the street frontage, the main building borders directly on the road. The vestibule is continued to the rear as an annexe. It is flanked by the hall and various exhibition rooms. The whole complex is of striking simplicity.

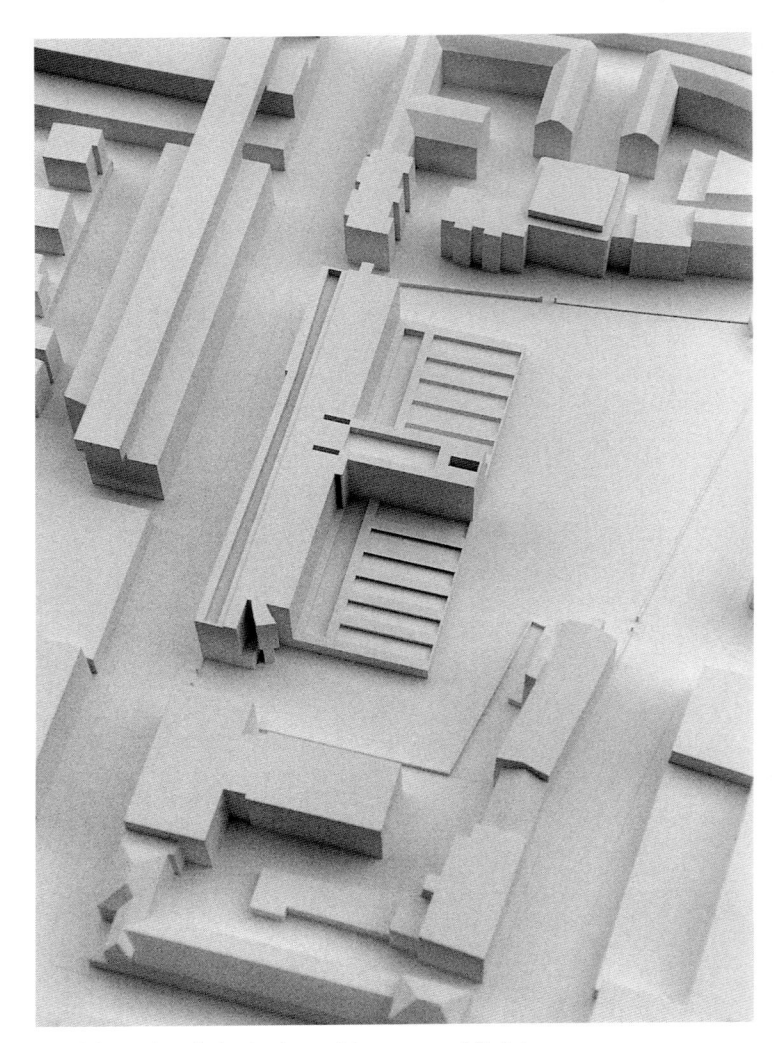

Modell des Wettbewerbseingabe, deren präzis zusammengefaßte Anlage eine kompakte Einheit bildet
Competition model showing compact, precise building complex

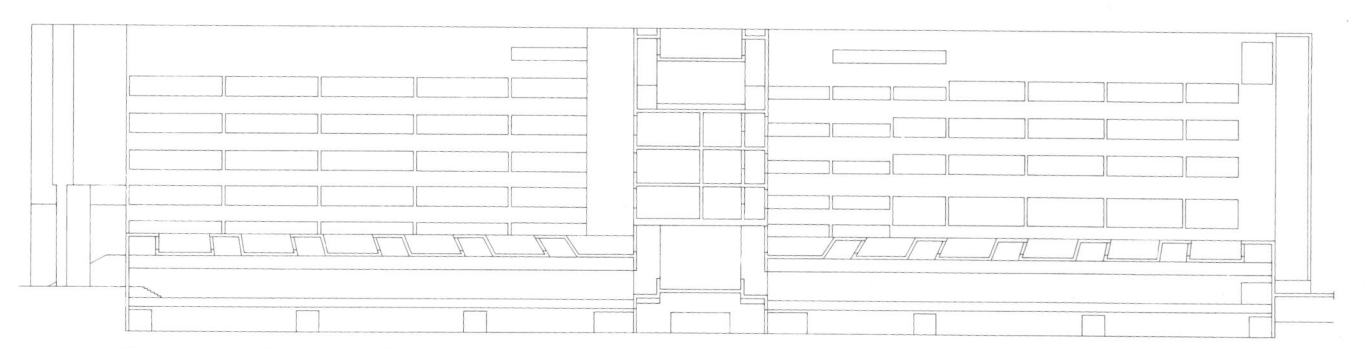

Längsschnitt durch die Aula und durch den Ausstellungsraum / Longitudinal section through the hall and exhibition room

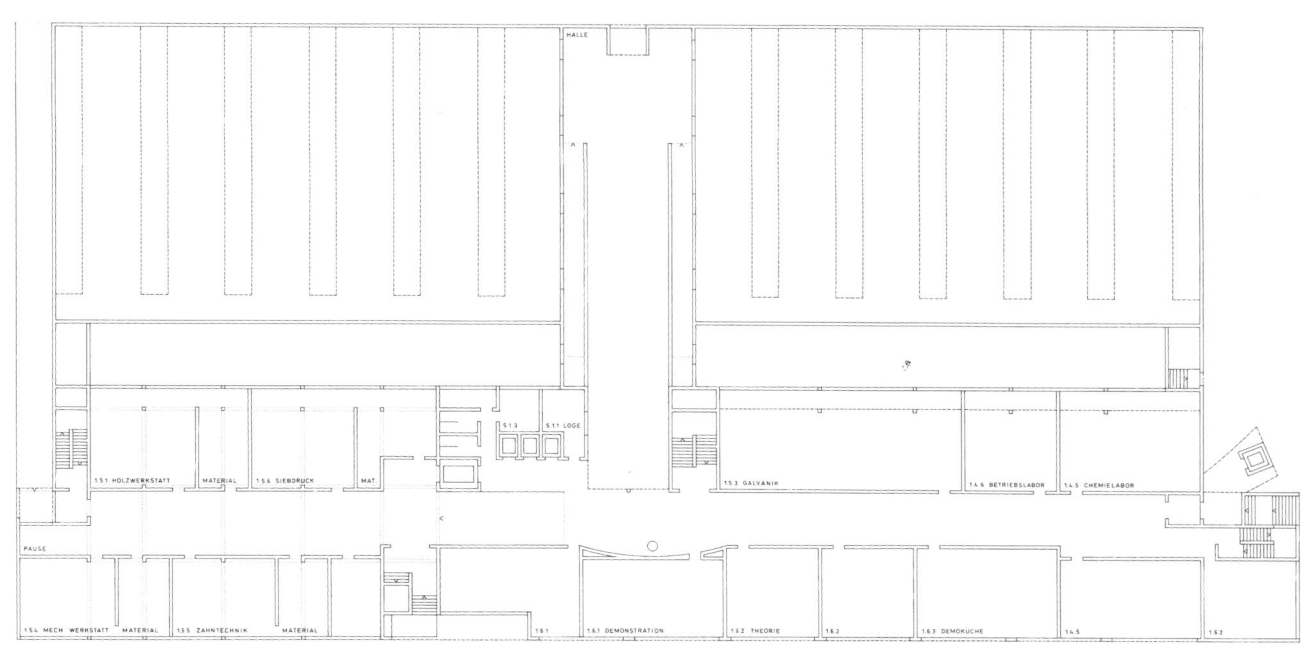

Grundriß Erdgeschoß / Ground floor plan

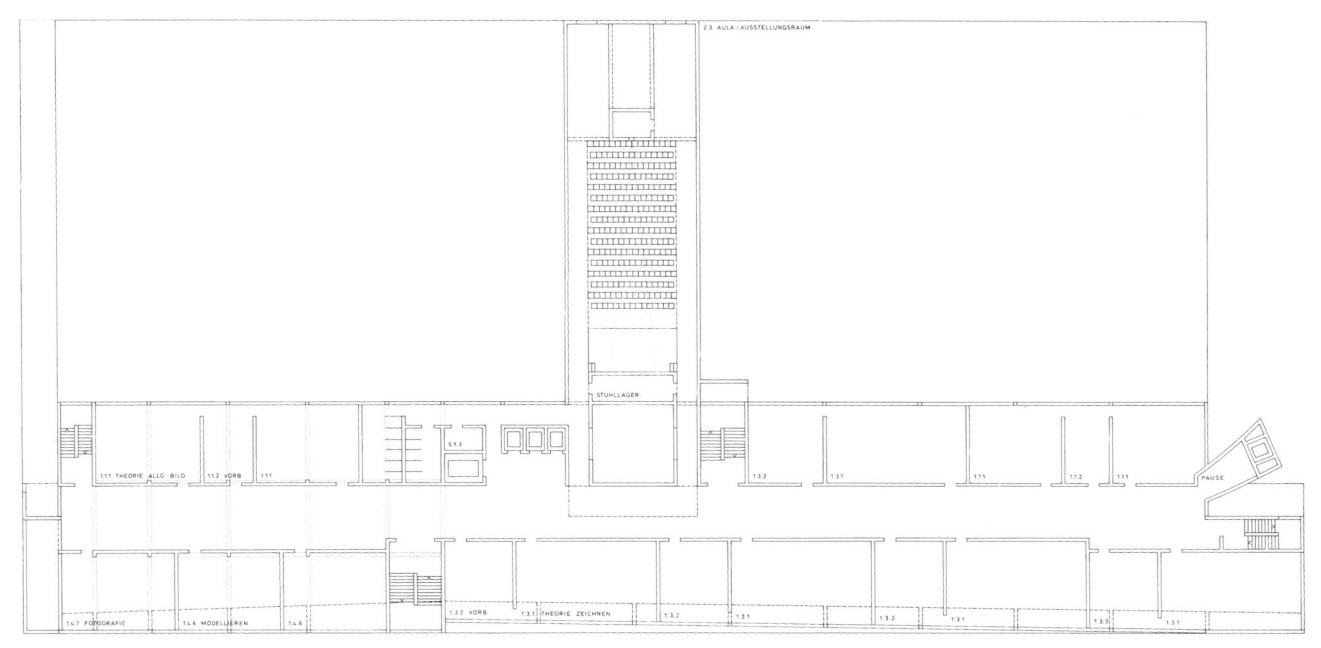

Grundriß erstes Obergeschoß / First floor plan

Rolf Furrer · François Fasnacht, Basel

Städtische Details

Es mag verwegen erscheinen, das Werk von Rolf Furrer und François Fasnacht mit der Tatsache in Verbindung zu bringen, daß in einer Welt zunehmender Widersprüche die Dinge wieder vermehrt im Detail liegen. Und doch bestätigt sich dieser erste Gesamteindruck auch nach eingehender Auseinandersetzung, und er kann deshalb als typisches Charakteristikum ihrer Denk- und Arbeitsweise angesehen werden. In ihrer Tätigkeit legen die beiden Architekten auch bei kleinsten Ausführungen großen Wert auf die Details und damit auf das Material und die Konstruktion. Diesem Anliegen werden sie zugleich in ästhetischer wie auch in funktionaler Hinsicht gerecht. Erkennbar ist diese Eigenheit besonders gut an den verschiedenen Bus- und Tramwartehallen in Basel. Ihre meist in der Stadt auffindbaren Realisationen bestechen durch die unprätentiöse Erscheinung und den gezielten Eingriff und lassen sich deshalb als städtische Details bezeichnen. Furrer und Fasnachts architektonische Haltung kann mit einem Gedanken Umberto Ecos umschrieben werden: «Die Abneigung, zwischen Ästhetik und Funktionalität zu unterscheiden, führt zu einer Einfügung des Ästhetischen in alle Lebensvorgänge; und sie ordnet weniger das Schöne dem Guten oder dem Nützlichen unter, als sie das Gute und das Nützliche dem Schönen unterstellt.»

Urban Details

It may seem audacious to bring Rolf Furrer's and François Fasnacht's work into relationship with the fact that, in a world of growing contradictions, meaning resides more and more in the details. Yet this first impression is confirmed by in-depth study, and can thus be seen as a typical characteristic of their mode of thinking and working. In even their smallest projects the two architects attach great importance to details, and therefore to materials and methods of construction. They satisfy this concern both aesthetically and functionally. This quality is seen especially clearly in the various waiting halls for buses and trams in Basle. The charm of their productions, mostly to be found in towns, lies in their unpretentious aspect and directness of approach. They can thus be described as details of the urban landscape. Furrer and Fasnacht's architectural attitude can be summed up by an idea of Umberto Eco's: "A reluctance to distinguish between aesthetics and functionality leads to the infusion of the aesthetic into all life processes; and this does not subject the beautiful to the good or useful so much as it subordinates the good and useful to the beautiful."

Biographie

Rolf Furrer

1955
Geboren in Basel.

1975–81
Architekturstudium an der ETH-Zürich und ETH-Lausanne.

1981
Diplom bei Professor Dolf Schnebli an der ETH-Zürich.

1981
Mitarbeit im Büro Silvia Gmür in Basel.

1982–83
Mitarbeit im Büro Marbach + Rüegg in Zürich.

1984–85
Mitarbeit im Büro Klaus Dolder in Zürich.

1985–86
Assistent bei Gastdozentin Silvia Gmür an der ETH-Zürich.

Seit 1988
Gemeinsames Büro mit François Fasnacht in Basel.

François Fasnacht

1957
Geboren in Zürich.

1980–86
Architekturstudium an der ETH-Zürich.

1986
Diplom bei Professor Dolf Schnebli an der ETH-Zürich.

1986
Mitarbeit im Büro Suter + Suter AG in Basel.

1987
Mitarbeit im Büro DeMartini-Fasnacht in New York.

1986-89
Assistent bei Professor Rolf Schaal an der ETH-Zürich.

Seit 1988
Gemeinsames Büro mit Rolf Furrer in Basel.

Auszeichnungen
1993
Eidgenössisches Kunststipendium.

Ausgewähltes Werkverzeichnis

1989
Tram- und Buswartehallen für die Basler Verkehrsbetriebe, Basel (1986–94)
Ausgeführte Projekte.
Normalwartehalle: Theaterplatz (1986);
Zusammenarbeit mit Peter Stiner, Basel.
Doppelhalle: Schützenhaus (1990)
Schmaltyp: Giba-Geigy (1992)
Rundtyp: Lachenweg in Riehen (1992)
Standortspezifisch: Kohlenberg (1991–93), Schifflände (1994), Riehen Dorf (1994), Hoffmann-La Roche (1994).

Helikopterbasis der REGA auf dem Kantonsspital Basel-Stadt (1989–91)
Bauprojekt.

Umbau und Sanierung Zollamt Lysbüchel in Basel (1989–92)
Elsäßerstraße 265
Ausgeführtes Projekt.

Einbau Informatikabteilung im ZLF Kantonsspital Basel-Stadt (1989–93)
Hebelstrasse 20
Ausgeführtes Projekt. Zusammenarbeit mit Kurt Nussbaumer, Basel.

1990
Amtsplatzüberdachung mit Inselpavillon, Zoll Lysbüchel in Basel
Bauprojekt.

Clubhaus Golf- und Countryclub in Hagental (Frankreich)
Bauprojekt.

Oberflächengestaltung und Verkehrsführung der Großbasler Innenstadt in Basel
Studienauftrag.

1991
Umbau und Erweiterung Einfamilienhaus in Bottmingen (Kanton Baselland)
Flurweg 8
Ausgeführtes Projekt.

Gestaltung und Verkehrsführung Wettsteinplatz in Basel
Studienauftrag.

Umbau und Erweiterung des Lützelhofes, Berufsfeuerwehr in Basel (1991–94)
Bauprojekt.

Augenklinik Polykliniktrakt 1 des Inselspitals in Bern (1991–94)
Arbeitsgemeinschaft mit I + B Architekten, Bern.
Ausgeführtes Projekt.

1992
Umbau Baukasse des Baudepartements in Basel
Münsterplatz 11
Ausgeführtes Projekt.

Blockheizkraftwerk-Kaminanlage Schulhaus Neubad in Basel
Kaltbrunnen Promenade
Ausgeführtes Projekt.

Ausbaupotential Schulanlagen in Basel
Studienauftrag.

Sanierung und Erweiterung der historischen Bauten des Baudepartements Basel-Stadt
Studienauftrag. Bauprojekt.

Um- und Neubau Bürohaus «Pro Optik» in Basel (1992–93)
Steinenvorstadt 62
Ausgeführtes Projekt.

1993
Veranda an ein Wohnhaus in Basel
Mittlere Straße 43
Ausgeführtes Projekt.

Fotoatelier in Allschwil (Kanton Baselland)
Bauprojekt.

1994
Fassadensanierung Villa in Oberrohrdorf (Kanton Aargau)
Haufroosstraße 11
Ausgeführtes Projekt.

Helikopterlandeplatz auf dem Kantonsspital in Basel
Bauprojekt.

Umbau Zöllnergebäude in Biel-Benken (Kanton Baselland)
Bauprojekt.

SBB Zentralstellwerk Personenbahnhof Basel
Studienauftrag.

Centre PasquART, Erweiterung Kunsthalle in Biel (Kanton Bern)
Studienauftrag.

Bürogebäude der Balimpex in Muttenz (Kanton Baselland)
Bauprojekt.

Biography

Rolf Furrer

1955
Born in Basle

1975–81
Studied architecture at the ETH, Zurich and the ETH Lausanne

1981
Graduated with diploma under Prof. Dolf Schnebli at the ETH Zurich

1981
Worked at the Silvia Gmür architectural office in Basle

1982–83
Worked at the Marbach & Rüegg architectural office in Zurich

1984–86
Worked at the Klaus Dolder architectural office in Zurich

1985–86
Assistant to visiting lecturer Silvia Gmür at the ETH Zurich

Since 1988
Joint architectural office with François Fasnacht in Basle.

François Fasnacht

1957
Born in Zurich

1980–86
Studied architecture at the ETH Zurich

1986
Graduated with diploma under Prof. Dolf Schnebli at the ETH Zurich

1986
Worked at the Suter + Suter AG architectural office in Basle

1987
Worked at the DeMartini-Fasnacht architectural office in New York

1986–89
Assistant to Prof. Rolf Schaal at the ETH Zurich

Since 1988
Joint architectural office with Rolf Furrer in Basle.

Awards

1993
Swiss state art scholarship

Selected list of work

1989
Tram and bus waiting halls for Basle transport services, Basle (1986–94)
Completed projects.
Standard waiting hall: Theaterplatz (1986); in collaboration with Peter Stiner, Basle.
Double hall: Schützenhaus (1990)
Narrow type: Ciba-Geigy (1992)
Round type: Lachenweg in Riehen (1992)
Location-specific: Kohlenberg (1991–93), Schifflände (1994), Riehen Dorf (1994), Hoffmann-La Roche (1994).

REGA helicopter pad on Kantonsspital, City of Basle (1989–91)
Final project.

Conversion and refurbishment of customs office at Lysbüchel in Basle (1989–92)
Elsässerstrasse 265
Completed project.

Incorporation of data processing department in the ZLF Kantonsspital, Basel-Stadt (1989–93)
Hebelstrasse 20
Completed project. Collaboration with Kurt Nussbaumer, Basle.

1990
Roof over Amtsplatz with island pavilion, customs post at Lysbüchel in Basle
Final project.

Clubhouse for golf and country club in Hagental (France)
Final project.

Land use and traffic route plan for centre of Greater Basle
Study commission.

1991
Conversion and extension of family house in Bottmingen
(Canton of Basel-Land)
Flurweg 8
Completed project.

Design and traffic plan for Wettsteinplatz in Basle
Study commission.

Conversion and extension of Lützelhof, fire service, Basle (1991–94)
Final project.

Eye clinic in Polykliniktrakt 1 at Inselspital in Berne (1991–94)
In partnership with I + B Architekten, Berne.
Completed project.

1992
Conversion of Baukasse of Building Department, Basle
Münsterplatz 11
Completed project.

Block–type thermal power station and chimney at Neubad Schulhaus in Basle
Kaltbrunnen Promenade
Completed project.

Investigating potential for expansion of Basle schools
Study commission.

Refurbishment and enlargement of historic buildings of the Building Department Basel-Stadt
Study commission.
Final project.

Conversion and addition to the the "Pro Optik" office building in Basle (1992–93)
Steinenvorstadt 62
Completed project.

1993
Veranda on a residence in Basle
Mittlere Strasse 43
Completed project.

Photographic studio in Allschwil (Canton of Basel-Land)
Final project.

1994
Refurbishment of façade of villa in Oberrohrdorf (Canton of Aargau)
Haufroosstrasse 11
Completed project.

Helicopter pad on the Kantonsspital in Basle
Final project.

Conversion of customs building in Biel-Benken (Canton of Basel-Land)
Final project.

SBB central signal box, passenger station, Basle
Study commission.

Centre PasquART, extension to Kunsthalle in Biel (Canton of Berne)
Study commission.

Office building for Balimpex in Muttenz (Canton of Basel-Land)
Final project.

Einbau Informatikabteilung im Zentrum für Lehre und Forschung, Kantonsspital Basel-Stadt 1989–1993

Die Aufgabenstellung: Einbau der Informatikabteilung in die bestehende Baustruktur. Die bereits ungenügend natürlich belichtete Vorhalle durfte nicht weiter verdunkelt oder räumlich verstellt werden. Die gegebene Raumhöhe erlaubte die Aufhängung eines Galeriegeschosses an der Decke, stabilisiert durch eine Stützenreihe aus abgekanteten Stahlblechen. Konstruktiv dient dieselbe Stützenreihe zur Aufhängung einer Treppe und im Hallenbereich einer teilweise leicht gekrümmten, raumtrennenden, im obersten Teil transparenten Glaswand.

Incorporation of Data Processing Department at the Teaching and Research Centre, Cantonal Hospital of Basle City 1989–1993

The set task was to incorporate the data processing department in the existing buildings. The vestibule, already with insufficient natural lighting, was not to be further darkened of spatially distorted. The given room height allowed a gallery storey to be suspended from the floor deck above, stabilised by a row of columns of bent steel plate. The same row of columns also supports a staircase and, in the vestibule area, a slightly angled glass partition, transparent in its upper part.

Eingangspartie, die durch eine gekrümmte, raumtrennende Glaswand besonders artikuliert ist
Entrance section, with curved, room-dividing glass wall

Aus Stahl gefertigte Treppe, die ins Galeriegeschoß führt
Steel steps leading to the gallery level

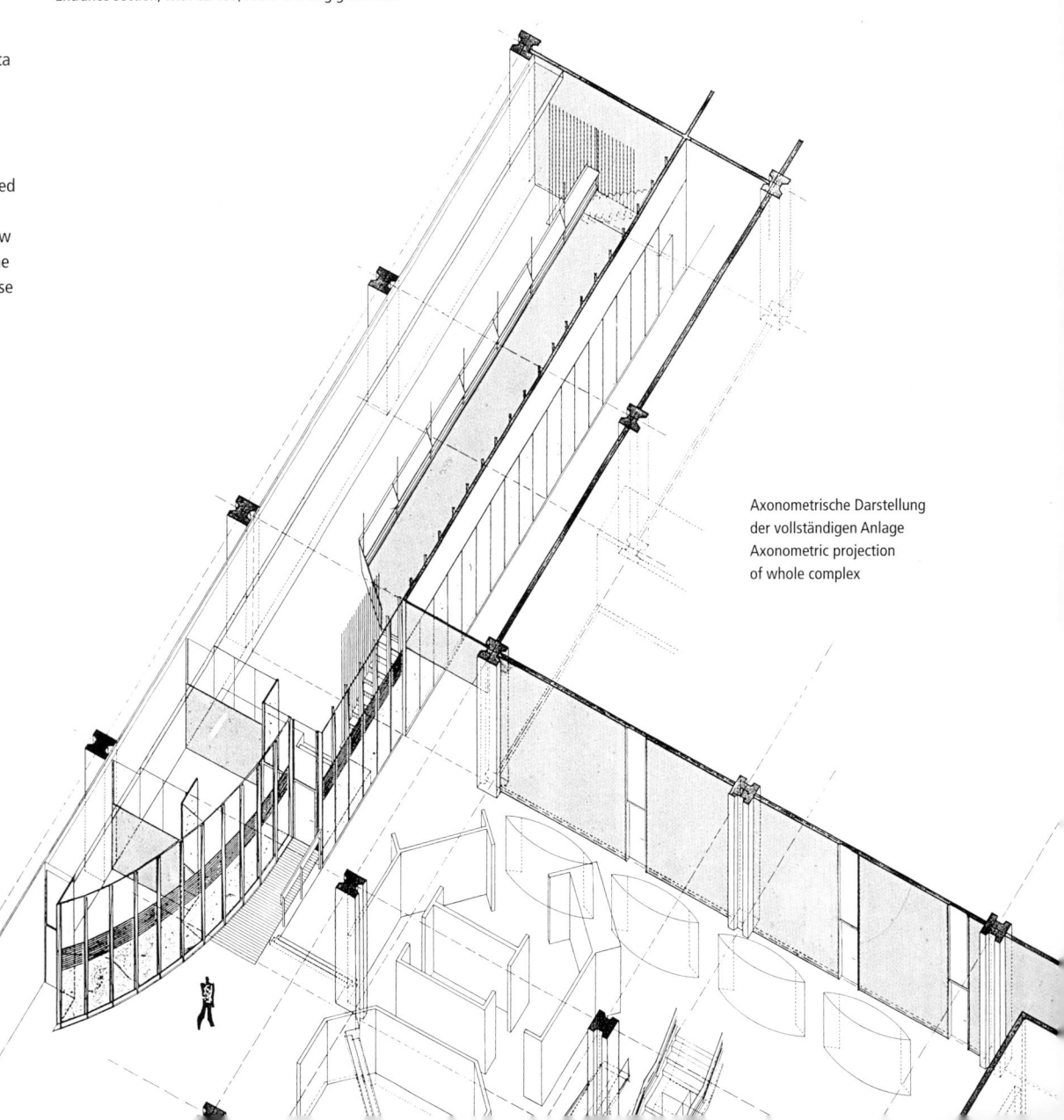

Axonometrische Darstellung der vollständigen Anlage
Axonometric projection of whole complex

Längsschnitt durch den doppelgeschossigen Raum
Longitudinal section through double-height room

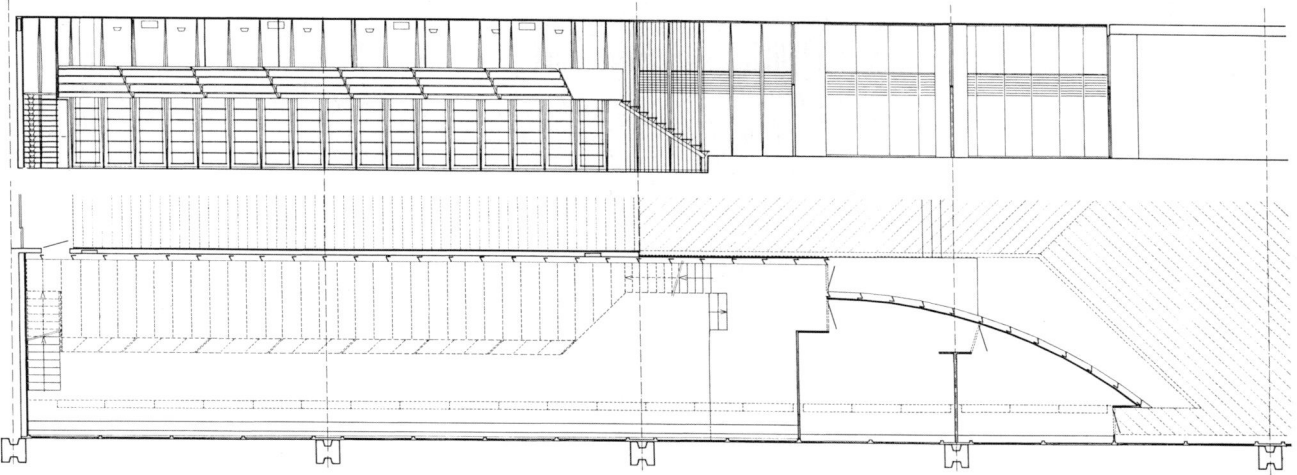

Grundriß Erdgeschoß / Ground floor plan

Teil des Längsschnittes durch den doppelgeschossigen Raum
Part longitudinal section through the double-height room

Querschnitt durch die Galerie
Cross section through gallery

Amtsplatzüberdachung mit Inselpavillon, Zoll Lysbüchel in Basel 1990

Zwischen den beiden Zollgebäuden der Schweiz und Frankreichs sollte eine gemeinsame Überdachung mit Inselpavillon erstellt werden. Das Dach aus wellenfömig verleimten Brettschichtträgern und den längsseitig verglasten Randbereichen ist an einem Dreigelenkträger aus Stahl von 25 Metern Höhe aufgehängt. Im darunterliegenden, schmalen Inselpavillon sind die schweizerische und französische Kontrollstelle mit der jeweiligen Publikumszone untergebracht, getrennt durch die diagonal verlaufende Wand entsprechend der Landesgrenze.

Roof over Amtsplatz with Island Pavilion, Customs Post Lysbüchel in Basle 1990

A common roof, with an island pavilion, was to span the area between the Swiss and French customs buildings. The roof, of undulating bonded laminated timber girders and with glazed areas along the long edges, is suspended from a steel three-pin girder 25 metres high. In the narrow island pavilion below it the Swiss and French control points are accommodated, separated by a diagonal wall running along the frontier.

Modell der Überdachung und des darunterliegenden Pavillons / Model of roof and pavilion below

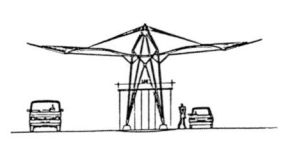

Querschnitt durch die Dachkonstruktion und durch den Pavillon

Cross section through the roof construction and pavilion

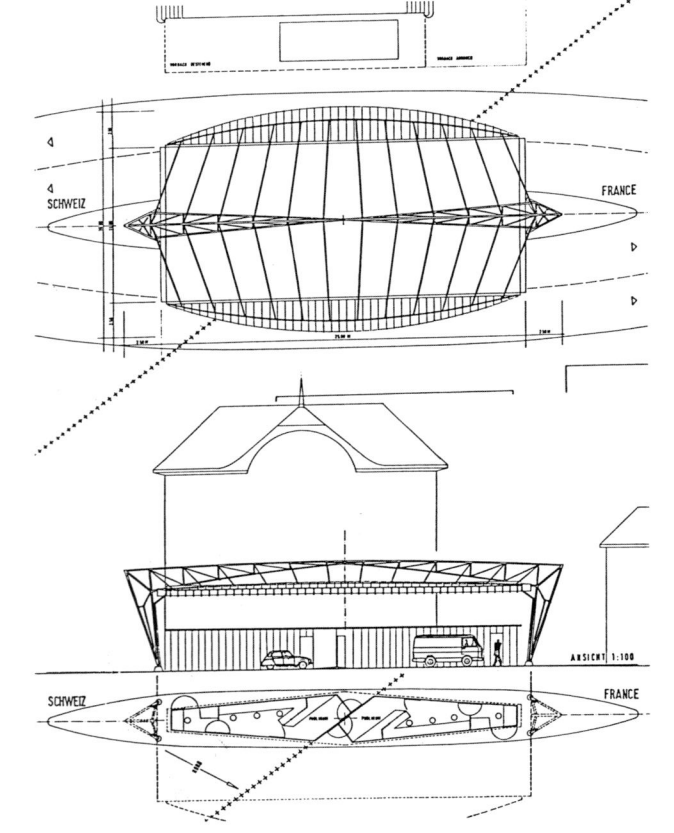

Aufsicht auf die Dachkonstruktion / Top view of roof construction

Ostfassade / East façade

Grundriß / Ground plan

Tramwartehalle für die Basler Verkehrsbetriebe in Basel
1991–1993

Für die Basler Verkehrsbetriebe haben Furrer & Fasnacht ein flexibles Baukastensystem entwickelt, um aus standardisierten Elementen je nach städtebaulichen oder verkehrstechnischen Erfordernissen größere oder kleinere Wartehallen zusammenzubauen. An zahlreichen Haltestellen in der Stadt Basel stehen bereits verschiedene Typen. So etwa an der steilen Straße, die zum Kohlenberg führt. Diese Wartehalle besteht aus zwei längsgerichteten, gegeneinander versetzten Volumen, deren jeweils flaches Dach von einer breiten U-förmigen Stütze – mit integrierter Telefonkabine – getragen ist. Die Hanglage erlaubt ebenso eine Staffelung im Schnitt.

Tram Waiting Hall for Basle Transport Services in Basle
1991–1993

For Basler Verkehrsbetriebe (Basle Transport Services), Furrer & Fasnacht developed a flexible modular system so that, depending on the planning or technical requirements, larger or smaller waiting rooms could be assembled from standardised elements. Various types are already installed at numerous stopping points in the city of Basle – for example, on the steep road leading to the Kohlenberg. This waiting hall consists of two longitudinal blocks, offset to each other, each with a flat roof supported by a wide U-shaped column with an integral telephone booth. The sloping site also allows a staggered cross-section.

Tramwartehalle mit integrierter Telefonkabine an steiler Straße
Tram waiting hall with integrated telephone booth on a steeply inclined street

Südfassade / South façade

Nordfassade / North façade

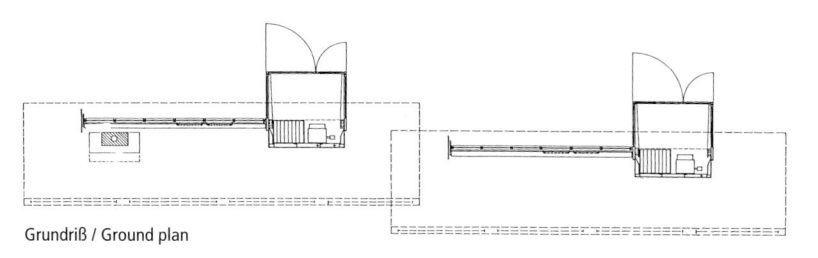

Grundriß / Ground plan

Augenklinik Polykliniktrakt 1 des Inselspitals in Bern 1991–1994

Strenge Rahmenbedingungen bestimmten das Entwurfskonzept. Wegen der geringen Belastbarkeit des darunterliegenden Geschosses mußte die Tragstruktur auf dem bestehenden Stützenraster aufgebaut werden. Ferner erforderte die Notwendigkeit der raschen Realisierbarkeit sowie der Leicht- und Trockenbauweise eine vorfabrizierte Stahlkonstruktion. Das Gebäude besteht aus zwei Teilen: einerseits die speziell entwickelte, umlaufende Glasfassade, und andererseits das herausragende, gewölbte Volumen aus Titanzinkblech. Die Auswahl der Materialien erfolgte nach betrieblichen und unterhaltsgerechten sowie, wo immer möglich, auch nach ökologischen Aspekten.

Eye Clinic in Polykliniktrakt 1 at the Inselspital in Berne 1991–1994

The design concept was determined by rigorous basic conditions. Because of the low load capacity of the storey below, the support structure had to be built up on the existing structural grid. In addition, the need for rapid erection and for a light and dry construction system called for a prefabricated steel structure. the building consists of two parts: on one hand, the specially developed glass façade running round the perimeter, and on the other the projecting, vaulted block made of titanium-zinc steel sheet. The materials were selected according to commercial criteria and for easy maintenance, but also, where possible, on ecological grounds.

Außenansicht der umlaufenden, mit Siebdrucken gestalteten Glasfassade
Exterior elevation of the encircling, screen-printed glass façade

Drei herausragende gewölbte Volumen aus Titanzinkblech
Three projecting vaulted volumes of titanium zinc-sheet

Innenraum des Durchganges
Interior of corridor

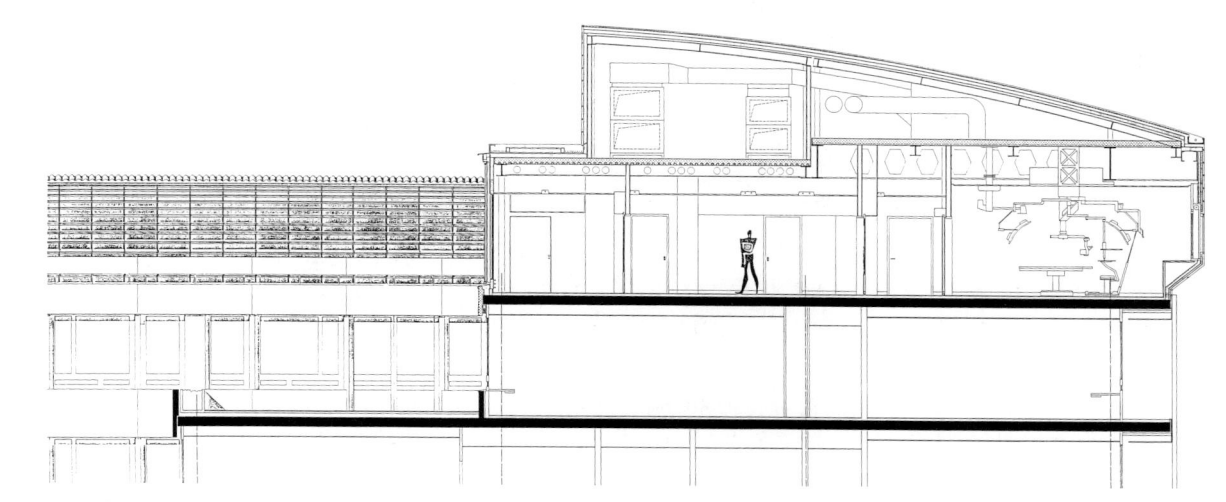

Längsschnitt durch die bestehenden und durch die neuen Räume
Longitudinal section through the existing and new rooms

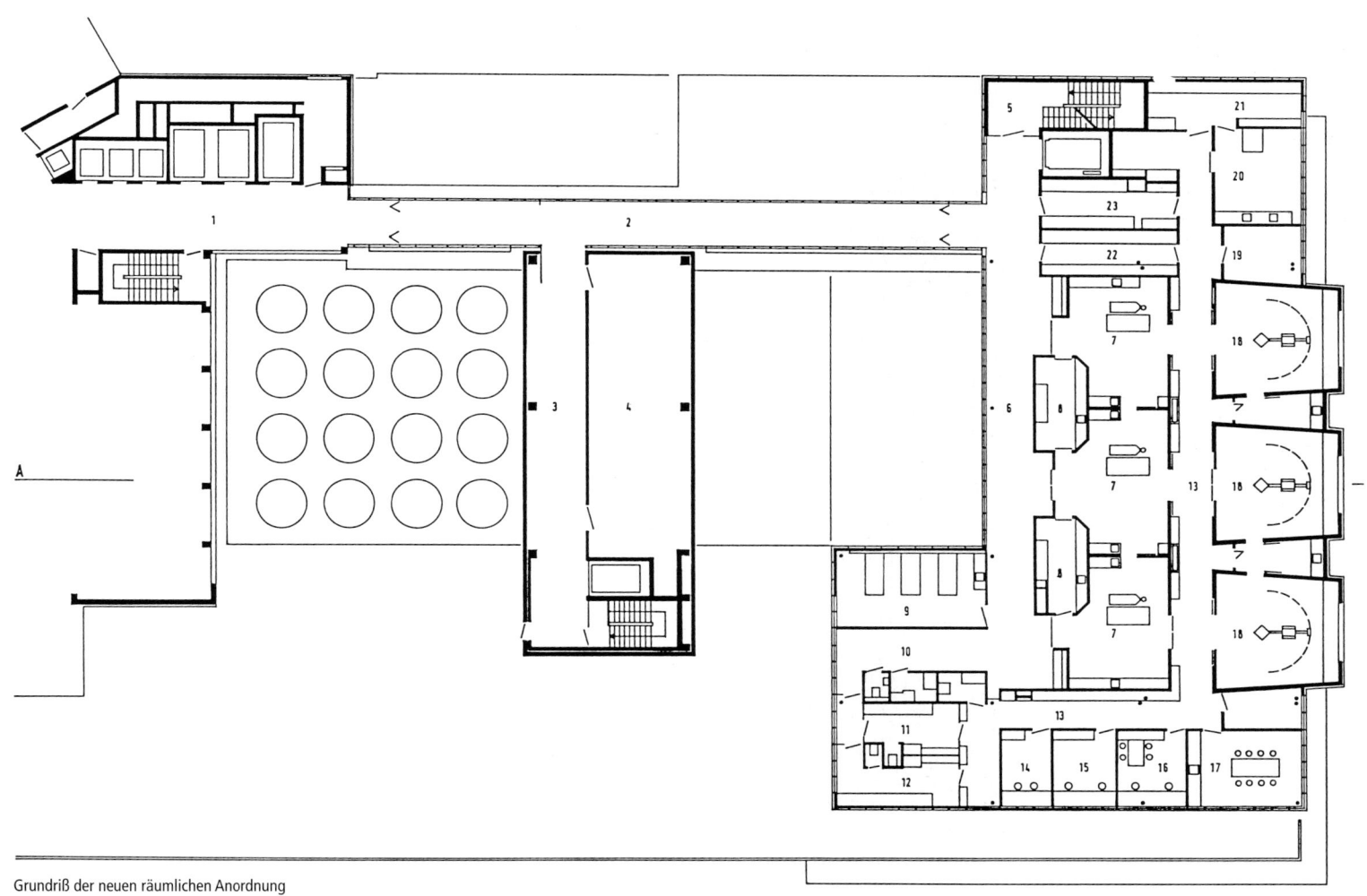

Grundriß der neuen räumlichen Anordnung
Ground plan of new spatial arrangement

Um- und Neubau Bürohaus «Pro Optik» in Basel 1992–1993

Das Projekt klärt die städtebaulich schwierige und bisher ungelöste Situation an einem Ort mit ehemaliger Stadtbefestigung. Die neue vorgelagerte Stützmauer erlaubt die gewünschte Freistellung des Baukörpers sowie den direkten Zugang zum nahen Parking. Bemerkenswert ist die horizontale, nach oben immer weiter auskragende, filigrane Rohrstruktur, die eine Funktion als primärer Sonnenschutz ausübt. Dieses besonders einfache, präzise gefertigte konstruktive Detail wirkt zudem als starker städtischer Akzent. Das Volumen faßt Büro- und Wohnräume.

Conversion and Addition to the "Pro Optik" Office Building in Basle 1992–1993

The project clarifies a difficult and hitherto unresolved planning situation at a site of former town fortifications. The new supporting wall set in front of the structure allows the desired clearance from the building and direct access to the nearby car park. A noteworthy feature is the horizontal, filigree tubular structure, cantilevered further and further out towards the top, which acts as a primary sun screen. This extremely simple and precisely finished constructional detail also acts as a strong accent on the urban skyline. The building includes offices and residential areas.

Horizontale, nach oben immer weiter auskragende filigrane Rohrstruktur
Horizontal, filigree tubular structure, projecting further out towards the top

Ansicht des gesamten Gebäudes
Elevation of whole building

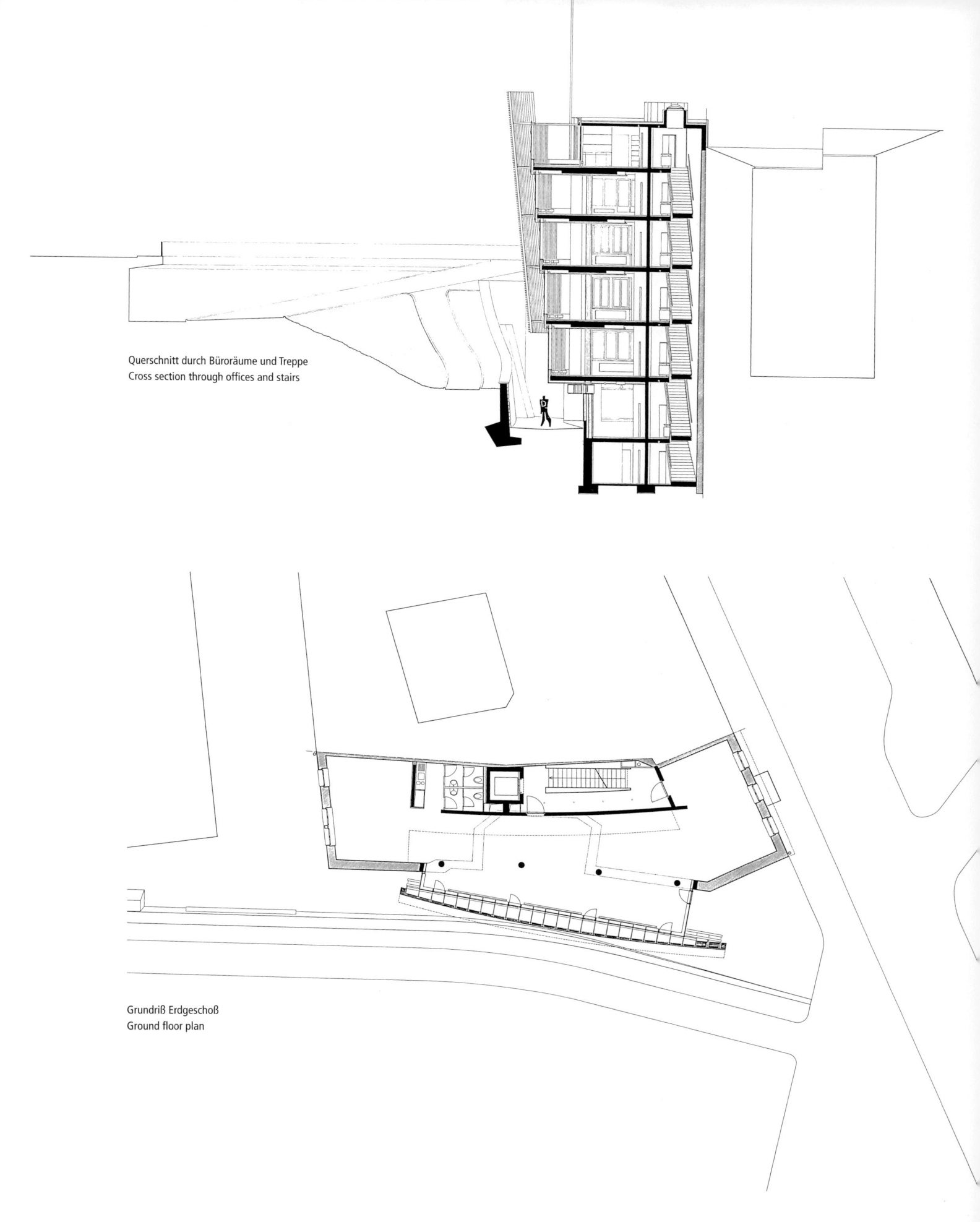

Querschnitt durch Büroräume und Treppe
Cross section through offices and stairs

Grundriß Erdgeschoß
Ground floor plan

Nick Gartenmann · Mark Werren · Andreas Jöhri, Bern

Integrales Denken

Die Denkweise Nick Gartenmanns, Mark Werrens und Andreas Jöhris geht über architektonische und städtebauliche Aspekte hinaus. Als Fachleute sehen sie sich eingebunden in eine Welt der fortdauernden gesellschaftlichen und politischen Veränderungen und Erneuerungen. Die wesentliche Anregung zum kreativen Schaffen liegt, ihrer Auffassung nach, im Aufspüren einer überzeugenden Vision, die zum verläßlichen Wertmaßstab im Arbeitsprozeß wird und die zum Prüfen und Hinterfragen der bisher entwickelten Lösungsansätze anregt. Kenntnisse und Erfahrungen mit neuen Arbeitsweisen und Energietechniken sowie mit umweltschonenden Baumethoden fließen in die Überlegungen ein und lassen so vielschichtige Projekte entstehen. Als ein herausragendes Beispiel sei das Wohnhaus Roethlisberger in Langnau genannt, das dank der gewählten Trockenbauweise eine Rohbauphase von nur zwei Tagen benötigte. Herausforderungen annehmen und klar Stellung beziehen im Spannungsfeld politischer und gesellschaftlicher Diskussionen bedeutet für diese Architekten auch ein Engagement außerhalb der schweizerischen Landesgrenze. So beispielsweise mit ihrem Entwurf für das neue Regierungsviertel in Berlin, für den sie unter 835 Teilnehmern und Teilnehmerinnen mit dem dritten Preis ausgezeichnet wurden. Diese anspruchsvolle Intention nennen sie selber integrales Denken. Diesem annähernd gerecht werden zu wollen, erfordert das kontinuierliche Wahrnehmen der sich im Arbeitsfeld stets ändernden Bedingungen und anschließend das Einfließenlassen in die tägliche Entwurfsarbeit.

Integral Thinking

The way of thinking of Nick Gartenmann, Mark Werren and Andreas Jöhri goes beyond architectural and town planning concerns. As specialists, they find themselves tied into a world of continuous social and political changes and innovations. In their view, the real stimulus for creative work lies in evolving a convincing vision which can act as a reliable criterion of value in the work process and which spurs them to test and retrospectively question the solutions they have begun to develop. Knowledge and experience of new working practices and energy technologies, and of building methods that respect the environment, play a part in their deliberations, giving rise to multi-layered projects. An outstanding example is the Roethlisberger residence in Langnau which, thanks to the dry construction method selected, needed a bare carcase stage of only two days. To accept challenges and take up clear positions in relation to political and social issues means, for these architects, to commit themselves outside the Swiss frontier. One example is their design for the new government quarter in Berlin, for which, of 835 entries, they were awarded third prize. These ambitious aims they themselves call integral thinking. To come close to satisfying its demands means being continuously aware of the constantly changing conditions in the work situation, and bringing them to bear on the daily task of designing.

Biographie

Nick Gartenmann

1958
Geboren in Bern.

1980–86
Architekturstudium an der ETH-Zürich.

1987
Diplom bei Professor Dolf Schnebli an der ETH-Zürich.

1987–88
Mitarbeit im Büro Gerber + Hungerbühler in Zürich.

Seit 1989
Gemeinsames Büro mit Mark Werren und Andreas Jöhri in Bern.

Mark Werren

1960
Geboren in Bern.

1980–86
Architekturstudium an der ETH-Zürich.

1987
Diplom bei Professor Mario Campi an der ETH-Zürich.

1987–88
Mitarbeit im Büro Burckhardt + Partner in New York und Zürich.

Seit 1989
Gemeinsames Büro mit Nick Gartenmann und Andreas Jöhri in Bern.

Andreas Jöhri

1961
Geboren in Thusis.

1981–87
Architekturstudium an der ETH-Zürich.

1987
Diplom bei Professor Alexander Henz an der ETH-Zürich.

1987–88
Nachdiplomstudium Energie an der Ingenieurschule beider Basel.

Seit 1989
Gemeinsames Büro mit Nick Gartenmann und Mark Werren in Bern.

Ausgewähltes Werkverzeichnis

1989
Umbau Mehrfamilienhaus Styner in Bolligen (Kanton Bern)
Brunnenhofstraße 37
Ausgeführtes Projekt.

Gesamtsanierung Migros Breitenrain in Bern (1989–90) Breitenrainplatz 37
Ausgeführtes Projekt.

Örtliche Bauleitung Ingenieurschule in Burgdorf (Kanton Bern; 1989–91)
Pestalozzistraße 20
Ausgeführtes Projekt.

1990
Anbau Ferienhaus Werren in Praz (Kanton Freiburg)
Chemin sous la Forge
Ausgeführtes Projekt.

Höhere Technische Lehranstalt in Chur
Wettbewerb, erster Ankauf.

Generaldirektion PTT in Worblaufen (Kanton Bern)
Wettbewerb, dritter Preis.

1991
Umbau Ingenieurschule Burgdorf (Kanton Bern), CIM-Labor
Pestalozzistraße 20 Ausgeführtes Projekt.

Mehrfamilienhaus Graf in Meikirch (Kanton Bern) Bauprojekt.

Altersresidenz in Burgdorf (Kanton Bern) Vorprojekt.

Verwaltungsgebäude Schweizerischer Bankverein in Ittigen (Kanton Bern; 1991–etwa 97)
Wettbewerb, erster Preis.
Ausführungsprojekt.

1992
Umbau Industriegebäude Fronsit in Zollikofen (Kanton Bern)
Industriestraße 35
Ausgeführtes Projekt.

Dienstleistungs- und Gewerbezentrum in Zollikofen (Kanton Bern)
Bauprojekt.

Mitarbeit am Programm DIANE beim Bundesamt für Energiewirtschaft in Bern. Beratung.
Projektbearbeitung.

Spitalstudien für Aigle (Kanton Waadt) und Olten (Kanton Solothurn) Studie.

Nullenergie-Bürohaus GAE und GWJ in Bern (1992–93) Bauprojekt.

Wohnüberbauung Tiger Käse AG in Langnau (Kanton Bern; 1992–etwa 96)
Wettbewerb, erster Preis.
Ausführungsprojekt.

1993
Übergangsheim für Strafentlassene BeVGe Felsenau in Bern
Vorprojekt.

Regierungsviertel in Berlin
Internationaler Ideenwettbewerb, dritter Preis.

Gewerbe- und Dienstleistungsbetriebe in Gümligen (Kanton Bern)
Wettbewerb, erster Ankauf.

Wohnüberbauung in Ostermundigen (Kanton Bern)
Wettbewerb, dritter Preis.

Alter Schlachthof in Berlin
Städtebauliches Gutachten, zweiter Preis.

Entwicklungsstandort in Ausserholligen (Kanton Bern) Studie.

Naherholungsgebiet in Gurten Kulm (Kanton Bern) Studie.

Wohnhaus Roethlisberger in Langnau (Kanton Bern; 1993–94)
Dorfbergstraße
Ausgeführtes Projekt.

1994
Anbau Ferienhaus Borer in Praz (Kanton Freiburg)
Chemin sous la Forge
Ausgeführtes Projekt.

Deutscher Bundestag in Berlin
Studie für Dorotheenblöcke.

Gesamtsanierung Migros Neuhausplatz in Köniz (Kanton Bern; 1994–95)
Ausgeführtes Projekt.

Umbau Mehrfamilienhaus in Bern (1994–95)
Ausgeführtes Projekt.

«Spreebogen Berlin, Internationaler städtebaulicher Wettbewerb. Eine Auswahl von Schweizer Beiträgen», Ausstellungsbeitrag für ETH-Hönggerberg, Zürich.

«Neue Bären» Ausstellungsbeitrag für das Architektur Forum, Zürich.

Japanische Botschaft in Bern (1994–96).
Ausführungsprojekt.

Gaswerkareal in Zug
Studienauftrag.

Biography

Nick Gartenmann

1958
Born in Berne

1980–86
Studied architecture at the ETH Zurich

1987
Graduated with diploma under
Prof. Dolf Schnebli at the ETH Zurich

1987–88
Worked at the Gerber + Hungerbühler
architectural office in Zurich

Since 1989
Joint architectural office with
Mark Werren and Andreas Jöhri in Berne.

Mark Werren

1960
Born in Berne

1980–86
Studied architecture at the ETH Zurich

1987
Graduated with diploma under
Prof. Mario Campi at the ETH Zurich

1987–88
Worked at the Burckhardt + Partner
architectural office
in New York and Zurich

Since 1989
Joint architectural office with Nick Gartenmann and Andreas Jöhri in Berne

Andreas Jöhri

1961
Born in Thusis

1981–87
Studied architecture at the ETH Zurich

1987
Graduated with diploma under
Prof. Alexander Henz at the ETH Zurich

1987–88
Postgraduate study of energy
at the Ingenieurschule in Basle

Since 1989
Joint architectural office with Nick
Gartenmann and Mark Werren in Berne.

Selected list of work

1989

Conversion of Styner multiple residence
in Bolligen (Canton of Berne)
Brunnenhofstrasse 37
Completed project.

Complete refurbishment of Migros
Breitenrain store in Berne (1989–90)
Breitenrainplatz 37
Completed project.

Local management of construction
of Ingenieurschule in Burgdorf
(Canton of Berne; 1989–91)
Pestalozzistrasse 20
Completed project.

1990

Extension to Werren holiday home
in Praz (Canton of Fribourg)
Chemin sous la Forge
Completed project.

Höhere Technische Lehranstalt in Chur
Competition, first purchased design.

Head office of PTT in Worblaufen
(Canton of Berne)
Competition, third prize.

1991

Conversion of Ingenieurschule
in Burgdorf (Canton of Berne),
CIM laboratory
Pestalozzistrasse 20
Completed project.

Graf multiple residence in Meikirch
(Canton of Berne)
Final project.

Old people's home in Burgdorf
(Canton of Berne)
Preliminary project.

Administrative building of the
Schweizerischer Bankverein in Ittigen
(Canton of Berne; 1991–approx. 97)
Competition, first prize. Final project.

1992

Conversion of Fronsit industrial building
in Zollikofen (Canton of Berne)
Industriestrasse 35
Completed project.

Commercial and services centre
in Zollikofen (Canton of Berne)
Final project.

Collaboration in DIANE programme
for Department of Energy in Berne
Consultancy. Project development.

Hospital studies for Aigle
(Canton of Vaud) and Olten
(Canton of Solothurn)
Study.

Zero-energy office block for GAE
and GWJ in Berne (1992–93)
Final project.

Residential development
for Tiger Käse AG in Langnau
(Canton of Berne; 1992–approx. 96)
Competition, first prize. Final project.

1993

Rehabilitation centre for released
prisoners for BeVGe Felsenau in Berne
Preliminary project.

Government quarter in Berlin
International ideas competition,
third prize.

Commercial premises in Gümligen
(Canton of Berne)
Competition, first purchased design.

Residential development in Ostermundigen (Canton of Berne)
Competition, third prize.

Old slaughterhouse in Berlin
Town-planning proposal, second prize.

Development zone in Ausserholligen
(Canton of Berne)
Study.

Recreation area in Gurten Kulm
(Canton of Berne)
Study.

Roethlisberger residence in Langnau
(Canton of Berne; 1993–94)
Dorfbergstrasse
Completed project.

1994

Extension to Borer holiday residence
in Praz (Canton of Fribourg)
Chemin sous la Forge
Completed project.

German Bundestag in Berlin
Study for Dorotheenblöcke buildings.

General refurbishment of
Migros Neuhausplatz store in Köniz
(Canton of Berne; 1994–95)
Completed project.

Conversion of multiple residence
in Berne (1994–95) Completed project.

«Spreebogen Berlin, international urban
design competition. A selection of Swiss
entries», exhibition entry for the ETH-
Hönggerberg, Zurich.

«Neue Bären» (New Bears) Exhibition
entry for the Architektur Forum, Zurich.

Japanese Embassy in Berne (1994–96).
Final project.

Gas works site in Zug. Study project.

Verwaltungsgebäude Schweizerischer Bankverein in Ittigen 1991-etwa 1997

Der viergeschossige, im Grundriß rechteckige Baukörper ist innen durch drei markante, geschoßübergreifende Räume gegliedert: die gedeckte Halle des Eingangsbereichs, der offene Innenhof mit freiem Übergang zum umliegenden Grünbereich und der galerieartige Lichtschlitz. Die verschiedenen vertikalen und horizontalen Bezüge ergeben eine weitgehende innere Transparenz und gewähren so eine optimale Orientierung. Einfach verschiebbare Trennwandelemente ermöglichen in allen drei identischen Obergeschossen, die den Büros vorbehalten sind, größtmögliche Flexibilität.

Administrative Building of the Schweizerischer Bankverein in Ittigen 1991–approx. 1997

The four-storey building with a rectangular ground plan is structured internally by three striking spaces which cut across floor levels: the covered hall at the entrance, the open inner courtyard with a free transition to the surrounding green areas and the gallery-like light shaft. The different vertical and horizontal relationships spread a feeling of transparency throughout the interior and make for optimal orientation. Easily moved partitions on all three identical upper storeys, which are reserved for offices, allow maximum flexibility.

Modell der Fassadenkonstruktion / Model of façade construction

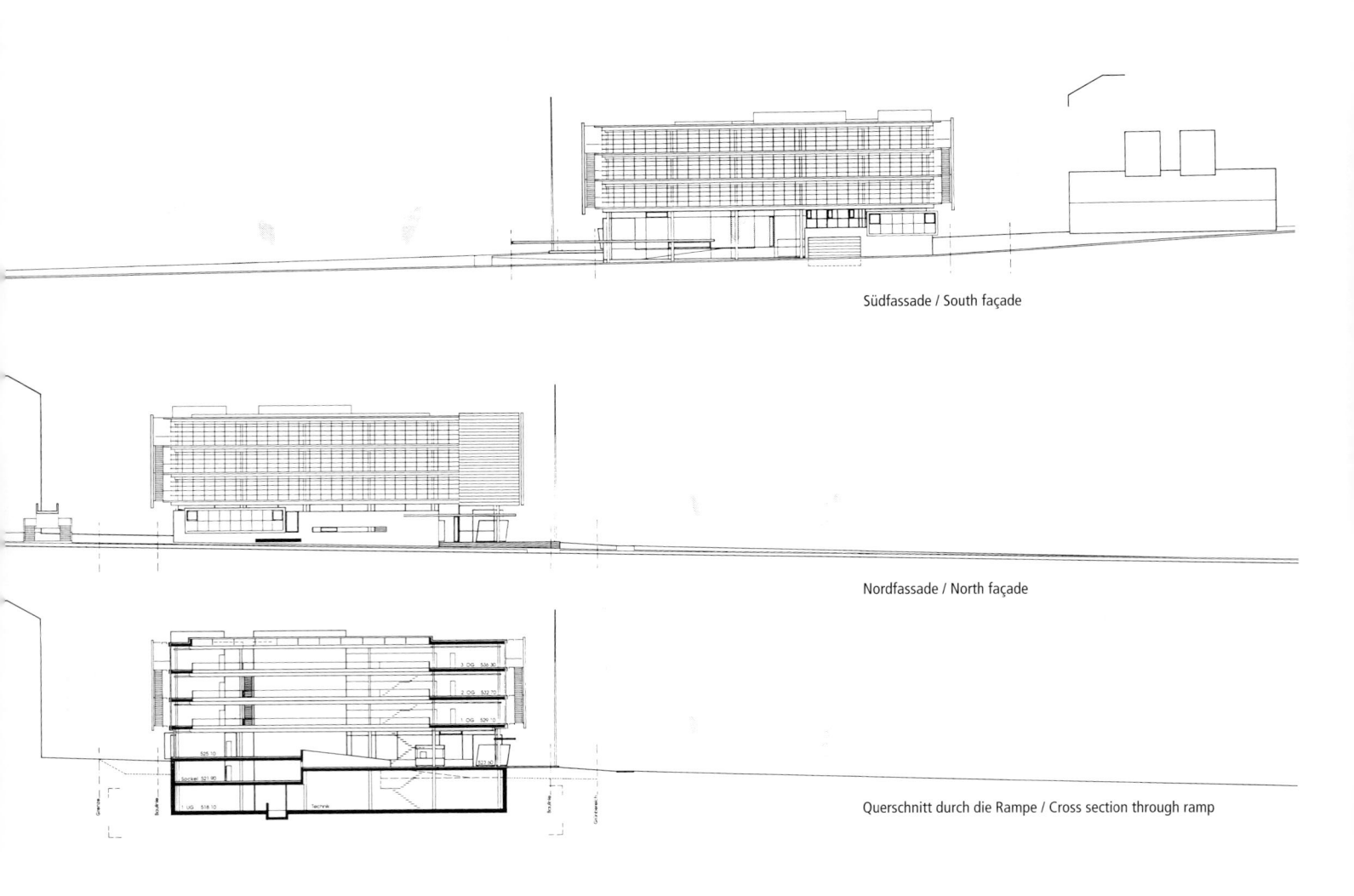

Südfassade / South façade

Nordfassade / North façade

Querschnitt durch die Rampe / Cross section through ramp

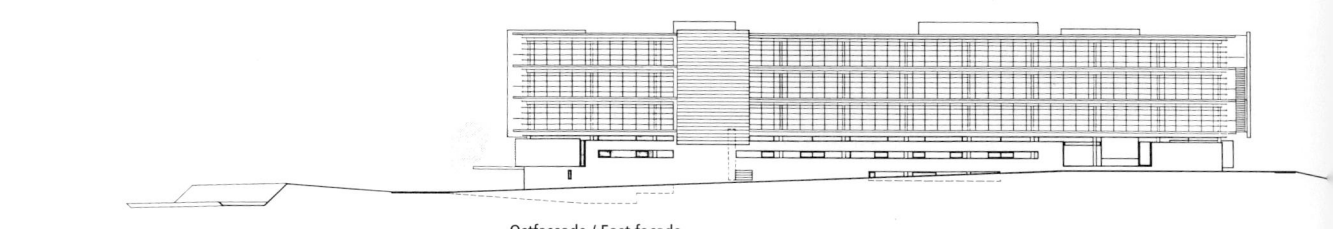

Ostfassade / East façade

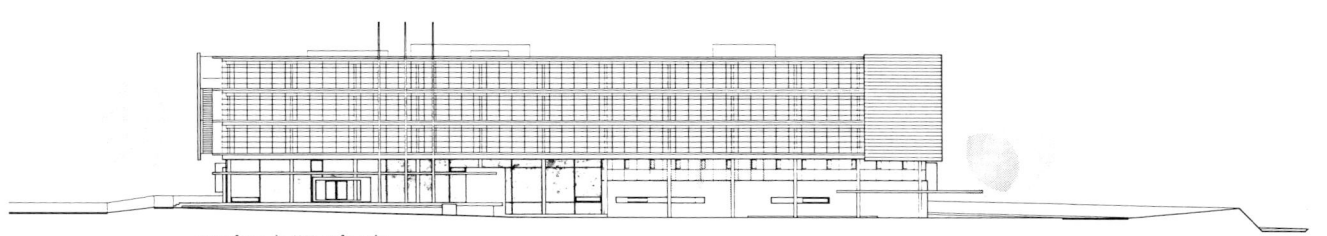

Westfassade / West façade

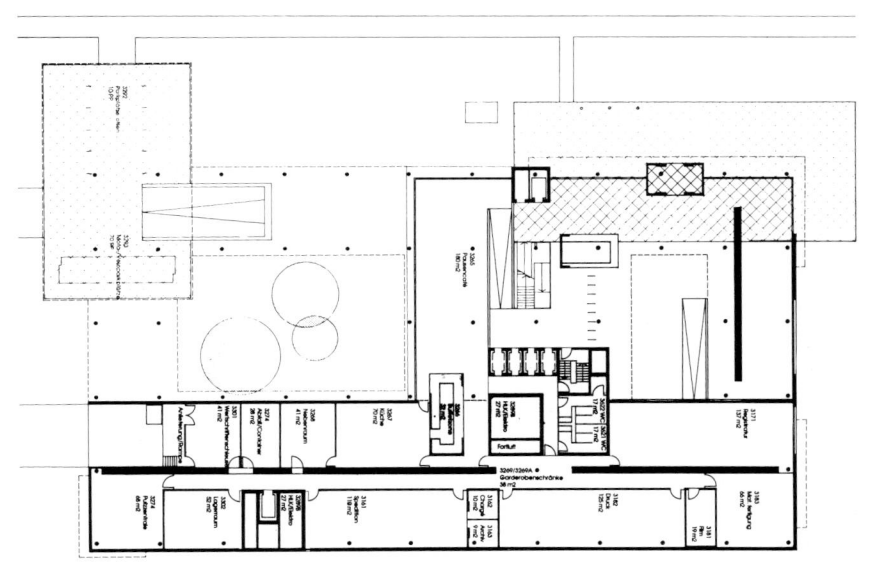

Grundriß Sockelgeschoß / Ground plan of base level

83

Höhere Technische Lehranstalt in Chur 1990

Die Lage außerhalb des Stadtzentrums, inmitten des Industriequartiers und in unmittelbarer Nähe einer lärmigen Straße ist ein prägender Faktor. Eine gekrümmte Wand entlang der Straße definiert einen rückwärtigen geschützten Raum, in welchem sich winkelförmig angeordnet drei verschiedene Volumen befinden: die Bibliothek mit einer Cafeteria im ersten Obergeschoß, das doppelgeschossige Foyer mit den darüberliegenden Dozentenzimmern sowie das Gebäude mit den einzelnen Unterrichtsräumen. An die lose Komposition der verschiedenen Kuben, die durch ihre unbeschwerte Art gefällt, fügen sich interessante Außenbereiche an.

Höhere Technische Lehranstalt in Chur 1990

The situation outside the town centre, in the middle of the industrial district and directly beside a noisy road, was a decisive factor. A curved wall along the road defines a protected space behind it, in which three different blocks are arranged at an angle: the library with a cafeteria on the first storey, the two-storey foyer with the lecturers' offices above it and the building containing the teaching rooms. The loose composition of the different cubes has a pleasingly uncomplicated quality and gives rise to interesting exterior spaces.

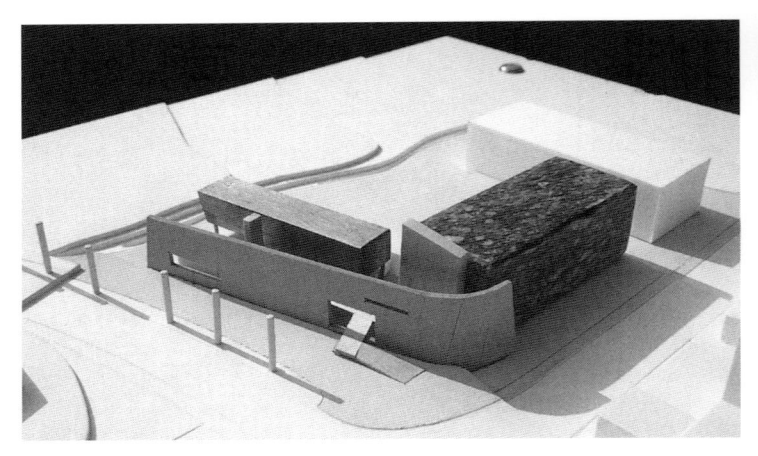

Modell der Wettbewerbseingabe / Competition model

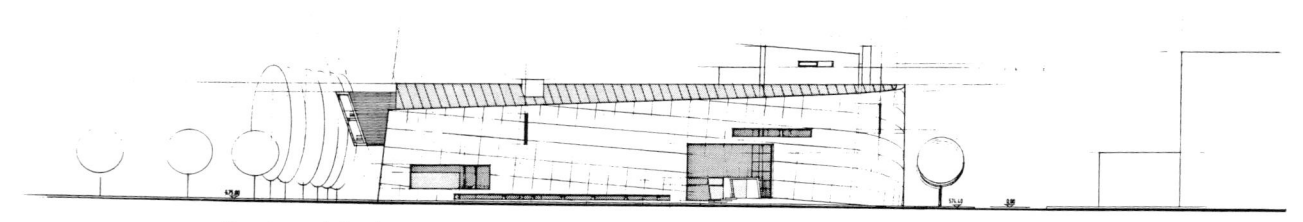

Nordfassade / North façade

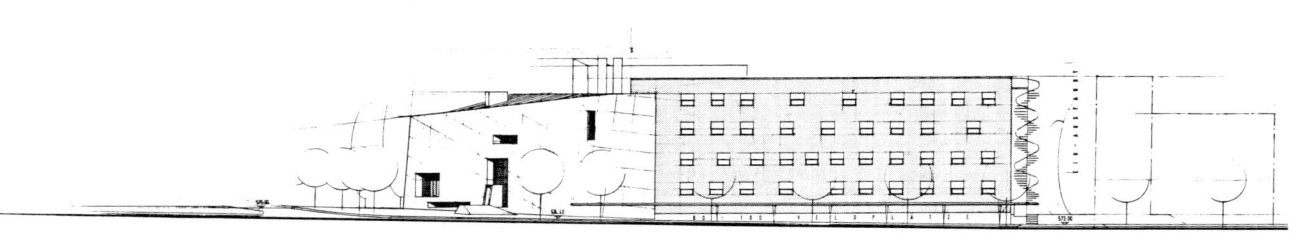

Westfassade / West façade

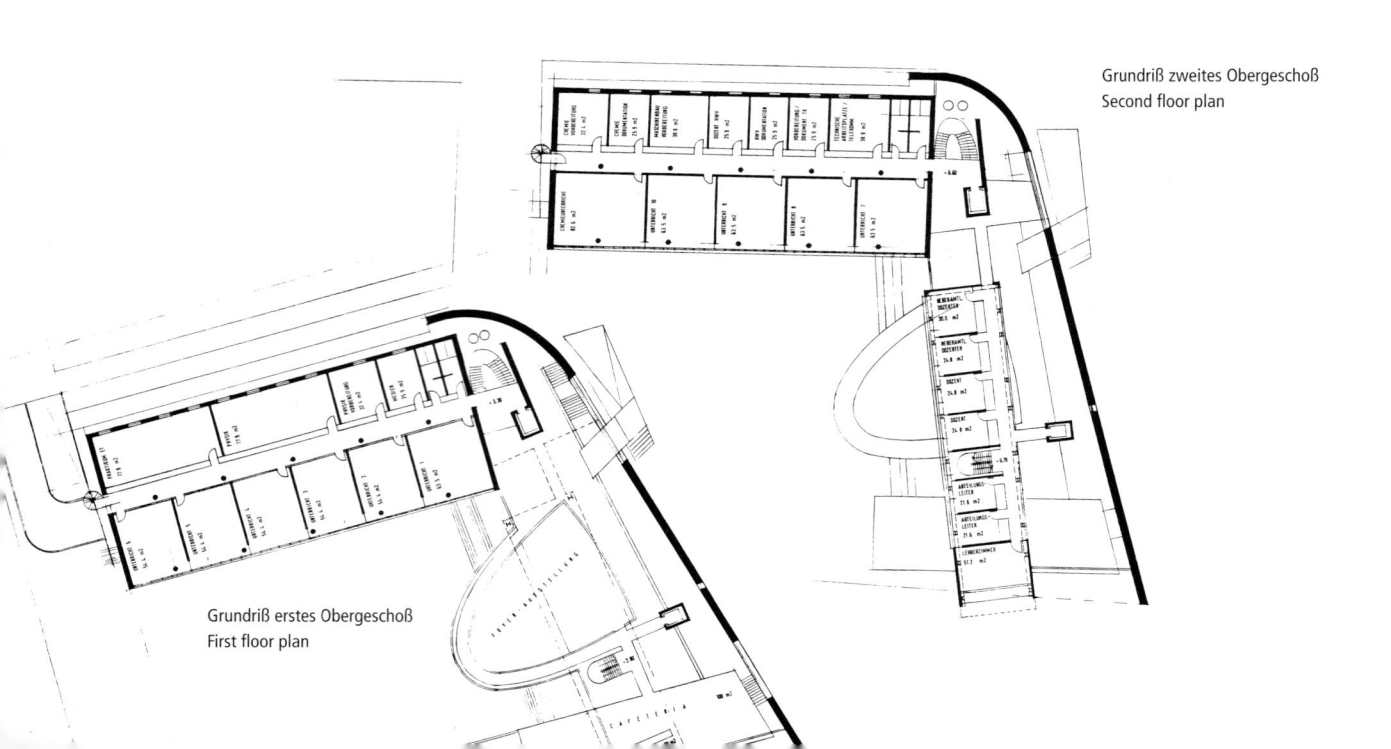

Grundriß zweites Obergeschoß
Second floor plan

Grundriß erstes Obergeschoß
First floor plan

Wohnüberbauung Tiger Käse AG in Langnau
1992–etwa 1996

Die Aufgabenstellung beinhaltete zum einen die Integration der neuen Überbauung in das bestehende, ländliche Ortsbild, zum anderen die Bereitstellung von attraktivem, aber kostengünstigem Wohnraum. Drei kleinere Volumen quer zum Hang markieren den Übergang vom steilen zum flachen Teil, drei größere stehen parallel zur gegebenen Topographie. Die unterschiedlich gestalteten Wohnungen gewähren, trotz einfachster Konstruktionen als Folge des großen Kostendrucks, eine bemerkenswerte räumliche Vielfalt und eine flexible Nutzungsdisposition.

Residential Development for Tiger Käse AG in Langnau
1992–approx. 1996

The commission involved, on one hand, integrating the new development with the existing rural milieu and, on the other, providing attractive but low-cost accommodation. Three smaller blocks placed across the slope mark the transition from the steep to the flatter section, while three larger ones are placed parallel to the given topography. The apartments, of varying floor plans, offer noteworthy spatial diversity and flexibility of use despite their very simple construction resulting from tight cost constraints.

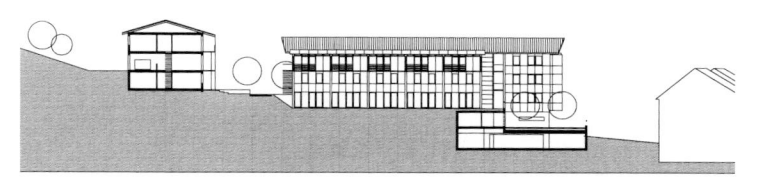

Querschnitt durch die kleineren Volumen quer zum Hang
Cross section through the smaller volumes across the slope

Grundriß Erdgeschoß aller Wohnungen
Ground floor plan of all apartments

Grundriß einer Duplex-Wohnung beziehungsweise einer Geschoßwohnung
Ground plan of a maisonette apartment and single-level apartment

Regierungsviertel in Berlin
1993

In ihrer Vision für das neue Regierungsviertel integrierten die Architekten den Staat in die Stadt, um keine Ghettoatmosphäre, sondern neuen Lebensraum für die Öffentlichkeit zu schaffen. So standen die Thematisierung der demokratischen Staatsform und ihre städtebauliche Formulierung im Zentrum ihrer Überlegungen. Das Konzept geht von einer prozeßhaften Stadtentwicklung und nicht vom momentanen Zustand aus. Der Entwurf zeigt einen strengen orthogonalen Raster, der drei große städtische Freiräume besonders akzentuiert und der zukünftige Entwicklungen – politische, gesellschaftliche und wirtschaftliche – schöpferisch aufnehmen kann.

Government Quarter in Berlin
1993

In their vision for the new government quarter the architects integrated state and city, to avoid creating a ghetto atmosphere but instead to provide new living space for the public sphere. Their central concern was to find a way of formulating the democratic state form in town-planning terms. Their concept starts from urban development as a process rather than a momentary state. The design shows a grid, based on strict right-angles, giving special emphasis to three main urban spaces and capable of creatively assimilating future developments – in politics, society and economics.

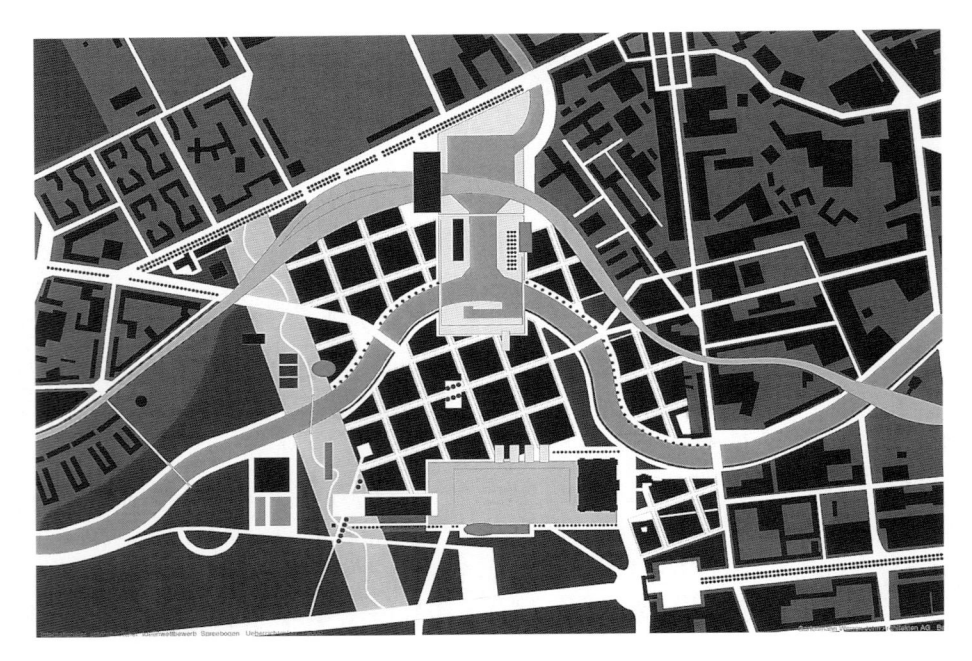

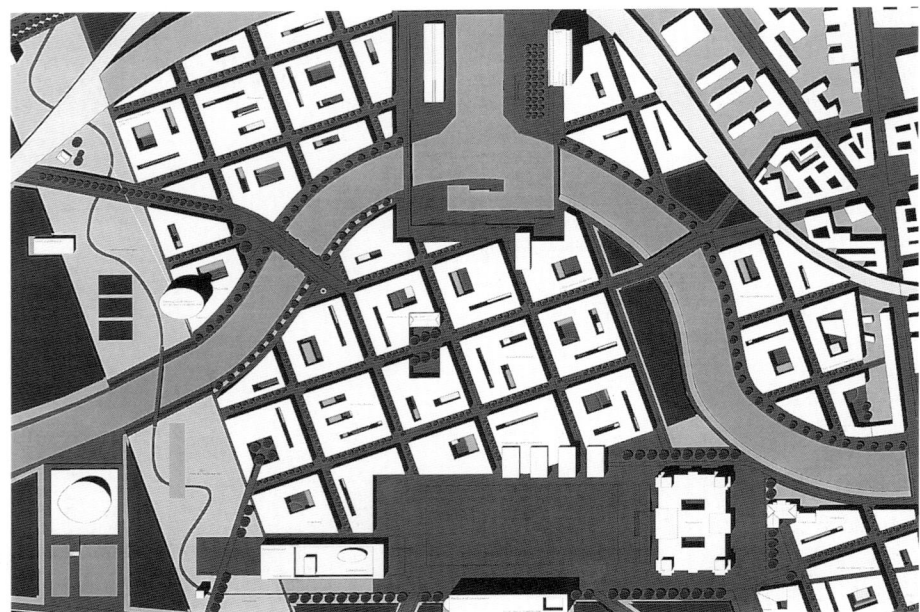

Situation des strengen orthogonalen Rasters / Situation of the strict orthogonal grid

Innerhalb des Rasters werden drei große städtische Räume sowie zahlreiche kleinere Höfe gebildet
Three large urban spaces and many smaller courtyards are formed within the grid

Perspektivische Darstellungen der vorgeschlagenen Stadtentwicklung / Perspective drawings of the proposed urban development

Wohnhaus Roethlisberger in Langnau 1993-1994

Ausschlaggebend für die Wahl des Holzrahmenbaus war der besonders kurze Zeitraum, der für die Ausführung zur Verfügung stand. Die Wahl der Trockenbauweise sowie der hohe Anteil an vorfabrizierten Bauteilen, der eine äußerst sorgfältige Planung und Detaillierung erforderte, ermöglichte es, den eigentlichen Bau in nur zwei Tagen auszuführen. Trotz einfachster Konstruktionsarten ist im Innern eine große räumliche Vielfalt entstanden. Der zweigeschossige Baukörper ruht auf einer massiven Kellerplatte. Die hinterlüftete Fassade und der unbeheizte Dachraum wirken als energetisch optimierte Pufferzonen. Das offen gestaltete Erdgeschoß ist dem Wohnen vorbehalten. Das Obergeschoß umfaßt verschiedene Schlafräume und einen Kinderhort. Die Veranda bildet einen eigenständigen Außenraum.

Roethlisberger Residence in Langnau 1993–1994

A decisive factor in selecting timber-frame construction was the very short time available for executing the project. The choice of dry construction, and the high proportion of prefabricated components, calling for extremely careful planning and detailing, made it possible to erect the structure itself in only two days. Despite the simple construction methods the interior has great spatial diversity. The two-storey building rests on a solid basement slab. The ventilated façade and the unheated attic area, act as buffer zones to optimise energy conservation. The open-plan ground floor is set aside as a living area. The upper storey contains various bedrooms and a children's area. The veranda forms a separate outer space.

Ansicht des Wohnhauses, das aus gleichformatigen Brettern, abwechselnd in Birken- und Zedernholz, gebaut ist
Elevation of the house with alternating, beech and cedar cladding in equal-sized formats

Veranda als räumlich eigenständiges Element, das den Übergang von innen nach außen bildet
The veranda as a spatially distinct element forming the transition from outside to inside

Markante Schrankzone im Obergeschoß
Storage area in upper storey

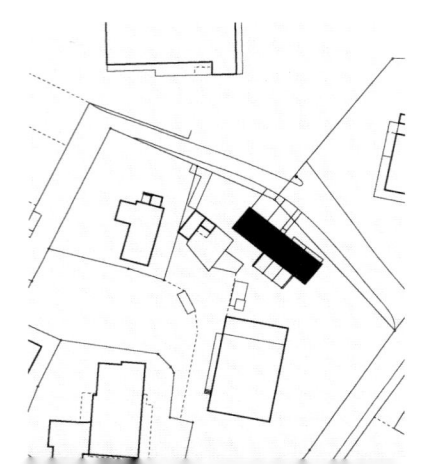

Situation innerhalb des Kontextes
Contextual situation

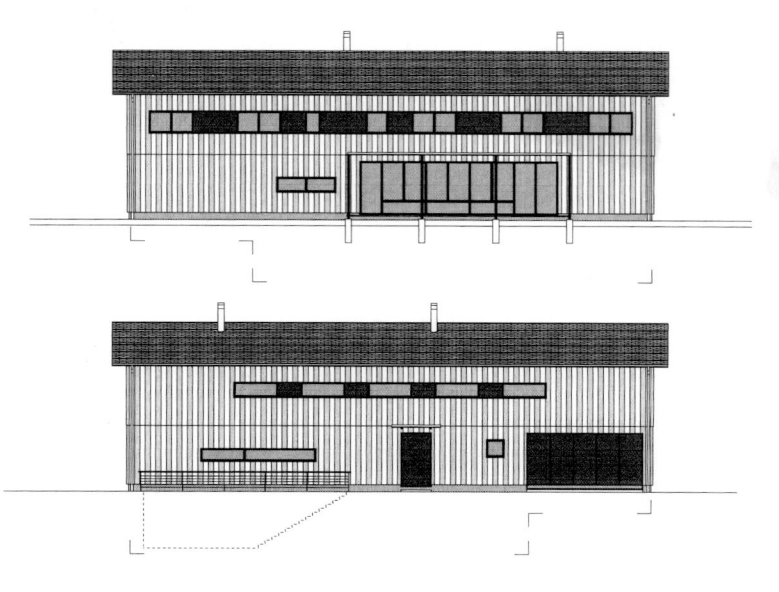

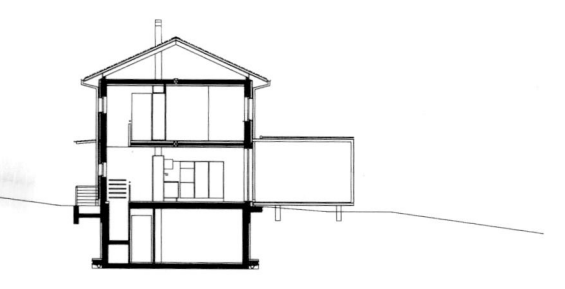

Querschnitt durch das Wohnhaus mit der Veranda
Cross section through house with veranda

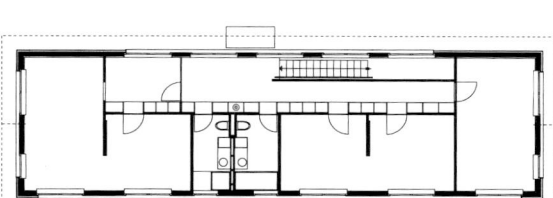

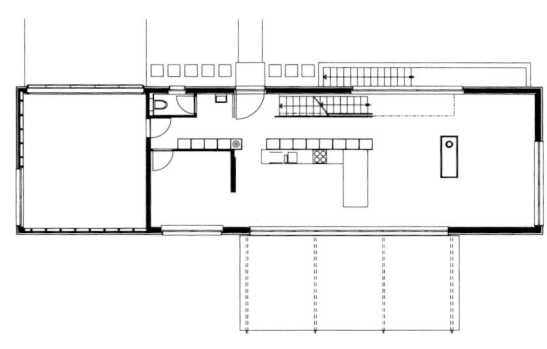

Südwestfassade / Southwest façade

Nordostfassade / Northeast façade

Grundriß Obergeschoß / Ground plan of upper floor

Grundriß Erdgeschoß / Ground floor plan

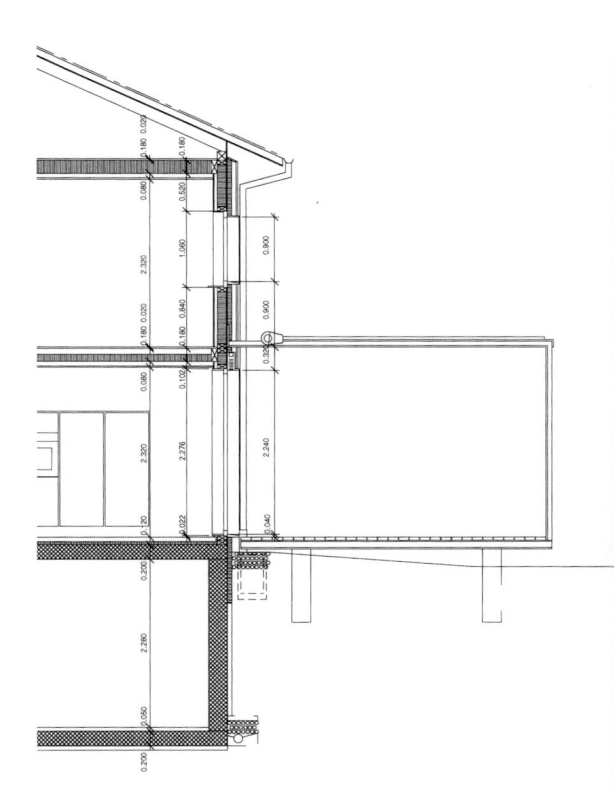

Konstruktive Ausführung der Holzbauweise
Timber construction

Gewerbe- und Dienstleistungsbetriebe in Gümligen 1993

Innerhalb eines zufällig ausgeschnittenen Grundstückes, in der Ebene tangential zu Autobahn und Hangfuß, nehmen die dynamisch angeordneten, langen, schmalen Baukörper Bezug auf die großräumigen Landschafts- und Siedlungselemente der Umgebung. Mit der unterschiedlichen Höhe der einzelnen Volumen antworten die Architekten auf das Spannungsfeld Hang/Ebene. Die dazwischenliegenden Räume differenzieren sich durch geographische Lage sowie räumliche Definition und nehmen entsprechend unterschiedliche Nutzungen auf.

Commercial Premises in Gümligen 1993

Within an arbitrarily shaped plot, on flat ground adjoining the motorway and at the foot of a slope, the long narrow blocks, dynamically interrelated, set up a relationship with their spacious surroundings, made up of countryside and built-up areas. The architects respond to the tension between slope and plain by the varying heights of the buildings. The spaces between them are differentiated both by geographical position and by spatial outline, and accept correspondingly diverse uses.

Modell der Wettbewerbseingabe / Competition model

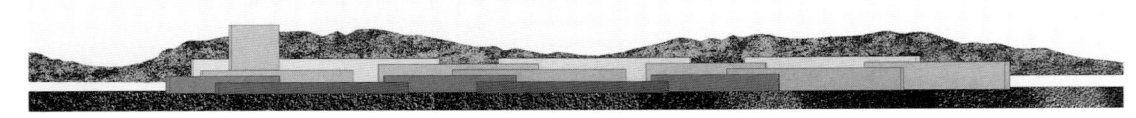

Ansicht der unterschiedlich hohen sowie verschieden langen schmalen Baukörper
Elevation of the different heights and the various, long, narrow building volumes

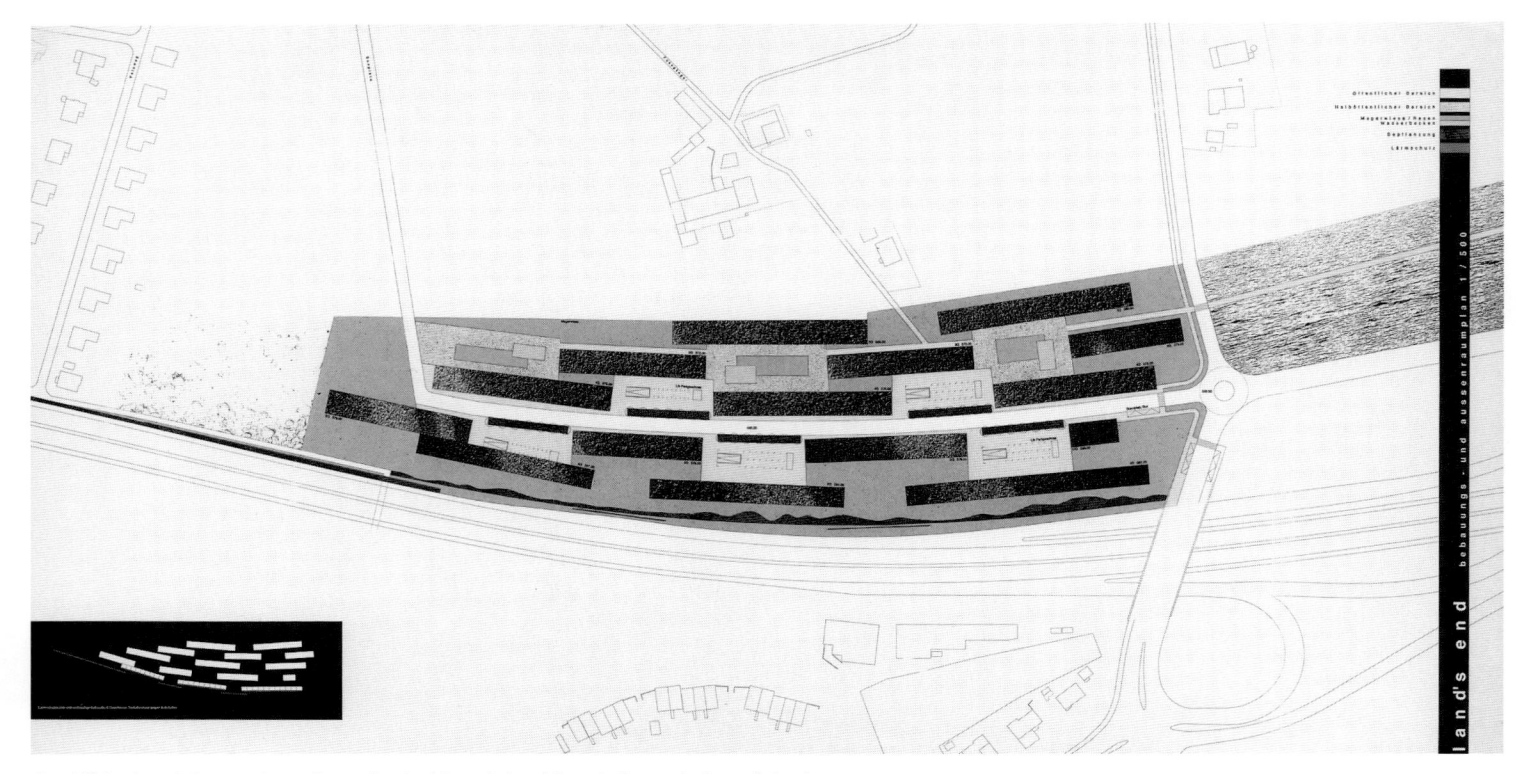

Grundriß der dynamisch angeordneten Gesamtsituation / Ground plan of dynamically organised overall situation

Anbau Ferienhaus Borer in Praz 1994

Der Wunsch nach mehr Raum und Licht führte zum zweistöckigen Anbau an das bestehende Ferienhaus. Die örtlichen klimatischen Verhältnisse – mildes Seeklima mit lokalen Winden – ließen die Idee einer Glaskonstruktion aufkommen. Die Orientierung des neuen Volumens nach Nordwesten sowie die horizontale und vertikale Querlüftung erlauben es, auf den sonst notwendigen Sonnenschutz zu verzichten, und ermöglichen so die feine, fast filigrane konstruktive Ausführung.

Extension to Borer Holiday Residence in Praz 1994

The desire for more space and light gave rise to the two-storey extension to the existing holiday residence. The local climatic conditions – mild lake climate with local winds – prompted the idea of a glass construction. The north-west orientation of the new part, and the horizontal and vertical air currents cutting across it, made it possible to do without the sun screening otherwise necessary and to use a delicate, almost filigree construction.

Ansicht des Glasanbaus an das bestehende Ferienhaus
Elevation of glass extension to existing holiday residence

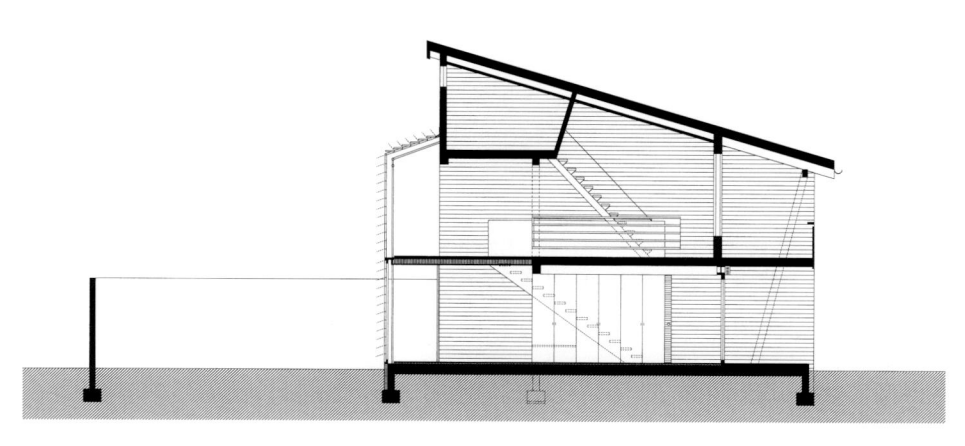

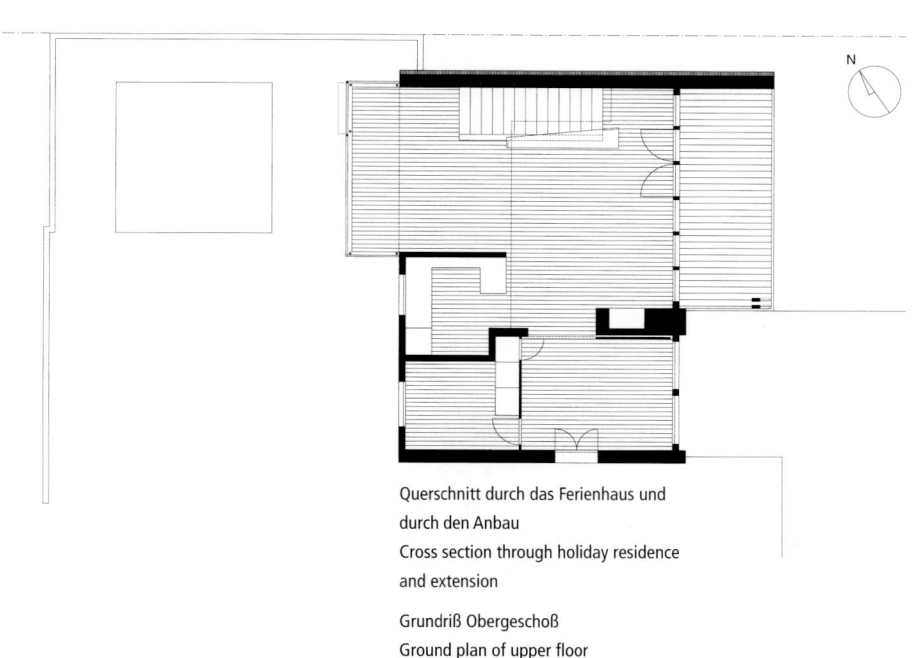

Querschnitt durch das Ferienhaus und durch den Anbau
Cross section through holiday residence and extension

Grundriß Obergeschoß
Ground plan of upper floor

Christian Gautschi · Marianne Unternährer, Zürich

Gesteuerte Interpretation

Seit rund vier Jahren führen Christian Gautschi und Marianne Unternährer ein gemeinsames Büro. In dieser Zeitspanne sind verschiedene Wettbewerbsprojekte und Studien sowie einige Umbauten entstanden. In ihrer Arbeit sind die beiden Architekten bestrebt – nachdem sie eine fundierte Analyse des Ortes geleistet haben –, die Frage zu beantworten: «Was braucht dieser bestimmte Ort im Zusammenhang mit dem neuen Programm?» Freie Felder werden kreiert, um gezielt mit individuellen Eingriffen zu wirken. Diese Interventionen können in ihren Dimensionen minimal sein, erreichen aber durch Maßstabsverfremdung, Materialisierung und Situierung ihre eigene Wirkung und ihren unverwechselbaren Ausdruck. Sie selber bezeichnen diesen Prozeß als gesteuerte Interpretation, da die Arbeit nach der Reflexion nie unvoreingenommen angegangen werden kann. Verformen, Anfügen und Weglassen sind Aktivitäten, die als Methode zur Interpretation der einzelnen Situationen im Kontext angewendet werden. Die beiden Architekten bewegen sich dabei in der Tradition der Moderne, allerdings entmystifiziert und neu entdeckt. Ihre Architektur formuliert Räume, die, klar und konsequent konzipiert und solide konstruiert, über ihren Gebrauchswert hinaus eine ihnen eigene poetische Ausstrahlung besitzen.

Controlled Interpretation

Christian Gautschi and Marianne Unternährer have run a joint architectural office for about four years. In this time they have produced various competition entries and studies, and completed a number of conversions. In their work the two architects are concerned – after carrying out an in-depth analysis of the location – to answer the question: "What does this particular place need in connection with the new programme?" Spaces are cleared to allow them to take purposeful measures. These measures may be minimal in size but, by dislocating proportions or by material use and placing, have their own unmistakable stamp. They themselves describe this process as controlled interpretation, since the work that follows reflection can never be approached without preconceptions. Re-forming, addition and omission are activities used as a method of interpreting the particular situation in its context. In this the two architects are working within the tradition of Modernism, although in a demystified and rediscovered form. Their architecture formulates spaces which, clearly and logically conceived and solidly constructed, have a poetic aura of their own over and above their utility value.

Biographie

Christian Gautschi

1957
Geboren in Thun.

1978–84
Architekturstudium an der ETH-Zürich.

1983/84
Diplom bei Professor Dolf Schnebli an der ETH-Zürich.

1984–86
Mitarbeit im Büro Schnebli + Ammann + Partner in Zürich.

1986
Selbständige Arbeiten in Zürich.

1986–88
Mitarbeit im Büro Burckhardt + Partner AG in Zürich.

1988–91
Eigenes Büro in Zürich.

1989-91
Assistent bei Professorin Flora Ruchat-Roncati an der ETH-Zürich.

Seit 1991
Gemeinsames Büro mit Marianne Unternährer in Zürich.

Marianne Unternährer

1958
Geboren in Willisau.

1979–85
Architekturstudium an der ETH-Zürich.

1984/85
Diplom bei Professor Dolf Schnebli an der ETH-Zürich.

1985–86
Mitarbeit im Büro Bob Gysin in Dübendorf.

1986–91
Mitarbeit im Büro Ueli Zbinden in Zürich.

1993–94
Assistentin bei Gastdozent Ueli Zbinden an der ETH-Zürich.

Seit 1991
Gemeinsames Büro mit Christian Gautschi in Zürich.

Ausgewähltes Werkverzeichnis

1991
SBB-Areal Station Seen in Winterthur
Studie.

Sanierung Fassade Bürohaus in Zürich
Studienauftrag.

Erweiterung Technikum in Rapperswil (Kanton St. Gallen)
Wettbewerb, sechster Preis.

1992
Wohnüberbauung in Winterthur-Seen
Bauprojekt.

Bahnhofplatz in Herne-Wanne (Deutschland)
Wettbewerb. Zusammenarbeit mit Stefan Rotzler (Landschaftsarchitekt), Zürich, und Metron (Verkehrsplanung), Windisch.

SBB-Areal in Rüti (Kanton Zürich)
Studienauftrag. Zusammenarbeit mit Metron (Verkehrsplanung), Windisch.

Jonaviadukt SBB in Rüti (Kanton Zürich)
Wettbewerb. Zusammenarbeit mit Wolfseher + Partner AG (Materialtechniker und Ingenieure), Zürich.

Umbau Dreizimmer-Wohnung in Zürich
Hönggerstraße 31
Ausgeführtes Projekt.

Umbau Terrassenwohnung Troxler-Unternährer in Willisau (Kanton Luzern)
Stegenhalde 3c
Ausgeführtes Projekt.

Umbau Wohnhaus «Lanoë» in St-Martin sur Oust, (Frankreich; 1992–93)
La Fontaine
Ausgeführtes Projekt.

1993
Überbauung Hofacker in Knutwil (Kanton Luzern)
Studie, Wohnüberbauung in verschiedenen Konzeptvarianten.

Überbauung Würzenbach in Luzern
Studie, Wohnüberbauung in Etappen.

Madagaskarhalle, Zoo in Zürich (1993–etwa 98)
Machbarkeitsstudie. Vorprojekt. Bauprojekt. Zusammenarbeit mit Abt. NL, Stahlbau, Minikus, Witta, Voss (Ingenieure), Zürich, Basler + Hofmann (Medientechnik), Zürich, und Stöckli, Kienast, Koeppel (Landschaftsarchitektur), Zürich.

Umbau und Aufstockung Wohnhaus Bruggmatt in Willisau (Kanton Luzern)
Studie.

Ökumenisches Begegnungszentrum Au in Wädenswil (Kanton Zürich)
Wettbewerb, erster Preis.

1994
Wohnüberbauung «Im Park» in Schönenwerd (Kanton Aargau)
Wettbewerb.

Büro- und Wohnhaus in Winterthur
Studienauftrag.

Wohnüberbauung in Buchs (Kanton Zürich)
Studienauftrag.

Armee-Ausbildungs-Zentrum in Luzern
Wettbewerb.

Biography

Christian Gautschi

1957
Born in Thun

1978–84
Studied architecture at the ETH Zurich

1983/84
Graduated with diploma under
Prof. Dolf Schnebli at the ETH Zurich

1984–86
Worked at the Schnebli + Ammann +
Partner architectural office in Zurich

1986
Freelance work in Zurich

1986–88
Worked at the Burckhardt & Partner AG
architectural office in Zurich

1988–91
Own architectural office
in Zurich

1989–91
Assistant to Prof. Flora Ruchat-Roncati
at the ETH Zurich

Since 1991
Joint architectural office with Marianne
Unternährer in Zurich.

Marianne Unternährer

1958
Born in Willisau

1979–85
Studied architecture at the ETH Zurich

1984/85
Graduated with diploma under
Prof. Dolf Schnebli at the ETH Zurich

1985–86
Worked at the Bob Gysin architectural
office in Dübendorf

1986–91
Worked at the Ueli Zbinden architectural
office in Zurich

1993–94
Assistant to visiting Prof. Ueli Zbinden
at the ETH Zurich

Since 1991
Joint architectural office with Christian
Gautschi in Zurich

Selected list of work

1991
SBB site station Seen in Winterthur
Study.

Refurbishment of office building façade
in Zurich
Study commission.

Extension of college of technology
in Rapperswil (Canton of St. Gallen)
Competition, sixth prize.

1992
Residential development
in Winterthur-Seen
Final project.

Bahnhofplatz in Herne-Wann, (Germany)
Competition. In collaboration
with Stefan Rotzler (landscape architect),
Zurich, and Metron (traffic planning),
Windisch.

SBB site in Rüti (Canton of Zurich)
Study commission. In collaboration with
Metron (traffic planning), Windisch.

SBB Jona viaduct in Rüti
(Canton of Zurich)
Competition. In collaboration
with Wolfseher + Partner AG (Materials
technicians and engineers), Zurich.

Conversion of three-roomed apartment
in Zurich
Hönggerstrasse 31
Completed project.

Conversion of Troxler-Unternährer
terrace apartment in Willisau
(Canton of Lucerne)
Stegenhalde 3c
Completed project.

Conversion of "Lanoë" residence in St
Martin sur Oust (France; 1992–93)
La Fontaine
Completed project.

1993
Hofacker development in Knutwil
(Canton of Lucerne)
Study, residential development
with concept variations.

Würzenbach development in Lucerne
Study, residential development in stages.

Madagaskarhalle, Zurich Zoo
(1993–approx. 98)
Feasibility study. Preliminary project.
Final project. In collaboration with Abt.
NL, Stahlbau, Minikus, Witta, Voss
(engineers), Zurich, Basler &
Hofmann (media technology), Zurich,
and Stöckli, Kienast, Koeppel (landscape-
architects), Zurich.

Conversion and upward extension
of Bruggmatt residence in Willisau
(Canton of Lucerne)
Study.

Au Ecumenical meeting centre
in Wädenswil (Canton of Zurich)
Competition, first prize.

1994
"Im Park" residential development
in Schönenwerd (Canton of Aargau)
Competition.

Office and residential building
in Winterthur
Study commission.

Residential development in Buchs
(Canton of Zurich)
Study commission.

Army training centre in Lucerne
Competition.

Umbau Terrassenwohnung Troxler-Unternährer in Willisau 1992

Die Wohnung ist Teil einer typischen Terrassensiedlung. Die Entwurfsidee bestand in der Umdeutung der Raumverhältnisse, ohne Veränderung von bestehenden Öffnungen oder Erschließung. Die Architekten interpretieren die bestehende Küche als Körper im Raum. Die Außenabwicklung ist mit Behältern aus Ahornholz verkleidet, die Innenseiten sind mit Chromstahlblech ausgelegt. Auffallend ist die präzise Einteilung in klare Schichten sowie die Auswahl der Materialien und Farben. Wände, Decken, Rahmen und Türblätter sind als ruhiger Hintergrund in gebrochenem Weiß gestrichen. Der Boden ist durchgehend mit Parkett aus Ahornholz belegt.

Conversion of Troxler-Unternährer Terrace Apartment in Willisau 1992

The apartment is part of a typical estate with terraces. The design concept involved reinterpreting spatial relationships without altering existing openings or services. The architects interpret the existing kitchen as a body in space. On the outside are maple-clad containers, whereas on the inside stainless steel sheet was used. The precise arrangement in clear layers and the choice of materials and colours are striking features. The walls, ceilings, frames and doors are painted in broken white to provide a calm background. The floor is covered in maple-wood parquet throughout.

Außenabwicklung des Küchenraums mit Behältern aus Ahornholz
Exterior of kitchen area with maple-clad containers

Längsschnitt durch die Küche / Longitudinal section through kitchen

Ansicht der Außenabwicklung / Exterior elevation

Längsschnitt durch die Toilette / Longitudinal section through toilet

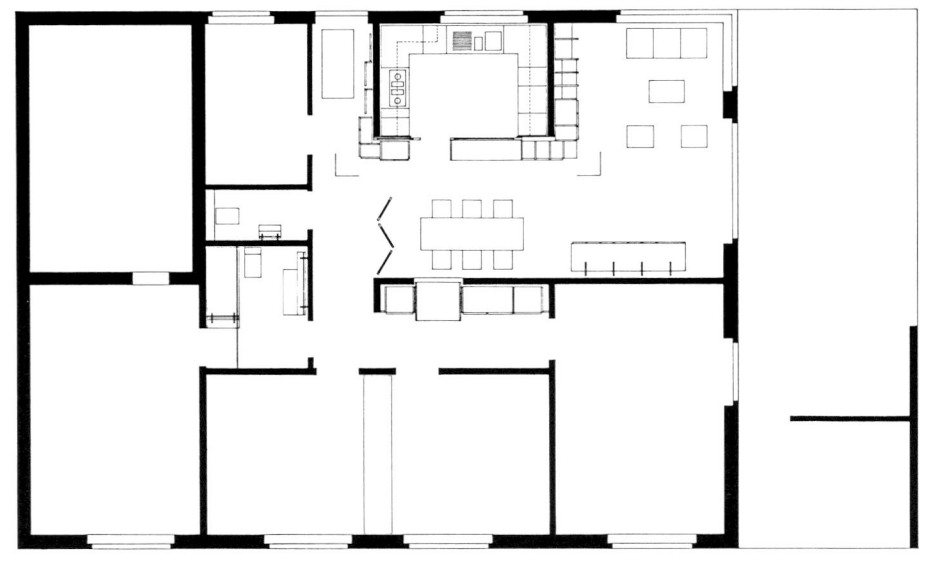

Grundriß der neuen Raumaufteilung / Ground plan of new spatial division

Umbau Wohnhaus «Lanoë» in St-Martin sur Oust, Frankreich 1992–1993

Das bestehende Wohnhaus weist die typischen Eigenschaften der bretonischen Einraumhäuser auf: Eingeschossig steht das Wohnhaus in einer Zeile, besitzt eine Feuerstelle an beiden Querseiten und in der Mitte der Längsseiten eine Tür, die seitlich von je einem Fenster flankiert ist. Der Dachraum, als Speicher benutzt, war früher nur von außen, über eine kleine Lukarne erreichbar. Zwei mächtige Eichenbalken mit darüberliegenden Querträgern gliedern den Raum. Im Erdgeschoß ist die Treppe als Körper in das schmale Mittelfeld gesetzt und unterteilt den Raum in einen Wohn- und einen Kochbereich. Dieses eingeschobene Volumen enthält im Dachgeschoß die Naßzelle und den Treppenaufgang. Zwei Schlafzimmer umgeben diesen Bereich.

Conversion of "Lanoë" Residence in St. Martin sur Oust, France 1992–1993

The existing residence has typical qualities of Breton single-room houses: it has one storey, is part of a row, has a hearth on both the transverse sides and a door in the middle of each longitudinal side, flanked on each side by a window. The attic, used for storage, was previously accessible only from outside, through a skylight. Two massive oak beams with transverse joists above them give the room structure. On the ground floor the staircase is placed as a separate body in the narrow centre section, dividing the room into a living and a kitchen area. On the attic floor this inserted element contains the bathroom and the top of the stairs. This area is enclosed by two bedrooms.

Treppe als im schmalen Mittelfeld plazierter Körper
Stairs placed in the narrow central section

Küche in einem seitlichen Feld angeordnet
Kitchen placed in side section

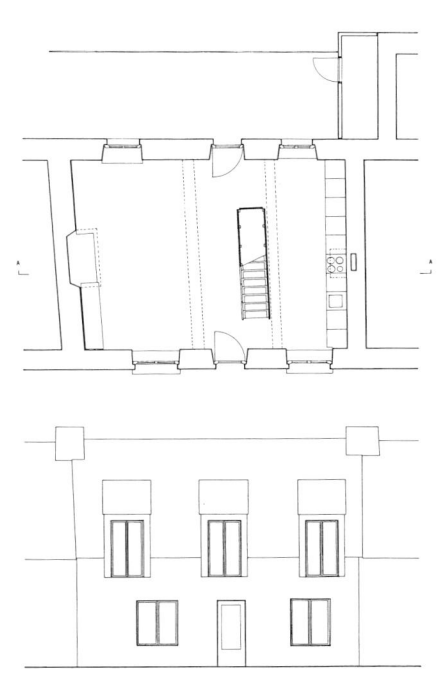

Grundriß Erdgeschoß
Ground floor plan

Südfassade
South façade

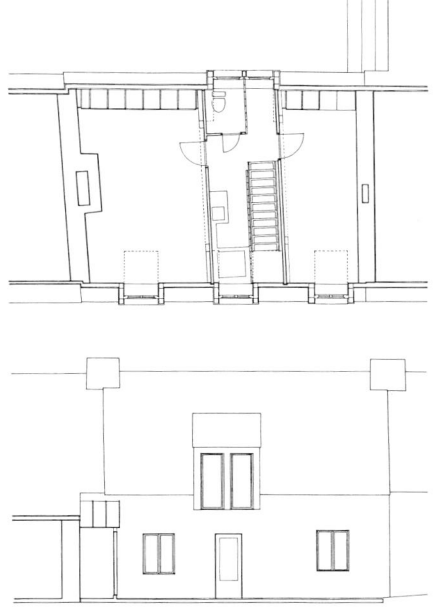

Grundriß Obergeschoß / Ground plan of upper floor

Nordfassade / North façade

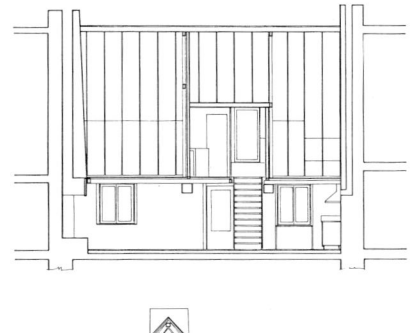

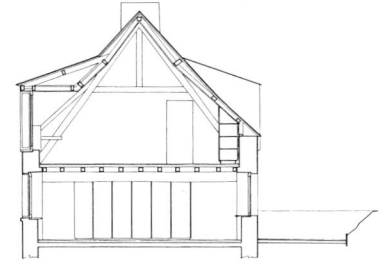

Längsschnitt durch die Naßzelle und durch die Treppe
Longitudinal section through bathroom unit and stairs

Querschnitt durch die Dachkonstruktion
Cross section through roof construction

**Madagaskarhalle, Zoo in Zürich
1993–etwa 1998**

Die Ökosystemhalle mit Regenwaldklima ist auf dem Erweiterungsgelände, nordöstlich des bestehenden Zoos, geplant. Die Parzelle ist von drei Seiten mit Wald umgeben und fällt gleichmäßig ab. Die architektonisch als neutrales Gefäß interpretierte Hülle folgt in ihrem Volumen ruhig der gegebenen Topographie. Zehn parallele, gedrungene Bogen aus Stahl, die sich teilweise in das Gelände eingraben, überspannen je eine Breite von 90 Metern und definieren so den Innenraum. Die einheitliche Materialisierung der Dacheindeckung und der Stirnseiten unterstützt die Illusion eines endlosen, introvertierten Raumes. Der Grundriß ist an den Stirnseiten ausgeklappt und nimmt über die Vorbauten räumlich und maßstäblich Bezug auf die unmittelbare Umgebung.

**Madagaskarhalle, Zurich Zoo
1993–approx. 1998**

The eco-system hall with rain-forest climate is planned to be built on the extension area north-east of the existing zoo. The plot is surrounded by woods on three sides and has an even descending slope. The volume of the casing, interpreted architecturally as a neutral container, follows the given topography without resistance. Each of ten squat, parallel steel arches, partly embedded in the soil, spans a width of 90 metres, thus defining the interior space. The uniform material used for ceiling and end faces reinforces the illusion of an endless, introverted space. The floor plan opens out at the ends, using the porches to set up a relationship, in terms of space and scale, with the immediate surroundings.

Machbarkeitsstudie: Modell mit der umliegenden Topographie
Feasibility study: model with surrounding topography

Perspektivische Darstellung des Restaurants / Perspective drawing of the restaurant

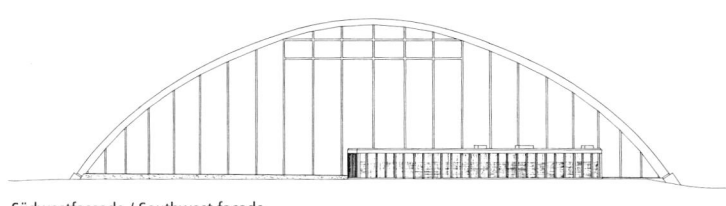

Südwestfassade / Southwest façade

Querschnitt durch den gedrungenen Stahlbogen / Cross section through compact steel arches

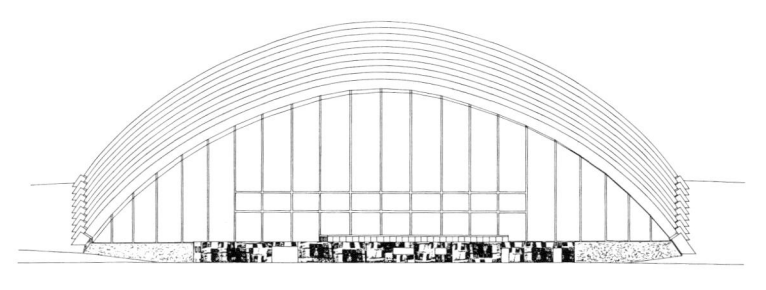

Nordostfassade / Northeast façade

Südostfassade / Southeast façade

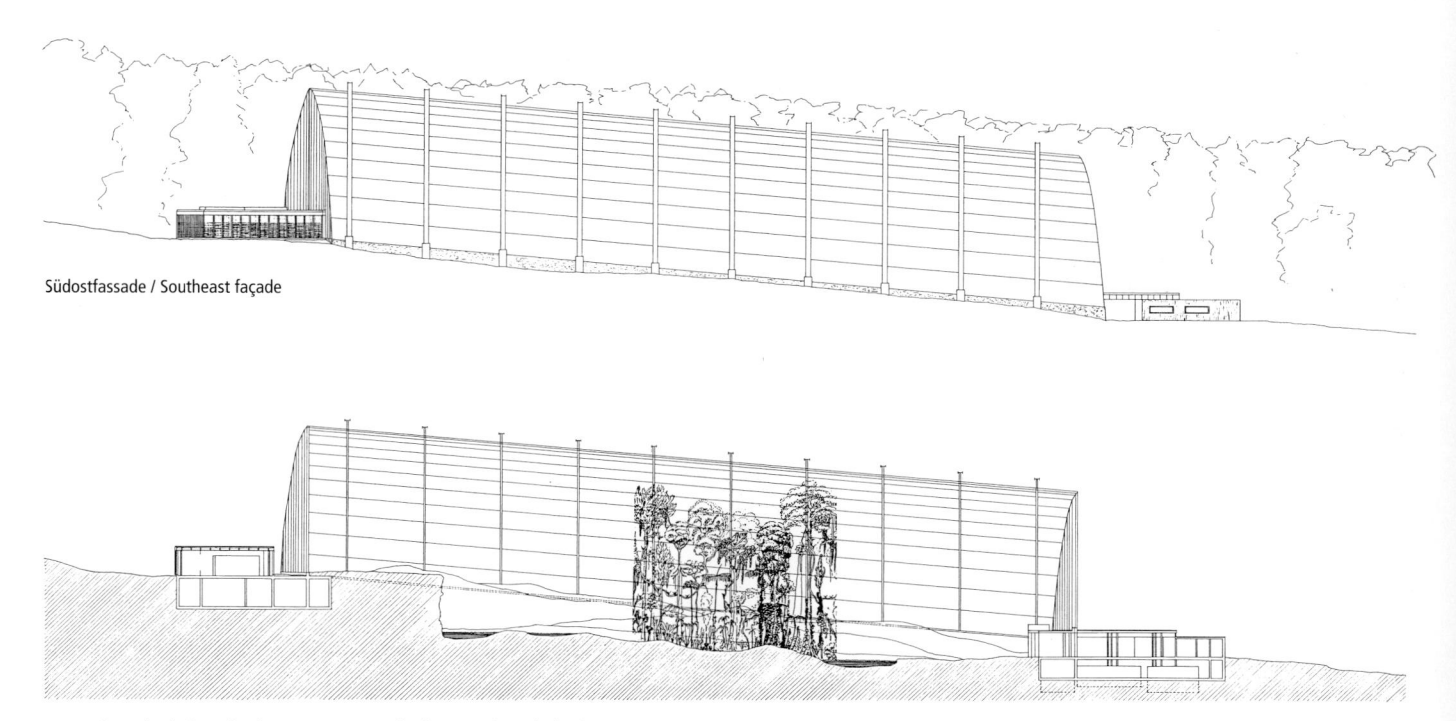

Längsschnitt durch die Geländeneigung / Longitudinal section through the sloping site

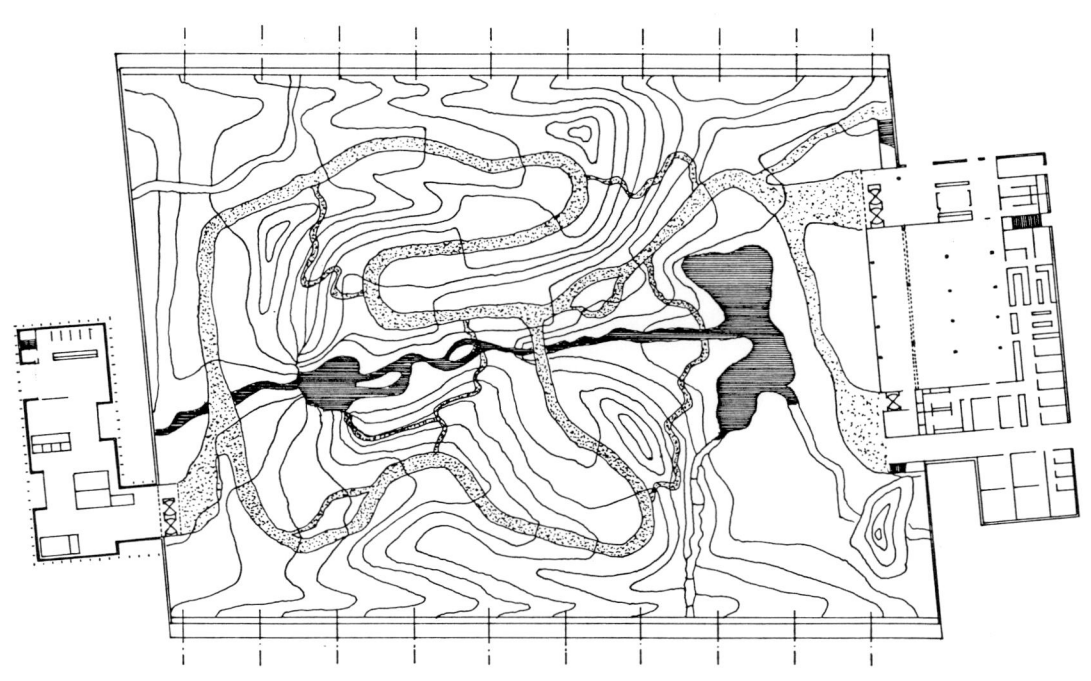

Grundriß mit den seitlichen Anbauten / Ground plan with lateral structures

Ökumenisches Begegnungszentrum Au in Wädenswil 1993

Das Projekt für das ökumenische Begegnungszentrum knüpft an die Typologie der umliegenden Bauernhöfe mit funktionsbestimmten Einzelgebäuden an. Verschieden große Volumen dienen den einzelnen Nutzungen. In ihrem Zusammenspiel bilden die Baukörper Außenräume von unterschiedlicher Ausdehnung und mit wechselnden Charakteristika. Die zu erhaltende, denkmalgeschützte alte Scheune ist als dominantes Element der Anlage lesbar. Der Gottesdienstraum, als würfelförmiges Volumen konzipiert, erlaubt verschiedene Möblierungen. Die Jugend- und Gruppenräume sind ihrem seriellen Auftreten in einem längsgerichteten Körper untergebracht, der sich halbgeschossig versetzt am Abhang entwickelt. Da die Kuben nur auf sich selbst verweisen, kommt durch ihre Verschiedenheit eine gegenseitige Verstärkung zustande.

Au Ecumenical Meeting Centre in Wädenswil 1993

The project for the ecumenical meeting centre connects with the typology of the surrounding farms by using functional, separate buildings. Volumes of various sizes meet the different needs. Through their interplay the buildings form external spaces of differing area and changing characteristics. The barn, which is to be preserved as a listed building, is clearly legible as the dominant element in the complex. The hall for worship, conceived as a cube, permits a range of different options in placing furniture. The rooms for youth and groups are housed serially in a longitudinal building which accommodates the slope by a half-floor offset. As the cubes refer only to themselves, their disparity produces an effect of reciprocal reinforcement.

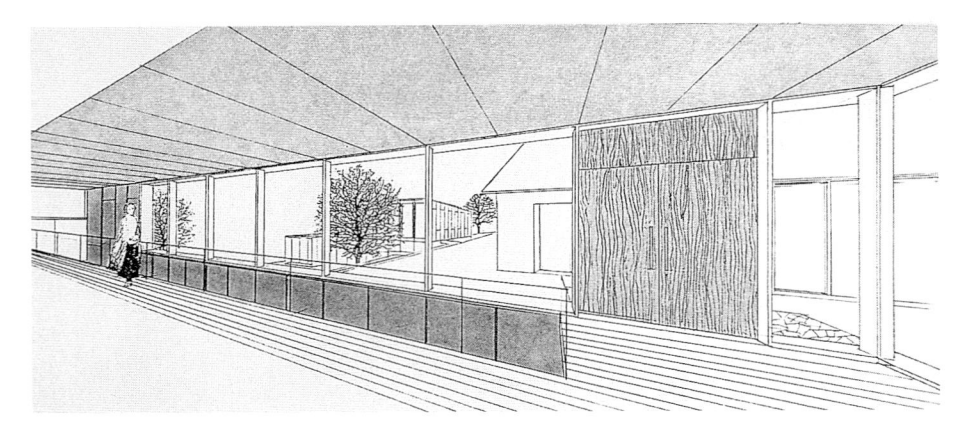

Perspektivische Darstellungen / Perspective drawings

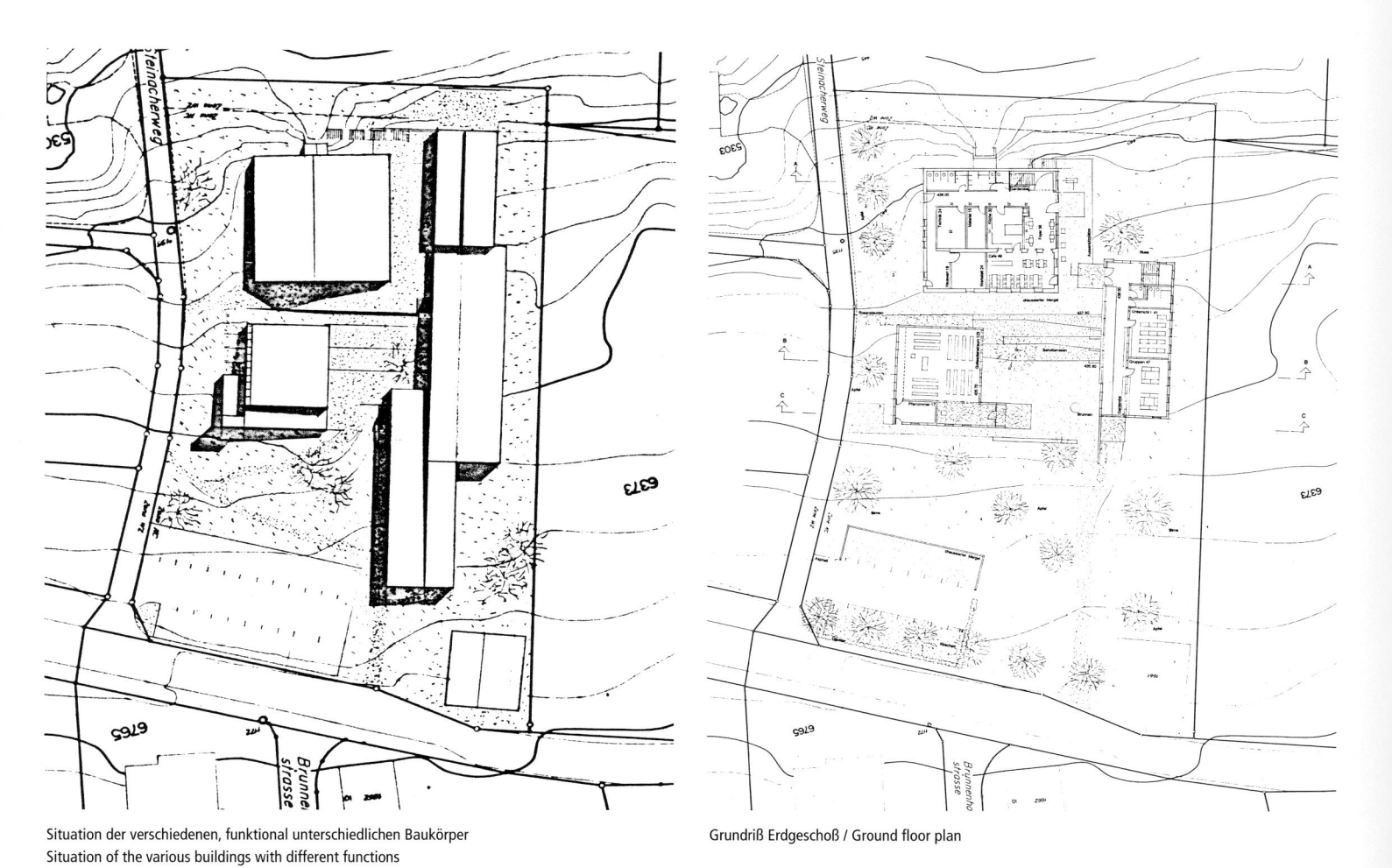

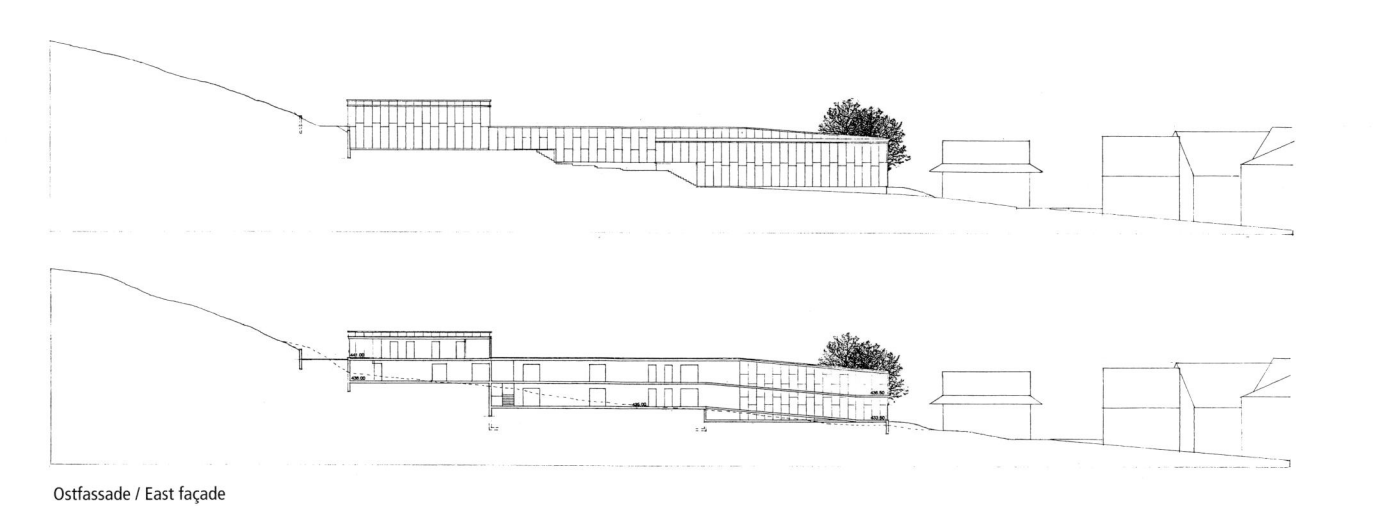

Situation der verschiedenen, funktional unterschiedlichen Baukörper
Situation of the various buildings with different functions

Grundriß Erdgeschoß / Ground floor plan

Ostfassade / East façade

Querschnitt durch die Jugend- und Gruppenräume
Cross section through youth and group rooms

Dieter Jüngling · Andreas Hagmann, Chur

Architektonisches Schichten

«Wir haben keinen Stil», so definieren Dieter Jüngling und Andreas Hagmann pragmatisch ihre Architektur. Die beiden arbeiten befreit von belastenden Konventionen und Ideologien. Ihr bisheriges Schaffen, zahlreiche Wettbewerbsprojekte sowie einige Ausführungen, ist nachhaltig geprägt durch eine präzise, glasklare und bis ins letzte Detail konsequente Denkweise. Sie selber beschreiben ihren entwerferischen Prozeß als ein akribisches Suchen nach einem adäquaten Thema, dem alles unterzuordnen sei. Das Thema ergebe sich aus dem jeweiligen Ort und der entsprechenden Aufgabenstellung. Aus der intensiven Interpretation des einmal formulierten Themas entwickle sich sodann der Bau losgelöst von individuellen Präferenzen. Auffallend in ihren bisher realisierten Bauten ist das architektonische Schichten; dies bezüglich einzelner Materialien, aber auch der Innen- und Außenräume. So etwa bei ihrem ersten gemeinsam projektierten und ausgeführten Bau: der Höheren Technischen Lehranstalt in Chur, bei dem sie die aus drei verschiedenen Baukörpern bestehende Anlage vollständig in rohe, industriell vorgestanzte Kupfertafeln kleiden und das Prinzip einer geschichteten Fassade thematisieren. Beim Schul- und Gemeindezentrum in Mastrils sind es nicht primär die Materialien, die geschichtet werden, sondern die Räume. Die Haltung von Jüngling und Hagmann ist mit jener der Architekten Herzog & de Meuron vergleichbar: «Wir nehmen alles, was erhältlich ist - Backstein und Beton, Stein und Holz, Metall und Glas, Wörter und Bilder. Das Material ist dazu da, den Bau zu bestimmen, aber der Bau ist in gleichem Maße da, um zu zeigen, aus was er gemacht ist.»

Architectural Layering

"We have no style" – this is Dieter Jüngling's and Andreas Hagmann's pragmatic definition of their architecture. They work unencumbered by conventions and ideologies. Their work to date, numerous competition entries and a number of completed projects, is lastingly influenced by a mode of thinking which is precise, crystal clear and logical down to its last detail. They themselves describe their design process as a meticulous search for an adequate theme under which everything can be subsumed. The theme emerges from the given place and the set task. The building then develops from the intensive interpretation of the theme, once formulated, independently of individual preferences. Architectural layering is a striking feature of their buildings completed so far, in relation both to individual materials and to the interior and exterior spaces of the buildings. This can be seen, for example, in their first jointly designed and executed building, the Höhere Technische Anstalt (college of technology) in Chur. The complex, consisting of three different blocks, is entirely clad in unfinished, industrially pre-stamped copper panels, embodying the principle of a layered façade. In the school and community centre in Mastrils it is not the materials that are layered, but the rooms. Jüngling's and Hagmann's attitude is comparable to that of the architects Herzog & de Meuron: "We take everything we can get hold of – brick and concrete, natural stone and wood, metal and glass, words and images. The material is there to determine the structure, but the structure is no less there to show what it is made of."

Biographie

Dieter Jüngling

1957
Geboren in Basel.

1978–79
Mitarbeit im Büro Herzog & de Meuron in Basel.

1979–82
Architekturstudium an der HTL in Muttenz.

1983–86
Mitarbeit im Büro Herzog & de Meuron in Basel.

1986–90
Mitarbeit im Büro Peter Zumthor in Haldenstein, Graubünden.

Seit 1990
Gemeinsames Büro mit Andreas Hagmann in Chur.

Andreas Hagmann

1959
Geboren in Luzern.

1980–87
Architekturstudium an der ETH-Zürich.

1985–87
Mitarbeit bei der Denkmalpflege Graubünden.

1987
Diplom bei Professor Fabio Reinhart an der ETH-Zürich.

1987–90
Mitarbeit im Büro Peter Zumthor in Haldenstein, Graubünden.

Seit 1990
Gemeinsames Büro mit Dieter Jüngling in Chur.

Auszeichnungen

1994
Eidgenössisches Kunststipendium.

1994
Auszeichnung guter Bauten im Kanton Graubünden (Höhere Technische Lehranstalt in Chur).

Ausgewähltes Werkverzeichnis

1990
Postgebäude in Zillis
(Kanton Graubünden)
Wettbewerb, dritter Preis.

Umbau und Sanierung Staatskeller in Chur (1990–91)
Reichsgasse
Ausgeführtes Projekt.

Höhere Technische Lehranstalt in Chur (1990–93)
Ringstraße/Pulvermühlestraße
Wettbewerb, erster Preis. Ausgeführtes Projekt.

1991
Ausbau Flabschießplatz in Brigels
(Kanton Graubünden)
Wettbewerb, erster Preis.

Zentrum in Heerbrugg
(Kanton St. Gallen)
Ideenwettbewerb, erster Preis.

Quartierplan Cunclas in Sils
(Kanton Graubünden)
Wettbewerb.

1992
Schulhaus und Gemeindezentrum in Molinis (Kanton Graubünden)
Wettbewerb.

Postgebäude in Lohn
(Kanton Graubünden)
Wettbewerb, dritter Preis.

Gestaltung Regierungsplatz in Chur
Wettbewerb. Zusammenarbeit mit Conradin Clavout, Chur, und Jürg Conzett, Chur.

Schulhaus und Gemeindezentrum in Mastrils (Kanton Graubünden; 1992–95)
Dalavo
Wettbewerb, erster Preis.
Ausgeführtes Projekt.

Ausbau und Sanierung Waffenplatz St. Luzisteig (Kanton Graubünden; 1992)
Arbeitsgemeinschaft mit Peter Zumthor, Haldenstein. Baufachorgan: Amt für Bundesbauten Baukreis 2 Lugano. Bauherrschaft: EMD, Stab GA AWP.

1993
Schulhaus und Mehrzweckhalle in Fanas (Kanton Graubünden)
Wettbewerb, zweiter Preis.

Umbau Mehrfamilienhaus in Felsberg (Kanton Graubünden; 1993–94)
Obere Gasse
Ausgeführtes Projekt.

Doppel-Einfamilienhaus in Felsberg (Kanton Graubünden; 1993–95)
Oberfeld
Ausgeführtes Projekt.

Umbau und Sanierung Schulhaus Peist (Kanton Graubünden; 1993–95)
Ausgeführtes Projekt.

1994
Schulhaus und Mehrzweckhalle in Vella (Kanton Graubünden)
Wettbewerb, zweiter Preis. Zusammenarbeit mit Reto Schaufelbühl, Chur.

Schulhaus und Mehrzweckhalle in Thusis (Kanton Graubünden)
Wettbewerb, erster Preis.

Schulhaus und Mehrzweckhalle in St. Peter (Kanton Graubünden)
Wettbewerb, dritter Preis. Zusammenarbeit mit Jürg Meister, Wien.

Kur- und Golfzentrum in Alvaneu
(Kanton Graubünden)
Wettbewerb, erster Preis.

Biography

Dieter Jüngling
1957
Born in Basle
1978–79
Worked at the Herzog & de Meuron architectural office in Basle
1979–82
Studied architecture at the HTL in Muttenz
1983–86
Worked at the Herzog & de Meuron architectural office in Basle
1986–90
Worked at the Peter Zumthor architectural office in Haldenstein, Grisons
Since 1990
Joint architectural office with Andreas Hagmann in Chur.

Andreas Hagmann
1959
Born in Lucerne
1980–87
Studied architecture at the ETH Zurich
1985–87
Worked at the Grisons Department for the Preservation of Monuments
1987
Graduated with diploma under Prof. Fabio Reinhart at the ETH Zurich
1987–90
Worked at the Peter Zumthor architectural office in Haldenstein, Grisons
Since 1990
Joint architectural office with Dieter Jüngling in Chur.

Awards
1994
Swiss State Art Scholarship
1994
Award for Good Buildings in the Canton of Grisons
(Höhere Technische Lehranstalt in Chur).

Selected list of work

1990
Post office building in Zillis
(Canton of Grisons)
Competition, third prize.

Conversion and refurbishment of Staatskeller in Chur (1990–91)
Reichsgasse
Completed project.

Höhere Technische Lehranstalt (College of Technology) in Chur (1990–93)
Ringstrasse/Pulvermühlestrasse
Competition, first prize.
Completed project.

1991
Development of Flabschiessplatz in Brigels (Canton of Grisons)
Competition, first prize.

Centre in Heerbrugg
(Canton of St. Gallen)
Ideas competition, first prize.

Cunclas district plan in Sils
(Canton of Grisons)
Competition.

1992
School and community centre in Molinis (Canton of Grisons)
Competition.

Post office building in Lohn
(Canton of Grisons)
Competition, third prize.

Design for Regierungsplatz in Chur
Competition. In collaboration with Conradin Clavout, Chur, and Jürg Conzett, Chur.

School and community centre in Mastrils
(Canton of Grisons; 1992–95)
Dalavo
Competition, first prize.
Completed project.

Development and refurbishment of Waffenplatz, St. Luzisteig
(Canton of Grisons; 1992)
In collaboration with Peter Zumthor, Haldenstein. Client: Federal Building Inspectorate, Baukreis 2 Lugano / EMD, Stab GA AWP.

1993
School and multipurpose hall in Fanas
(Canton of Grisons)
Competition, second prize.

Conversion of multiple dwelling in Felsberg (Canton of Grisons; 1993–94)
Obere Gasse
Completed project.

Pair of semi-detached houses in Felsberg (Canton of Grisons; 1993–95)
Oberfeld
Completed project.

Conversion and refurbishment of school in Peist (Canton of Grisons; 1993–95)
Completed project.

1994
School and multipurpose hall in Vella (Canton of Grisons)
Competition, second prize. In collaboration with Reto Schaufelbühl, Chur.

School and multipurpose hall in Thusis
(Canton of Grisons)
Competition, first prize.

School and multipurpose hall in St. Peter
(Canton of Grisons)
Competition, third prize. In collaboration with Jürg Meister, Vienna.

Health and golf centre in Alvaneu
(Canton of Grisons)
Competition, first prize.

Höhere Technische Lehranstalt in Chur
1990–1993

Inmitten eines typischen, wenig attraktiven Industriequartiers, unweit des Stadtzentrums, setzen die Architekten ihr Gebäude in Beziehung zu den heterogenen Außenräumen der Umgebung. Die aus naturbelassenen Kupfertafeln gefügte Fassade, auf der sich im Laufe der Zeit eine dunkle Patina bilden wird, thematisiert das Prinzip einer geschichteten, hängenden Metallhülle. Der geheimnisvollen Atmosphäre außen antwortet innen, zwischen dem Unterrichts- und dem Labortrakt, ein stiller, konzentrierter Raum, die polyfunktionale Aula. Die zenitale Lichtführung erfolgt über einen geschoßhohen, kassettenförmigen Trägerrost aus Sichtbeton, der gleichzeitig die Aufhängung eines verschiebbaren Wandsystems für verschiedene Nutzungsarten bildet.

Höhere Technische Lehranstalt (College of Technology) in Chur
1990–1993

Amid a typical, far from attractive industrial district not far from the town centre, the architects have placed their building in a relationship to the heterogeneous spaces visible around it. The façade, made of untreated copper panels on which a dark patina will form in the course of time, embodies the principle of a layered, hanging metal skin. The mysterious atmosphere on the outside is answered, on the inside, between the lecture rooms and the laboratory zone, by a still, concentrated space, the multi-functional hall. The light from the apex passes through a storey-high, coffered support grid of exposed concrete, which at the same time acts as a guide for a sliding partition system to allow different uses of the space.

Ansicht der aus naturbelassenen Kupfertafeln gefügten Außenfassade
Elevation of façade of untreated copper panels

Polyfunktionale Aula mit dem geschoßhohen kasettenförmigen Trägerrost aus Sichtbeton
Multipurpose hall with storey-high coffered support grid of exposed concrete

Grundriß Erdgeschoß / Ground floor plan

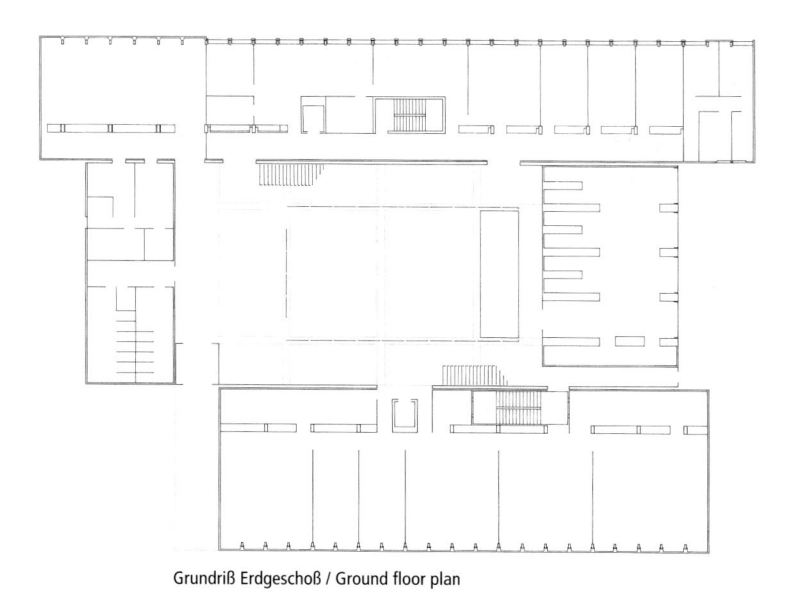

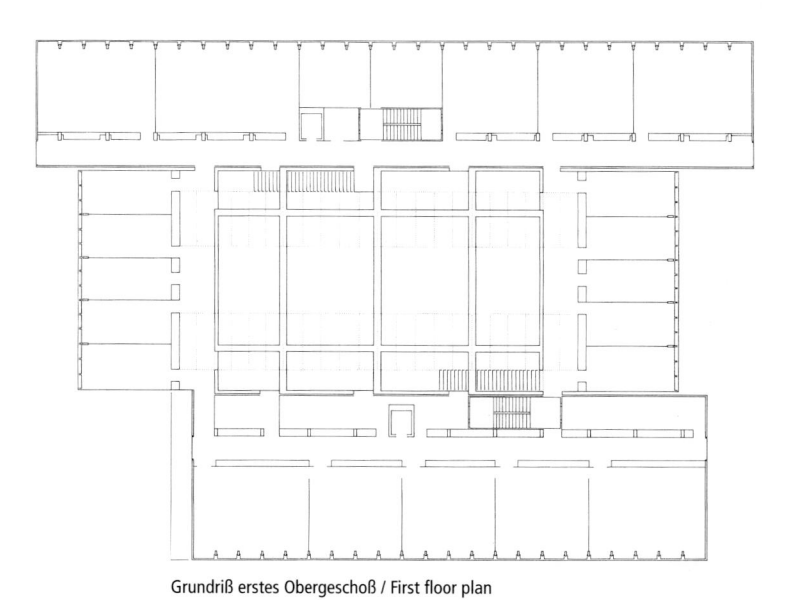

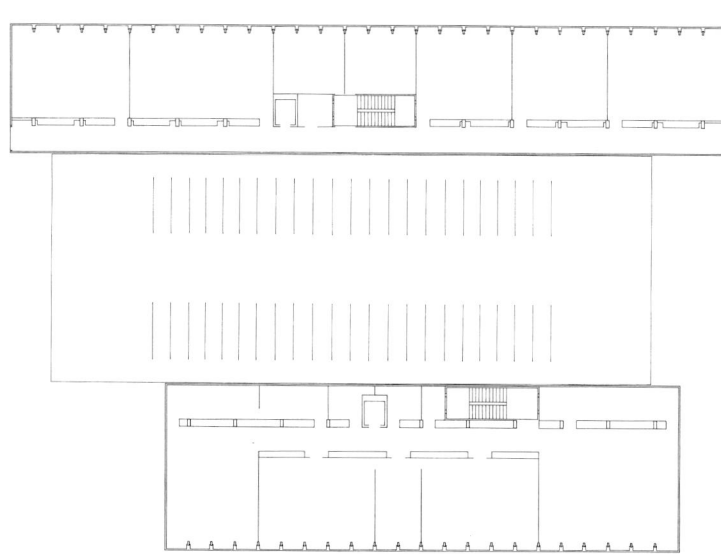

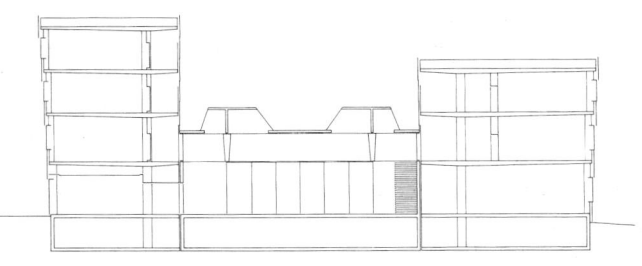

Querschnitt durch die gesamte Anlage / Cross section through whole complex

Grundriß erstes Obergeschoß / First floor plan

Grundriß zweites Obergeschoß / Second floor plan

Schulhaus und Gemeindezentrum in Mastrils 1992–1995

Um die markante Geländekammer im geographischen Mittelpunkt des Dorfes, zwischen einer Felskuppe und einem Bachtobel, zu unterstützen, stellen die Architekten ihren Baukörper senkrecht zur gegebenen Topographie. Die daraus resultierende Höhendifferenz bewältigen sie mit der Aufeinanderschichtung von fünf geschoßweise versetzten Trakte, die mit einem asymmetrischen Satteldach abgeschlossen sind. Innen ist dieses Thema durch eine über alle Geschosse verlaufende Kaskadentreppe mit stirnseitigen Ausblicken weitergeführt. Diese Baustruktur erlaubt es, verschiedene Nutzungen – wie Klassenzimmer, Kindergarten, Mehrzweckanlage, Wohnung und Gemeindeverwaltung – in eine kompakte Anordnung aufzunehmen.

School and Community Centre in Mastrils 1992–1995

To reinforce the distinctive landscape feature, at the geographical centre of the village, between a cliff and a stream gulley, the architects place their building at right angles to the given topography. They accommodate the resulting height difference by juxtaposing five successive sections, each offset to the next by the height of one storey and covered by an asymmetrical saddle roof. Inside the building this theme is carried over by a cascade staircase connecting all storeys, with views out from the end wall. This structure allows different functions – such as classrooms, kindergarten, multipurpose centre, living accommodation and local authorities administration – to be embraced in a compact arrangement.

Ostfassade / East façade

Nordfassade / North façade

Querschnitt durch das dritte, aufeinandergeschichtete Volumen, das die Klassenzimmer beherbergt
Cross section through the third, layered volume containing the classrooms

Längsschnitt durch die Kaskadentreppe
Longitudinal section through the cascading steps

Grundriß Erdgeschoß Gemeindeverwaltung
Ground floor plan of local authority administration offices

Grundriß erstes Obergeschoß: Klassenzimmer
Plan of first floor with classrooms

Grundriß zweites Obergeschoß: Klassenzimmer
Plan of second floor with classrooms

Grundriß drittes Obergeschoß: Mehrzweckhalle und Wohnung
Plan of third floor with multipurpose hall and apartment

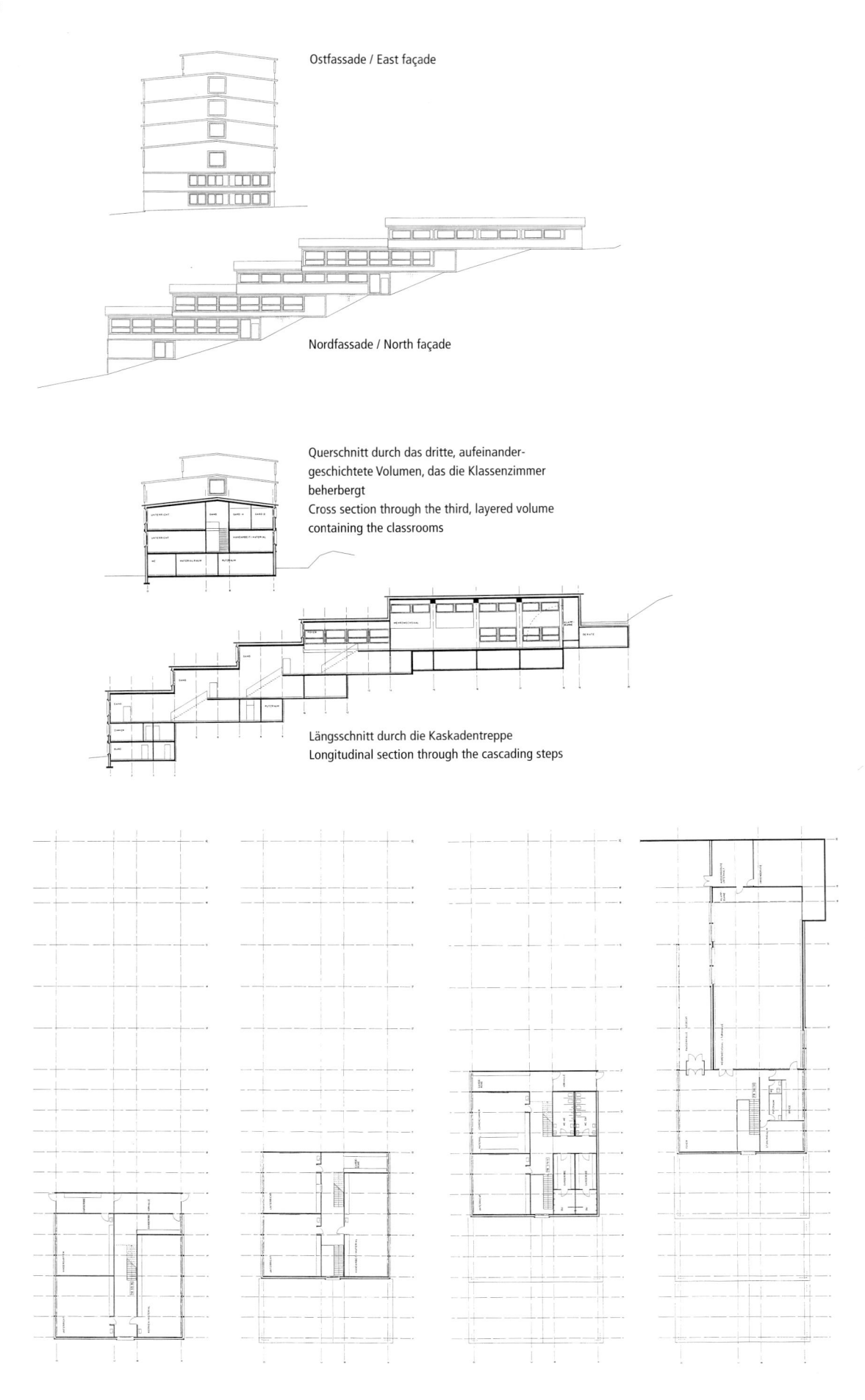

Ausbau und Sanierung Waffenplatz St. Luzisteig 1992

In Arbeitsgemeinschaft mit Peter Zumthor restaurieren die Architekten die historische Bausubstanz der kunstgeschichtlich bedeutenden militärischen Befestigungsanlage St. Luzisteig, die einzige vollständig erhaltene Sperranlage in der Schweiz aus der ersten Hälfte des neunzehnten Jahrhunderts. Die Anlage wird zudem mit Neubauten ergänzt und so den modernen Anforderungen angepaßt. Der Raum zwischen den historisch wertvollen Teilen ist in markante Geländekanten aufgefächert, denen die neuen Baukörper zugeordnet sind. Von dieser Terrainmodellierung bestimmt, ordnen sie sich zusammen mit der bestehenden Bausubstanz in eine geschlossene Gesamtanlage ein. Die neuen Bauten werden in Sichtbeton und mit markanter Differenzierung von Sockel und weit auskragenden Obergeschossen erstellt.

Development and Refurbishment of Waffenplatz, St. Luzisteig 1992

In collaboration with Peter Zumthor, the architects are restoring the historic fabric of the fortifications at St. Luzisteig. The site is of art-historical significance, being the only completely preserved barricade from the first half of the nineteenth century in Switzerland. New buildings are also being added, to adapt the site to modern requirements. The area between the parts of historic interest is divided into striking, fan-like terraces on which the new buildings are arranged. Determined by this modelling of the terrain, they combine with the existing buildings to form a closed complex. The new buildings are built of exposed concrete with sharp differentiation between the socle and the projecting upper storeys.

Modell der historischen und neuen Bausubstanz / Model of historic and new building substance

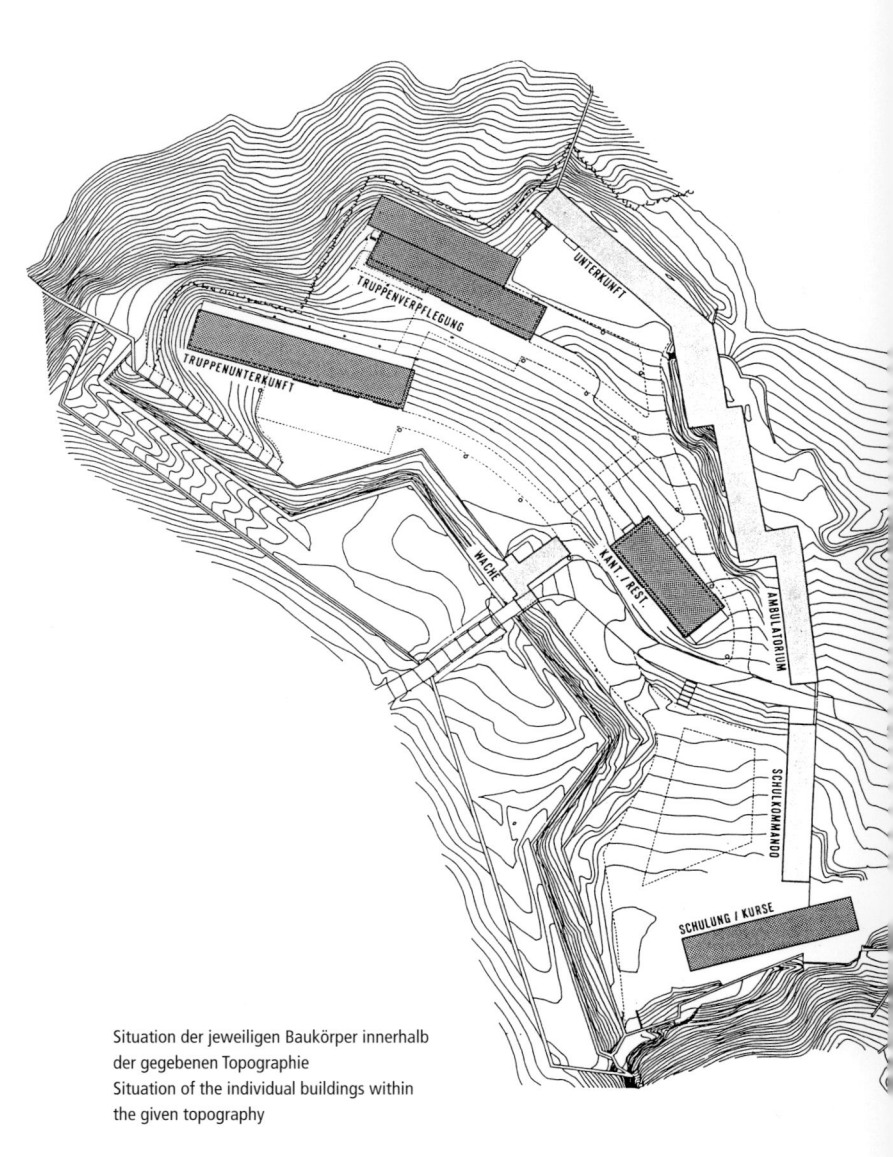

Situation der jeweiligen Baukörper innerhalb der gegebenen Topographie
Situation of the individual buildings within the given topography

Schulhaus und Mehrzweckhalle in Thusis 1994

Die Identität des Ortes ergibt sich aus der weiten Ebene mit steil abfallender Geländekante zur tiefer gelegenen Landschaft des Rheins. Diese prägnante topographische Eigenheit wird mittels parkähnlichen, längsgerichteten Außenräumen erfahrbar gemacht. Typologisch sucht die neue Anlage ein Gleichgewicht zwischen den räumlichen und physiologischen Vorzügen einer Pavillonschule und der teilweisen Verdichtung einer mehrgeschossigen Bauweise. Die einzelnen Baukörper sind durch innere Gärten, die der Orientierung, Belichtung und Belüftung dienen, gegliedert. Eine übersichtliche und einfache Baustruktur unterstützt eine rationelle Bauweise.

School and Multipurpose Hall in Thusis 1994

The identity of the village is created by the wide plain with a steep slope down to the lower-lying landscape of the Rhine. This striking topographical feature is further emphasised by park-like, longitudinal outdoor spaces. Typologically, the new complex seeks to strike a balance between the spatial and physiological advantages of a pavilion school and partial concentration in a multi-storey structure. The different buildings are structured by inner gardens, which facilitate orientation, lighting and ventilation. The simple, clear layout is reinforced by rational constructional techniques.

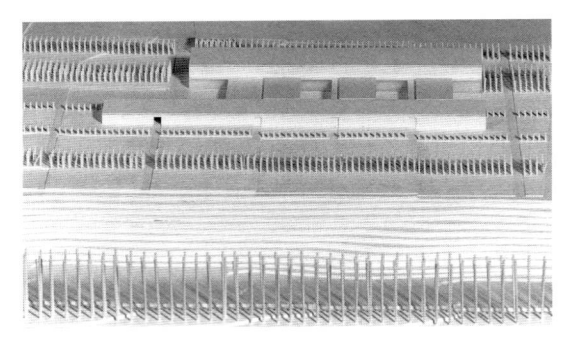

Modell der Wettbewerbseingabe / Competition model

Längsschnitt durch die mittlere Partie / Longitudinal section through central part

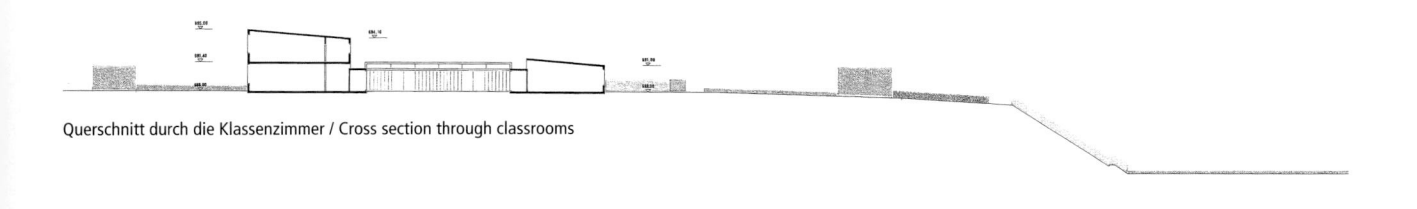

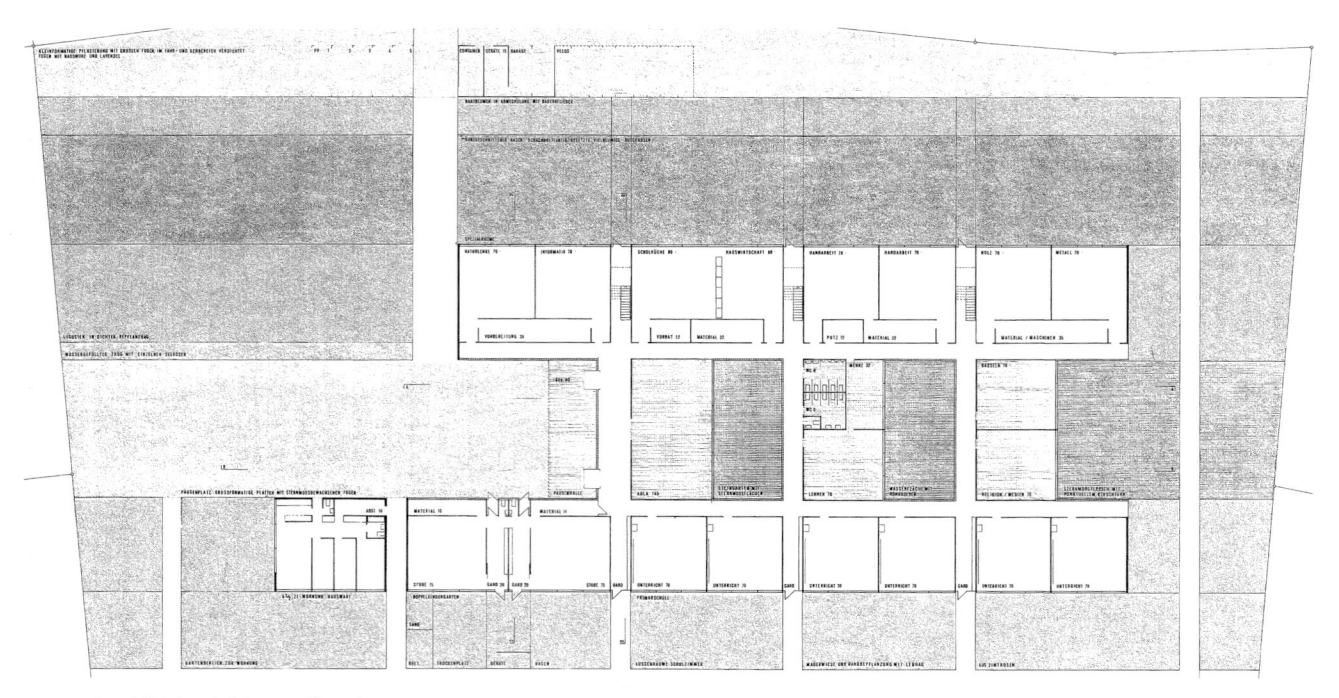

Querschnitt durch die Klassenzimmer / Cross section through classrooms

Grundriß Erdgeschoß / Ground floor plan

Kur- und Golfzentrum in Alvaneu 1994

Innerhalb der bestehenden Topographie zwischen Hangfuß und Flußlauf sieht das komplexe Bauprogramm verschiedene Hotelbauten, Bade- und Gemeinschaftsanlagen als Ergänzung eines geplanten Golfareals vor. Fünf verschiedene Baukörper sind so angeordnet, daß sie als Gesamtkomposition, aber auch als Einzelbauten etappiert in Erscheinung treten können. Die Hotelbauten sind als einbündige Längszeilen konzipiert. Gemeinschaftseinrichtungen wie Bad und Golfklub stehen pavillonartig vor dieser Kulisse. Der Golfplatz zieht sich als kontinuierlich fließender Grünraum durch die Anlage und verbindet die einzelnen Volumen mit der Landschaft zu einer Einheit.

Health and Golf Centre in Alvaneu 1994

Within the existing topography between the foot of a slope and a river, the complex building programme envisages various hotel buildings and bathing and community facilities to supplement a planned golf course. Five different buildings are arranged that they can appear both as a total composition and, in stages, as separate structures. The hotel buildings are conceived as linear blocks with rooms on one side of the corridor. Community facilities such as the spa and the golf clubhouse are arranged like pavilions in front of this backdrop. The golf course runs through the complex as a continuous flow of greenery, unifying the different buildings with the landscape.

Modell der Wettbewerbseingabe mit der umliegenden Situation
Competition model with surrounding situation

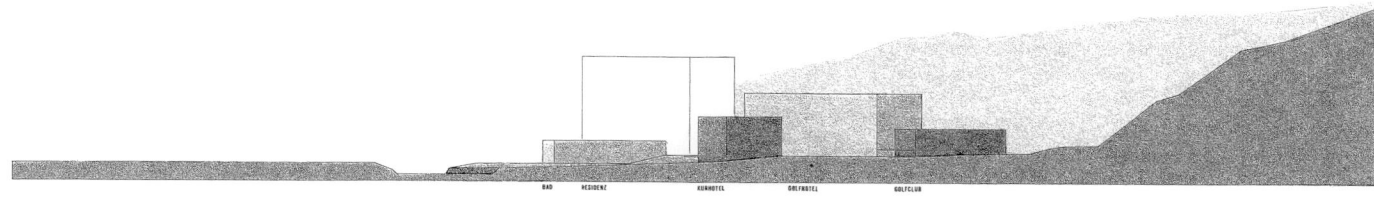

Ostfassade der verschiedenen Volumen / East façade of the different volumes

Grundriß Erdgeschoß / Ground floor plan

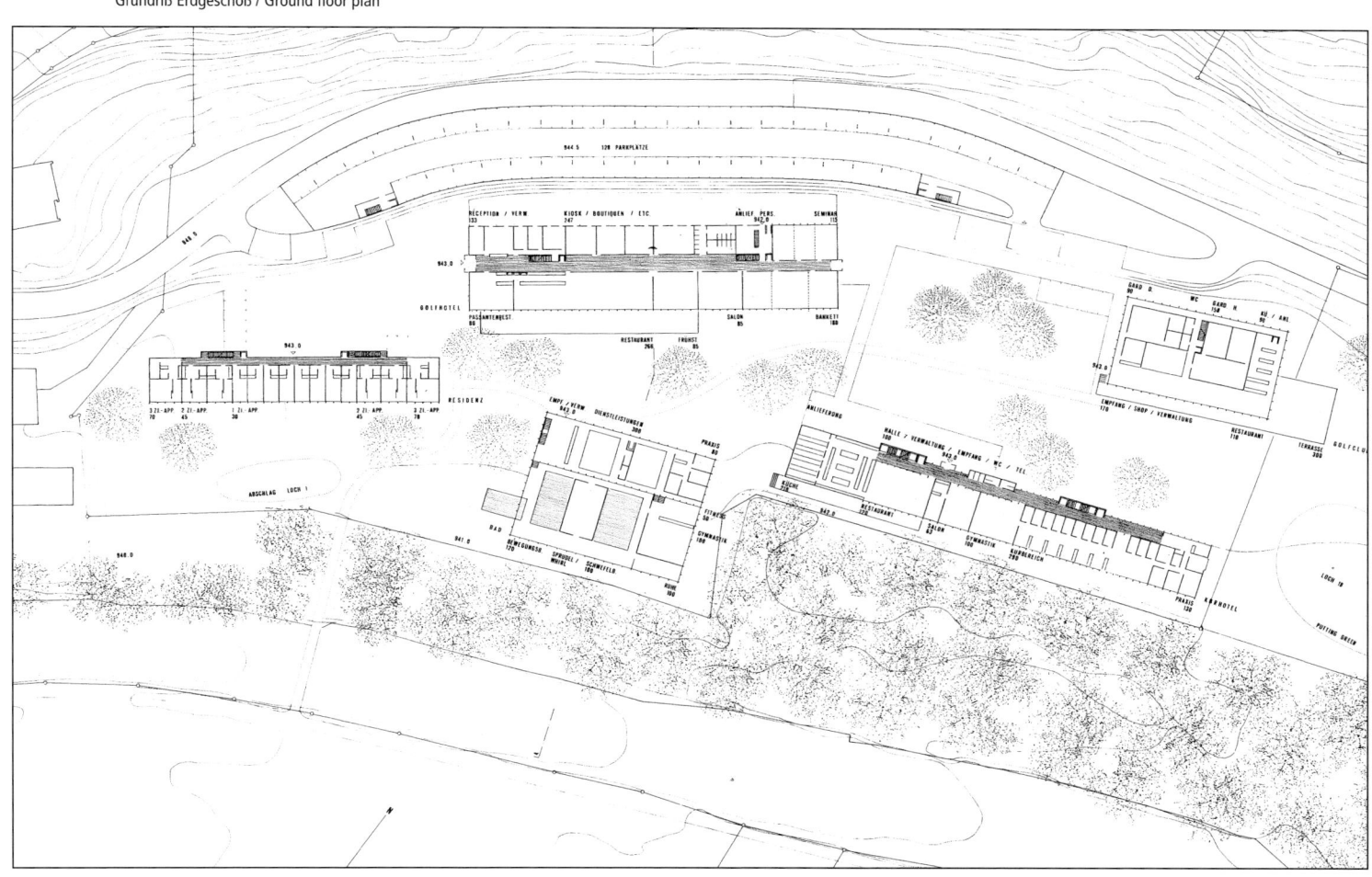

Claudine Lorenz · Florian Musso, Sitten

Spannungsvolle Räume

Die unterschiedlichen kulturellen Wurzeln scheinen die Arbeit von Claudine Lorenz und Florian Musso zu befruchten: Seit rund sechs Jahren arbeiten sie gemeinsam in Sion und haben eine ganze Anzahl wichtiger Wettbewerbsprojekte entworfen, von denen sie das neue Verwaltungsgebäude in Monthey, einen soliden, handwerklich sorgfältig ausgeführten Bau, 1994 fertigstellen konnten. Im selben Jahr wurde die Baustelle des Kontrollturms für den Flugplatz Sion eröffnet. Dazwischen realisieren die beiden Architekten kleinere Bauaufgaben wie den Pavillon Tabin-Darbellay in Savièse oder den Umbau der Buchhandlung «La Liseuse» in Sion. Vielen ihrer Projekte gemein ist die starke Beziehung von innen und außen sowie die wohlüberlegte räumliche Bestimmung. Diese Eigenschaften lassen spannungsvolle Räume entstehen. Die klaren Volumen werden so plaziert, daß sie gleichzeitig präzise, qualitätsvolle Außenräume definieren. Diese Charakteristik fällt besonders beim Verwaltungsgebäude in Monthey auf, wo der neuerstellte Baukörper zusammen mit den alten bestehenden einen neuen städtischen Außenraum bildet. Bemerkenswert ist das breite architektonische Interesse von Lorenz und Musso, das vom Wohnungs- zum Schulhaus- und Verwaltungsbau reicht und auch technisch komplizierte Aufgaben miteinschließt. So konnten sie vor kurzem zusammen mit weiteren Fachleuten in Basel den Wettbewerb für die zweite Rheinbrücke-Verbindungsbahn Basel Bahnhof SBB - Basel Badischer Bahnhof für sich entscheiden.

Tension-Filled spaces

Their different cultural roots seem to fertilise the work of Claudine Lorenz and Florian Musso. They have worked together in Sion for about six years and have designed a good number of important competition projects, of which they were able to build the new administrative building in Monthey, a solid, carefully crafted building, in 1994. In the same year the site of the control tower for Sion airfield was opened. Alongside this work the two architects carry out smaller projects such as the Tabin-Darbellay pavilion in Savièse or the conversion of the "La Liseuse" bookshop in Sion. Common to many of their projects is the strong relationship between interior and exterior space and the well-thought-out allocation of space. These qualities give rise to tension-filled spaces. The clear volumes are so placed that they define at the same time precise, high-quality external spaces. This characteristic is especially striking in the administrative building in Monthey, where the newly-constructed building forms a new urban space with the existing old one. The breadth of Lorenz and Musso's architectural interests is noteworthy, stretching from houses to schools and administrative buildings, and including technically complex tasks. For example, with other specialists in Basle they recently won the competition for the second Rhine-bridge link line between SBB station and the Badischer Bahnhof in Basle.

Biographie

Claudine Lorenz

1960
Geboren in Pully.

1979–85
Architekturstudium an der ETH-Lausanne.

1983
Praktikum im Büro Frei Otto in Warmbronn, Deutschland.

1985
Diplom bei Professor Pierre Foretay an der ETH-Lausanne.

1985
Mitarbeit im Büro Ivano Gianola in Mendrisio.

1986–89
Selbständige Arbeiten.

Seit 1989
Gemeinsames Büro mit Florian Musso in Sitten.

Florian Musso

1956
Geboren in Köln.

1974–77
Jurastudium an den Universitäten Freiburg i.Br. und München.

1977–82
Architekturstudium an der Universität Stuttgart und an der University of Virginia in Charlottesville, USA.

1982
Diplom bei Professor Wolfgang Knoll in Stuttgart.

1982
Mitarbeit im Büro Höfler, Kandel und Lienhardt in Stuttgart.

1982–84
Mitarbeit im Büro Fonso Boschetti in Lausanne.

1984–85
Assistent bei Professor Alain Tschumi an der ETH-Lausanne.

1985–88
Assistent bei Professor Wolfgang Döring an der RWTH in Aachen.

1988–89
Oberassistent bei Gastprofessorin Regina Gonthier an der ETH-Zürich.

Seit 1989
Lehrauftrag an der HTL in Freiburg.

Seit 1989
Gemeinsames Büro mit Claudine Lorenz in Sitten.

Veröffentlichungen von Musso:

1983
Büro für Entscheidungsvorbereitung und Bauforschung Stuttgart: «Baukosten-Sparfibel – Ein Ratgeber für kosten- und flächensparenden Eigenheimbau», Schriftenreihe des Bundesministers für Raumordnung, Bauwesen und Städtebau, Bonn 1983.

1989
M. Kleinen, W. Lewitzki, F. Musso: «Holzbaudetails, Baukonstruktionen, Bauphysik, Kosten, Beispiele», Werner-Verlag, Düsseldorf 1989.

Ausgewähltes Werkverzeichnis

1985
Marktplatz in Gladbeck (Deutschland)
Wettbewerb, vierter Preis.

1986
Park + Skilift «Ride Les Vignettes» in Montana (Kanton Wallis)
Wettbewerb, fünfter Preis.

1987
Deutsches Historisches Museum in Berlin
Wettbewerb, vierter Preis.

1988
Psychiatrisches Krankenhaus in Maleros Monthey (Kanton Wallis)
Wettbewerb, erster Preis.

Altersheim in Grimisuat (Kanton Wallis; 1988–91)
Wettbewerb, erster Preis.
Ausgeführtes Projekt.

1989
Sportzentrum in Sitten (Kanton Wallis)
Wettbewerb, erster Preis.

Regionalflughafen in Paderborn-Lippstadt (Deutschland)
Wettbewerb, Ankauf.

Stuag-Werkhöfe in Bern
Gutachterverfahren, erster Preis.

Gestaltung Bahnhofgebiet in Brig (Kanton Wallis)
Wettbewerb, achter Preis.

Verwaltungsgebäude in Monthey (Kanton Wallis; 1989–94)
Place de l'Hôtel de Ville
Wettbewerb, erster Preis.
Ausgeführtes Projekt.

1990
Roemer-Pelizaeus-Museum in Hildesheim
Wettbewerb, Ankauf.

Verdichteter Wohnungsbau in Saillon (Kanton Wallis)
Gutachterverfahren, zweiter Preis.

Hauptpost in Sitten (Kanton Wallis)
Wettbewerb, vierter Preis.

Pavillon Tabin-Darbellay in Savièse (Kanton Wallis)
Ausgeführtes Projekt.

1991
Sportzentrum Sankt Leonhard in Freiburg
Wettbewerb, erster Preis. Vorprojekt.

Hotel «Dents-du-Midi» in Champéry (Kanton Wallis)
Gutachterverfahren, erster Preis.

Schulhaus in Saxe-Fully (Kanton Wallis)
Wettbewerb, dritter Preis.

1992
Verwaltungsgebäude AVE in Sitten (Kanton Wallis)
Wettbewerb, fünfter Preis.

Schulhaus 4 in Zermatt (Kanton Wallis)
Wettbewerb, vierter Preis.

Bürogebäude Kantonspolizei in Lausanne
Wettbewerb, achter Preis.

Feuerwehrgebäude in Crans-Montana (Kanton Wallis)
Wettbewerb, zweiter Preis.

Schulhaus in Raron (Kanton Wallis)
Wettbewerb, zweiter Preis.

Ausbildungszentrum PTT-Telecom und Hotel in Martigny (Kanton Wallis; 1992–etwa 98)
Gutachterverfahren, erster Preis.
Vorprojekt.

1993
Umbau Buchhandlung «La Liseuse» in Sitten (Kanton Wallis)
Rue de la Dent Blanche 10
Ausgeführtes Projekt.

Kontrollturm Flugplatz in Sitten (1993–etwa 96)
Gutachterverfahren, erster Preis.
Bauprojekt.

Umbau des Bundeshauses in Bern
Machbarkeitsstudie.

1994
Sanierung und Umbau Wohnhaus Berclaz-Zermatten in Sitten (Kanton Wallis)
Ausgeführtes Projekt.

Zweite Rheinbrücke-Verbindungsbahn Basel Bahnhof SBB - Basel Badischer Bahnhof in Basel
Gutachterverfahren, erster Preis.
Zusammenarbeit mit: Professor Dr. Christian Menn, Chur; WGG-Ingenieure, Basel; CSD-Ingenieure, Liestal; Locher & Cie., Zürich.

Biography

Claudine Lorenz

1960
Born in Pully

1979–85
Studied architecture at the ETH Lausanne

1983
Practical work at the Frei Otto architectural office in Warmbronn, Germany

1985
Graduated with diploma under Prof. Pierre Foretay at the ETH Lausanne

1985
Worked at the Ivano Gianola architectural office in Mendrisio

1986–89
Freelance work

Since 1989
Joint architectural office with Florian Musso in Sitten.

Florian Musso

1956
Born in Cologne

1974–77
Studied law at the universities of Freiburg i.Br. and Munich

1977–82
Studied architecture at the University of Stuttgart and the University of Virginia in Charlottesville, USA

1982
Graduated with diploma under Prof. Wolfgang Knoll in Stuttgart

1982
Worked at the Höfler, Kandel & Lienhardt architectural office in Stuttgart

1982–84
Worked at the Fonso Boschetti architectural office in Lausanne

1984–85
Assistant to Prof. Alain Tschumi at the ETH Lausanne

1985–88
Assistant to Prof. Wolfgang Döring at the RWTH in Aachen

1988–89
Senior Assistant to Visiting Prof. Regina Gonthier at the ETH Zurich

Since 1989
Teaching post at the HTL in Fribourg

Since 1989
Joint architectural office with Claudine Lorenz in Sitten

Publications by Musso:
1983
Büro für Entscheidungsvorbereitung und Bauforschung Stuttgart: "Baukosten–Sparfibel – Ein Ratgeber für kosten- and flächensparenden Eigenheimbau" [Guide to cost and space saving when building one's own home], Schriftenreihe des Bundesministers für Raumordnung, Bauwesen and Städtebau, Bonn 1983.

1989
M. Kleinen, W. Lewitzki, F. Musso: "Holzbaudetails, Baukonstruktionen, Bauphysik, Kosten, Beispiele", Werner-Verlag, Düsseldorf 1989.

Selected list of work

1985
Market square in Gladbeck (Germany)
Competition, fourth prize.

1986
"Ride Les Vignettes" park and ski lift in Montana (Canton of Valais)
Competition, fifth prize.

1987
Deutsches Historisches Museum in Berlin
Competition, fourth prize.

1988
Psychiatric Hospital in Maleros Monthey (Canton of Valais)
Competition, first prize.

Old people's home in Grimisuat (Canton of Valais; 1988–91)
Competition, first prize
Completed project.

1989
Sports Centre in Sitten (Canton of Valais)
Competition, first prize.

Regional airport in Paderborn-Lippstadt (Germany)
Competition, purchased design.

Stuag works depots in Berne
Consultants' report, first prize.

Design for station district in Brig (Canton of Valais)
Competition, eighth prize.

Administrative building in Monthey (Canton of Valais; 1989–94)
Place de l'Hôtel de Ville
Competition, first prize.
Completed project.

1990
Roemer-Pelizaeus-Museum in Hildesheim
Competition, purchased design.

High-density apartment development in Saillon (Canton of Valais)
Consultants' report, second prize.

Main post office in Sitten (Canton of Valais)
Competition, fourth prize.

Tabin-Darbellay pavilion in Savièse (Canton of Valais)
Completed project.

1991
Sankt Leonhard sports centre in Fribourg
Competition, first prize.
Preliminary project.

Hotel "Dents-du-Midi" in Champéry (Canton of Valais)
Consultants' report, first prize.

School in Saxe-Fully (Canton of Valais)
Competition, third prize.

1992
AVE administrative building in Sitten (Canton of Valais)
Competition, fifth prize.

School 4 in Zermatt (Canton of Valais)
Competition, fourth prize.

Cantonal police office building in Lausanne
Competition, eighth prize.

Fire station in Crans-Montana (Canton of Valais)
Competition, second prize.

School in Raron (Canton of Valais)
Competition, second prize.

PTT-Telecom training centre and hotel in Martigny (Canton of Valais; 1992–approx. 98)
Consultants' report, first prize.
Preliminary project.

1993
"La Liseuse" bookshop conversion in Sitten (Canton of Valais)
Rue de la Dent Blanche 10
Completed project.

Control tower in Sitten airfield (1993–approx. 96)
Consultants' report, first prize.
Final project.

Conversion of the Federal Houses of Parliament in Berne
Feasibility Study.

1994
Refurbishment and conversion of Berclaz-Zermatten residence in Sitten (Canton of Valais)
Completed project.

Second Rhine bridge for link line between Basle SBB station and Badischer Bahnhof in Basle
Consultants' report, first prize.
In collaboration with: Professor Dr. Christian Menn, Chur; WGG engineers, Basle; CSD engineers, Liestal; Locher & Cie., Zurich.

Verwaltungsgebäude in Monthey 1989–1994

Als letztes von drei unterschiedlichen Gebäuden gliedert sich der neue Bau um einen kleinen Hügel und öffnet sich zum frontal gelegenen Platz, der durch das alte Rathaus und die Kapelle definiert ist. Der Komplex ist strikte in einen öffentlichen – mit einer großzügigen, verglasten Halle – und in einen privaten Bereich – als zweibündige Anlage – geteilt. Seinem repräsentativen Charakter entsprechend ist die gewichtige tragende Fassade des Baukörpers mit gestocktem Beton und mit Natursteinplatten in zwei verschiedenen Farben verkleidet. Die aus Holz und Aluminium gefertigten Fensterprofile wurden so konstruiert, daß ein außenliegendes Storensystem elegant integriert werden konnte.

Administrative Building in Monthey 1989–1994

The last of three different buildings, the new structure is arranged around a small hill and opens at the front on to a square defined by the old town hall building and the chapel. The complex is divided strictly into a public area, with a spacious, glazed hall, and a private one, with central corridor. In keeping with its public character the imposing, load-bearing façade is faced with bush-hammered concrete and natural stone slabs in two different colours. The window mouldings, of wood and aluminium, are so constructed that an external blind system has been elegantly integrated.

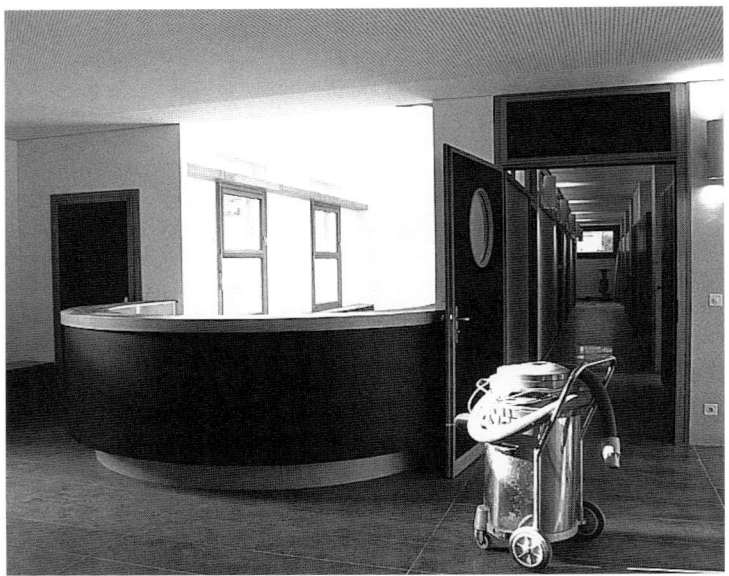

Ansicht des viergeschossigen Baus vom vorgelagerten Platz aus mit den eigens dafür gestalteten Lampen
Elevation of the four-storey buildings viewed from the square in front, with specially designed lamps

Innenraum der großzügigen Halle
Interior of large hall

Grundriß drittes Obergeschoß / Third floor plan
Grundriß zweites Obergeschoß / Second floor plan
Grundriß erstes Obergeschoß / First floor plan

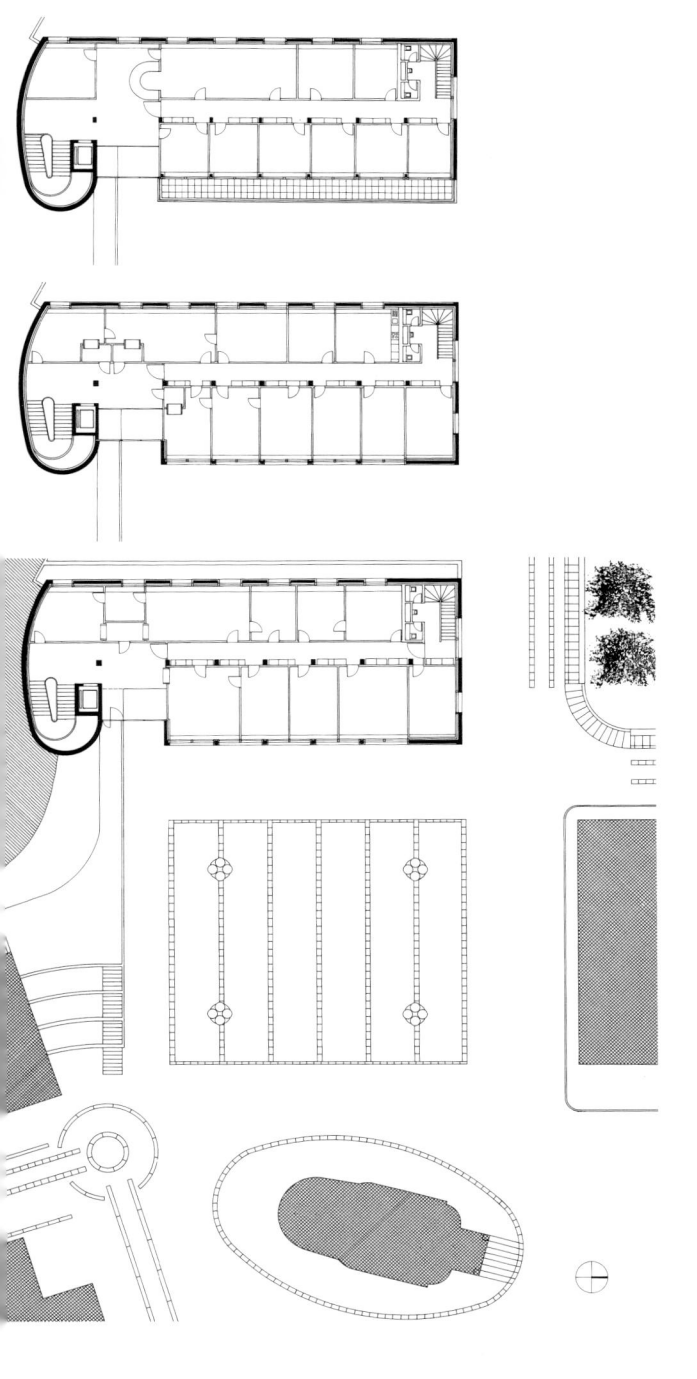

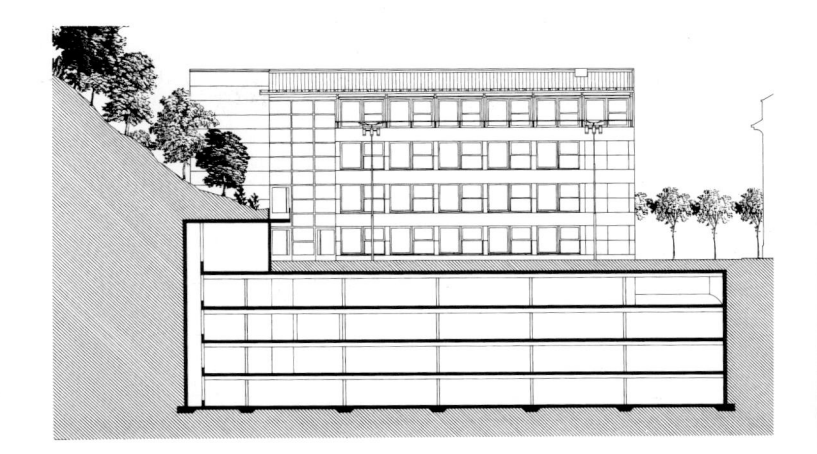

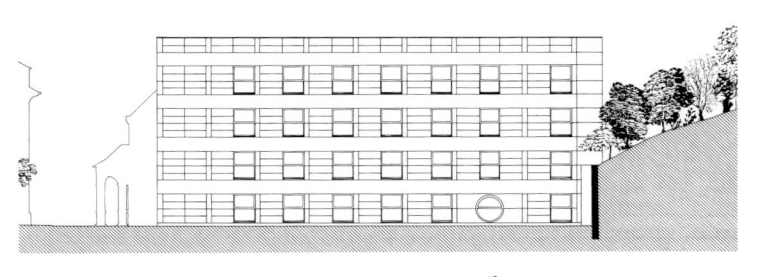

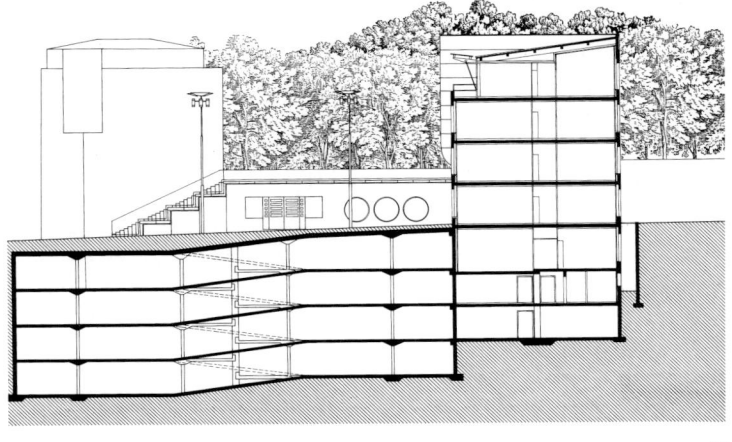

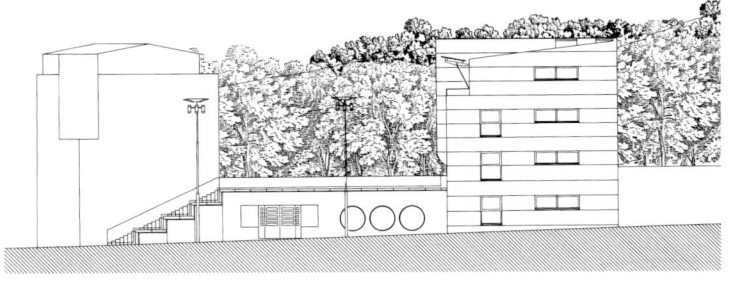

Ostfassade / East façade
Westfassade / West façade
Querschnitt durch das Verwaltungsgebäude und durch die unterirdische Garage
Cross section through the administration building and the basement car park
Nordfassade / North façade

117

Pavillon Tabin-Darbellay in Savièse 1990–1991

Inmitten eines mit mächtigen alten Bäumen bewachsenen Parks wünschte sich die Auftraggeberin, eine Malerin, neue Räumlichkeiten, um ihrer Beschäftigung in angenehmer Atmosphäre nachzugehen. Das neue Objekt steht als Solitär, gleichsam wie ein Möbelstück, in seiner Umgebung. Das Projekt weist zwei Bereiche auf – auf dem Rechteck beziehungsweise auf dem Achteck aufbauend –, die durch einen dritten, bei dem sich der Eingang befindet, miteinander verbunden werden. Von besonderer Bedeutung ist die innere Lichtqualität, die durch große vertikale Fenster gewährleistet ist. Der Pavillon ist auf Stützen gebaut und vollständig aus Holz gefertigt.

Tabin-Darbellay Pavilion in Savièse 1990–1991

In a park with mighty old trees the client, a painter, wanted new rooms enabling her to work in a pleasant atmosphere. The new building is placed as a free-standing unit – like a piece of furniture – in its surroundings. The project has two zones – built up on a rectangle or octagon – connected by a third containing the entrance. The interior light quality, guaranteed by large vertical windows, is especially important. The pavilion is built on posts and is made entirely of timber.

Ansicht des Pavillons innerhalb des Parks / Elevation of pavilion inside park

Oberlicht / Skylight

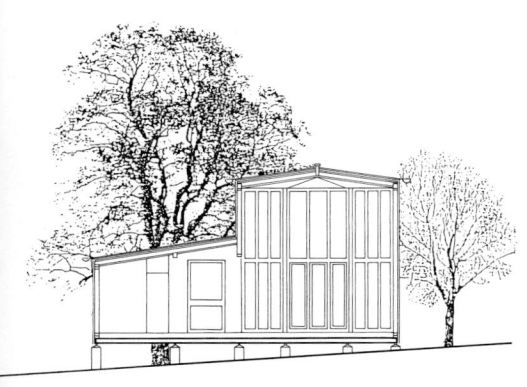

Längsschnitt durch beide Bereiche des Pavillons
Longitudinal section through both areas of the pavilion

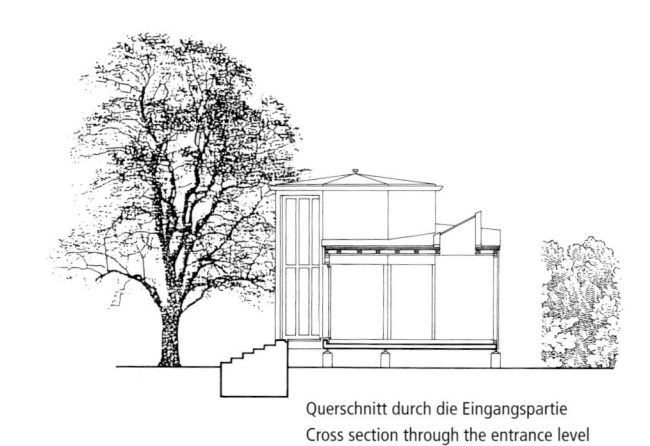

Querschnitt durch die Eingangspartie
Cross section through the entrance level

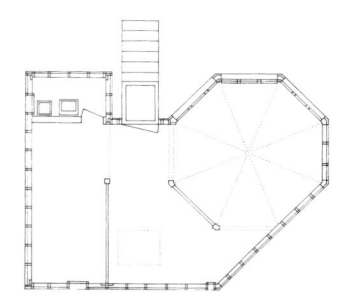

Grundriß / Floor plan

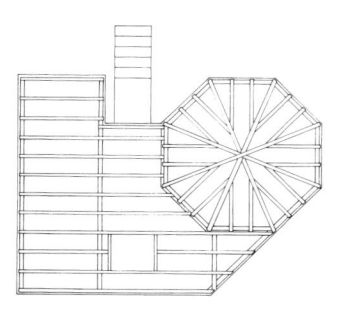

Dachkonstruktion / Roof construction

Schulhaus in Raron 1992

Auf der zur Verfügung stehenden flachen Parzelle lautete die komplexe Aufgabenstellung, Teile der bestehenden Primarschule zu erhalten, andere durch einen Neubau zu ersetzen. Um diese formal und funktional verschiedenen Elemente zusammenzuhalten, so daß sie als Einheit gelesen werden können, schlugen die Architekten eine übergeordnete, zweigeschossige Struktur vor: ein aus Stahl gefertigtes Dach. Darunter befinden sich sämtliche kompakt angeordneten Innen- und Außenräume wie Bühne, Turnhalle, verschiedene Werk- und Handarbeitsräume, zahlreiche Klassenzimmer sowie der gedeckte Pausenplatz. Das differenzierte Erschließungssystem ist klar formuliert.

School in Raron 1992

The complex commission required parts of the existing primary school on the available flat plot to be retained while others were replaced by a new building. To hold these formally and functionally disparate elements together, the architects proposed an overarching two-storey structure: a steel roof. Below it are all the compactly arranged indoor and outdoor spaces, such as the stage, gymnasium, various workshops and craft rooms, numerous classrooms and the covered playground. The differentiated access ways are clearly laid out.

Modell der Wettbewerbseingabe / Competition model

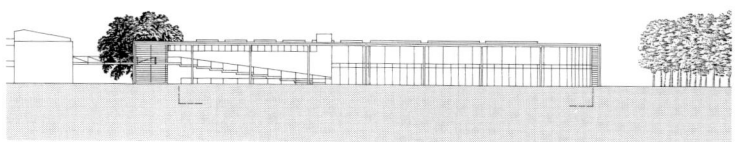

Westfassade / West façade

Nordfassade / North façade

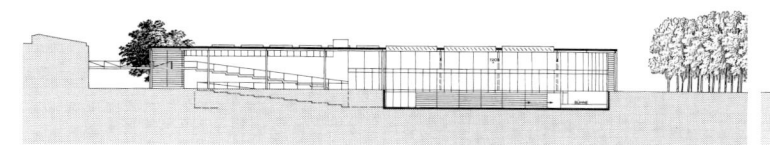

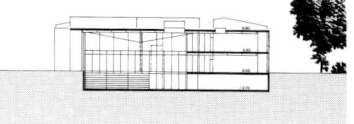

Längsschnitt durch die Turnhalle / Longitudinal section through gymnasium

Querschnitt durch die Turnhalle
Cross section through gymnasium

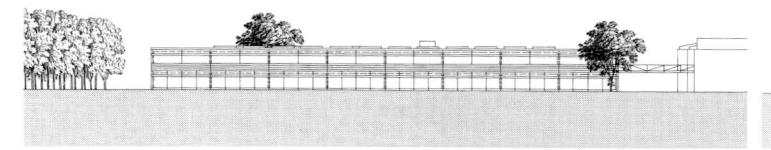

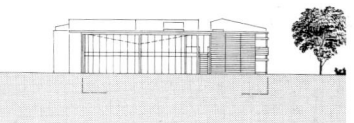

Ostfassade / East façade

Südfassade / South façade

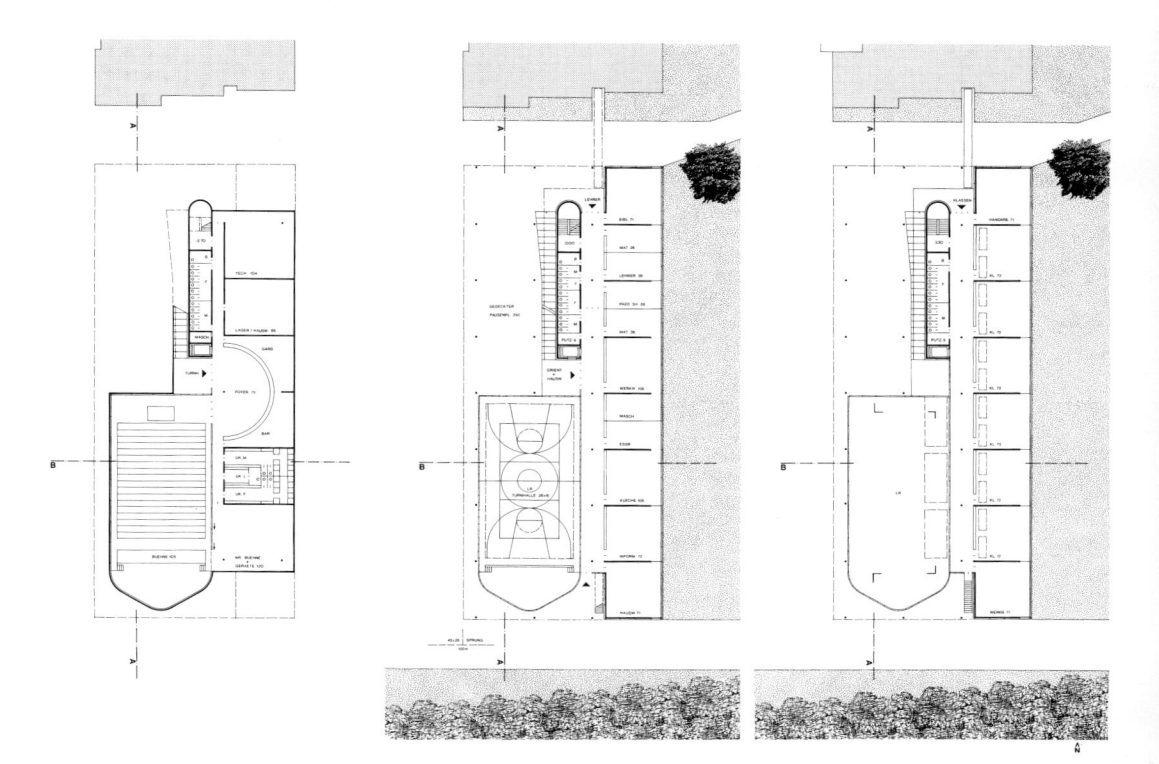

Grundriß Untergeschoß
Ground plan of basement level

Grundriß Erdgeschoß
Ground floor plan

Grundriß Obergeschoß
Ground plan of upper floor

Umbau Buchhandlung «La Liseuse» in Sitten 1993

Das bereits bestehende Buchgeschäft im Stadtzentrum, an einer befahrenen Straße gelegen, sollte den neuen Bedürfnissen angepaßt werden und außerdem vermehrt Aufmerksamkeit auf sich ziehen. Die Architekten entwickelten für die Unterbringung sämtlicher Bücher ein besonders einfaches, kostengünstiges System aus verzinktem Stahlblech. Diese Regale wurden den Wänden entlang sowie frei in den Raum gesetzt und erlauben durch ihre leichte, feine, transparente Konstruktion gewisse Durchblicke, so daß sie den Raum größer erscheinen lassen, als er eigentlich ist.

"La Liseuse" Bookshop Conversion in Sitten 1993

The existing bookshop in the town centre, on a busy road, was to be adapted to new needs and, in addition, made to attract more attention. To accommodate all the books the architects developed an especially simple, low-cost shelving system in zinc coated steel plate. The shelf units were placed along the walls as well as being used free-standing. Their light, delicate, transparent construction allows the gaze to pass through them in places, making the room seem larger than it actually is.

Ansicht Eckausbildung des Schaufensters
Elevation of corner with shop window

Innenraum mit den verzinkten Stahlblechregalen
Interior with zinc coated steel plate shelving

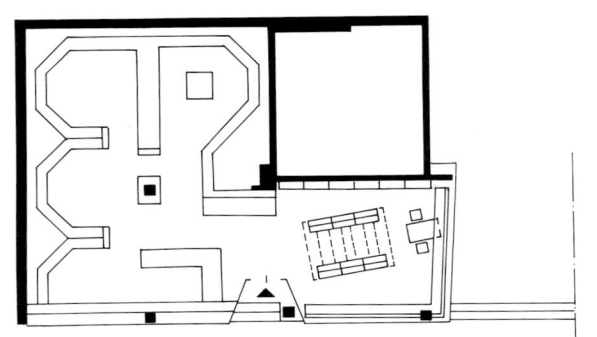

Grundriß Erdgeschoß des bestehenden und des neuen Teils
Ground floor plan of existing and new section

Kontrollturm Flugplatz in Sitten
1993–etwa 1996

Für die zivile und militärische Flugleitstelle mußten neue Räumlichkeiten geschaffen werden. Die vorgeschlagene Anlage besteht aus zwei verschiedenen aneinandergebauten Volumen: der horizontale, zweigeschossige, mit einem Pultdach versehene langgezogene Servicebereich für Technik und Büro sowie der vertikale Turm, der die Funktionen Überwachung und Kontrolle beherbergt. Dieser wurde so entworfen, daß optimale Sichtverhältnisse entstehen. Obwohl die beiden Baukörper aus denselben Materialkombinationen bestehen – Beton, Stahl und Glas –, treten sie in ein spannungsvolles Verhältnis zueinander.

Control Tower at Sitten Airfield
1993–approx. 1996

New accommodation had to be provided for the civil and military flight control centre. The proposed structure consists of two different, adjoining blocks: the horizontal, two-storey service area, with shed roof, for technical support and offices, and the vertical tower, housing the monitoring and control functions. This was designed to provide optimum vision. Although both blocks are made of the same combinations of materials – concrete, steel and glass – a relationship of tension is set up between them.

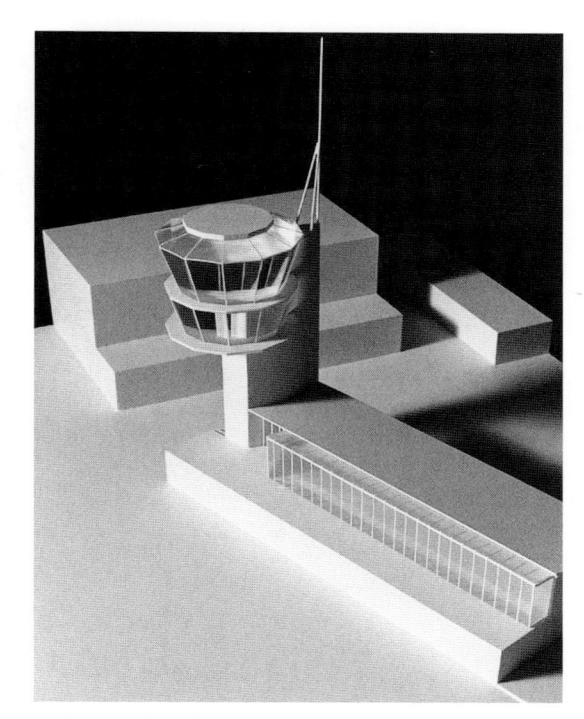

Modell der Wettbewerbseingabe mit den umliegenden Bauten
Competition model with surrounding buildings

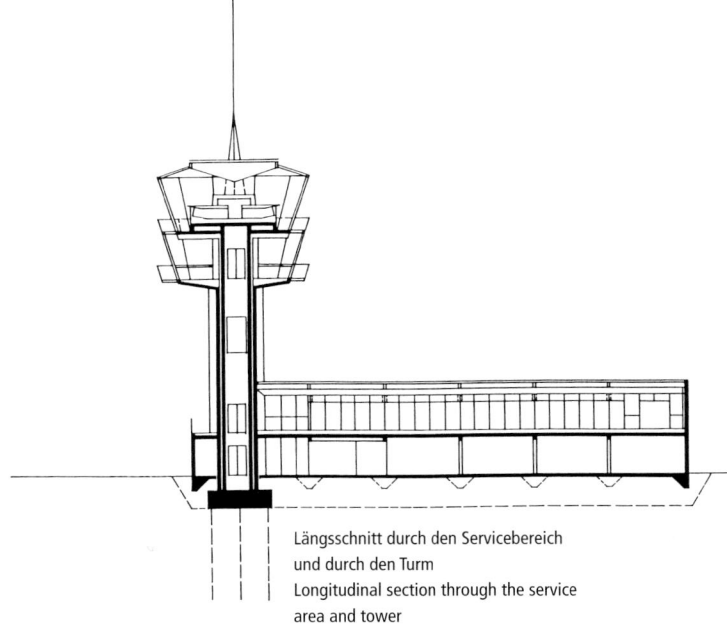

Längsschnitt durch den Servicebereich und durch den Turm
Longitudinal section through the service area and tower

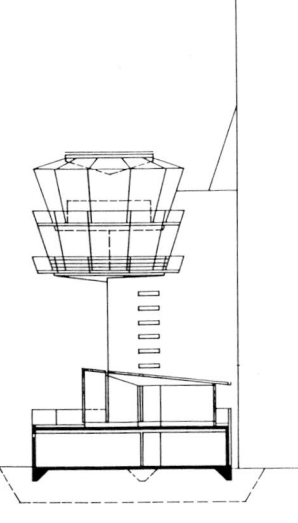

Querschnitt durch die Terrasse und durch den Servicebereich
Cross section through terrace and service area

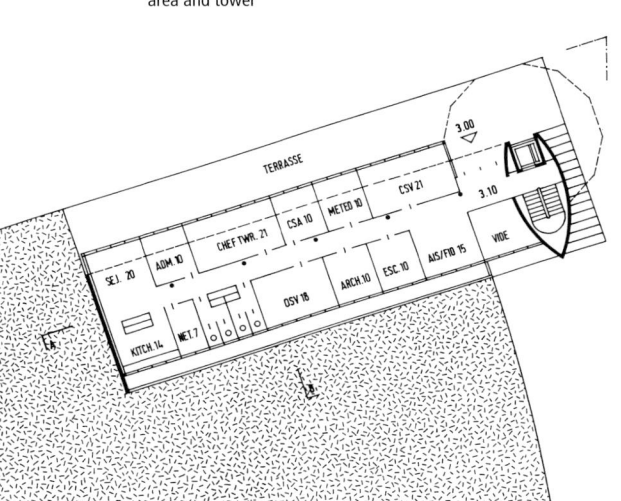

Grundriß Erdgeschoß
Ground floor plan

Meinrad Morger · Heinrich Degelo, Basel

Ästhetische Notwendigkeit

Als Antwort auf unsere heutige Kultur des totalen Überflusses und zweifelsohne geprägt durch das sogenannte Basler Klima (dessen Anfänge auf Ende der 20er Jahre zurückreichen) geht es bei der Architektur von Meinrad Morger und Heinrich Degelo um den sinnvollen Gebrauch materieller und geistiger Ressourcen. Ihre Intention ist es, die Architektur auf ihre elementare Substanz zu reduzieren. Die beiden Architekten propagieren ein gezieltes Beschränken auf das Wesentliche. In der Gestaltung der alltäglichen Umgebung heißt das eine Reduktion auf eine ästhetische Notwendigkeit, die ihre Erfüllung in einer natürlichen Einfachheit findet. Von besonderem Interesse ist für sie das Weiterdenken über den Bereich des allgemein Architektonischen hinaus. In ihrer Architektur ist Sinnlichkeit – Form, Material, Farbe – erst möglich nach dem Besinnen auf das absolut Notwendige. Auffallend in ihren Arbeiten sind die ideenreichen Anwendungen der Materialien, insbesondere von Holz: geschichtet, gestoßen, gefügt, roh, naturbehandelt, lasiert, deckend gestrichen, versiegelt, matt, glänzend ... Ihr Ziel ist es, das Material sichtbar und unverhüllt einzusetzen, nicht bloß materialgerecht, sondern vielmehr sachgerecht, der Aufgabe entsprechend, um angenehme, spannungsvolle Räume zu schaffen.

Aesthetic Necessity

In response to our present culture of total superfluity, and undoubtedly influenced by the so-called "Basle climate" (the origins of which go back to the end of the 1920s), the architecture of Meinrad Morger and Heinrich Degelo is concerned with the appropriate use of material and spiritual resources. Their aim is to reduce architecture to its elementary substance. The two architects advocate a deliberate confinement to the essential. In shaping our everyday environment this means reduction to an aesthetic necessity which finds fulfilment in a natural simplicity. They are especially interested in taking their reflections beyond the sphere of architecture. In their architecture, the sensuous element – form, material, colour – is only possible after reflection on what is absolutely necessary. A striking feature of their work is the inventive use of materials, especially wood: layered, butted, jointed, unfinished, natural or colour treated, painted, sealed, mat or shiny. Their aim is to use materials in a visible, exposed way, as is appropriate not only to the material but to its purpose, in order to create pleasant, tension-charged spaces.

Biographie

Meinrad Morger

1957
Geboren in St. Gallen.

1974–78
Lehre als Hochbauzeichner.

1978–80
Architekturstudium an der HTL in Winterthur.

1981–83
Fachhörer an der ETH-Zürich.

1984–85
Mitarbeit im Büro Michael Alder in Basel.

1985–88
Mitarbeit im Büro Metron Architekten in Brugg.

1993–94
Assistent bei Professor Wolfgang Schett an der ETH-Zürich.

Seit 1988
Gemeinsames Büro mit Heinrich Degelo in Basel.

Heinrich Degelo

1953
Geboren in Giswil.

1973–77
Lehre als Möbelschreiner.

1980–83
Fachklasse für Innenarchitektur an der Schule für Gestaltung in Basel.

1983–84
Studienaufenthalt in den Vereinigten Staaten und Mexiko.

1984–85
Mitarbeit im Büro Herzog & de Meuron in Basel.

Seit 1988
Gemeinsames Büro mit Meinrad Morger in Basel.

Auszeichnung

1992
Auszeichnung guter Bauten im Kanton Basel Stadt (Kindergarten in Basel).

Ausgewähltes Werkverzeichnis

1988
Kindergarten in Basel
Zähringerstraße
Ausgeführtes Projekt. Zusammenarbeit mit Gérard Prêtre, Basel.

Renovation Wohnhäuser in Basel (1988–89)
Rheinfelderstraße 34/Hammerstraße 9
Ausgeführtes Projekt. Zusammenarbeit mit Gérard Prêtre, Basel.

Anbau Wohnhaus in Basel (1988–90)
Gundeldingerstrasse 137
Ausgeführtes Projekt. Zusammenarbeit mit Gérard Prêtre, Basel.

1989
Wohnüberbauung Luzernerring in Basel
Wettbewerb, zweiter Preis. Zusammenarbeit mit Gérard Prêtre, Basel.

Kommunales Wohnhaus in Basel (1989–93)
Müllheimerstraße 138–140
Wettbewerb, erster Preis. Zusammenarbeit mit Gérard Prêtre, Basel. Ausgeführtes Projekt.

Claraschulhof in Basel (1989–etwa 96)
Wettbewerb, erster Preis. Zusammenarbeit mit Gérard Prêtre, Basel.

1990
Renovation «Zülle les Coiffures» in Basel
Pfluggäßlein 1
Ausgeführtes Projekt. Zusammenarbeit mit Gérard Prêtre, Basel.

Gestaltungsplan Westrand in Obermumpf (Kanton Aargau)
Wettbewerb, Ankauf. Zusammenarbeit mit Gérard Prêtre, Basel.

Sommerpavillon auf dem Seltisberg (Kanton Baselland)
Vorprojekt.

Wohnüberbauung in Schiers (Kanton Graubünden)
Wettbewerb.

Erweiterung Feuerwache in Basel
Studienauftrag für die Stadt Basel. Arbeitsgemeinschaft mit Ackermann Architekten SIA, Basel.

Anbau Wohnhaus in Basel (1990–91)
Arabienstrasse 27
Ausgeführtes Projekt.

1991
Hotel «Park im Grüene» in Rüschlikon (Kanton Zürich)
Wettbewerb, erster Preis. Arbeitsgemeinschaft mit Ackermann Architekten SIA, Basel.

Renovation Wohnhaus in Basel
Straßburgerallee 88
Ausgeführtes Projekt.

Renovation Wohnhäuser in Basel
Im Sesselacker 26 und 46
Ausgeführtes Projekt.

Renovation Pfarrhaus St. Joseph in Basel (1991–etwa 96)
Vorprojekt.

Überbauung Areal «Frauenhof» in Altstätten (Kanton St. Gallen; 1991–etwa 96)
Wettbewerb, erster Preis. Vorprojekt.

Dreifach-Turnhalle, Erweiterung Schulhaus und Wohnüberbauung in Basel (1991–etwa 96)
Bauprojekt. Projekt in Ausführung.

1992
Tagesheim in Basel
Vorprojekt.

Ausbaupotentiale Schulanlagen in Basel
Studie.

Wohnüberbauung «Melchrüti» in Wallisellen (Kanton Zürich)
Wettbewerb.

Coop-Areal in Basel
Wettbewerb, zweiter Preis.

Neue Bibliothek und Renovation der Ausstellungsräume 4,5,6 und 7 der Kunsthalle in Basel (1992–93)
Steinenberg 7
Ausgeführtes Projekt.

Innenrenovation Elisabethenkirche in Basel (1992–94)
Elisabethenstraße 14
Ausgeführtes Projekt. Arbeitsgemeinschaft mit Ritter/Nees/Beutler Architekten, Basel.

1993
Erweiterung Restaurant Stadtkeller in Aarau
Wettbewerb, zweiter Preis.

Keppler-Gymnasium in Freiburg im Breisgau
Wettbewerb, Ankauf.

«Hochhaus-Studie» Ausstellungsbeitrag für das Architektur Forum Zürich.

Dachausbau und neue verglaste Veranda in Basel (1993–94)
Thiersteinerrain 132
Ausgeführtes Projekt.

1994
Wohnüberbauung «Schloßmatte» in Grenzach-Wylen, Deutschland
Wettbewerb, zweiter Preis.

Mehrfamilienhaus in Binningen (Kanton Basellandschaft; 1994–etwa 96)
Rottmannsboden 20
Bauprojekt.

Biography

Meinrad Morger
1957
Born in St. Gallen
1974–78
Trained as architectural draughtsman
1978–80
Studied architecture at the HTL Winterthur
1981–83
Specialist study at the ETH Zurich
1984–85
Worked at the Michael Alder architectural office in Basle
1985–88
Worked at the Metron Architekten office in Brugg
1993–94
Assistant to Prof. Wolfgang Schett at the ETH Zurich
Since 1988
Joint architectural office with Heinrich Degelo in Basle.

Heinrich Degelo
1957
Born in Giswil
1973–77
Trained as cabinet maker
1980–83
Specialist course on interior design at the Schule für Gestaltung in Basle
1983–84
Study visits to the United States and Mexico
1984–85
Worked at the Herzog & de Meuron architectural office in Basle
Since 1988
Joint architectural office with Meinrad Morger in Basle

Awards
1992
Award for good buildings in the Canton of Basel-Stadt (kindergarten in Basle).

Selected list of work

1988
Kindergarten in Basle
Zähringerstrasse
Completed project. In collaboration with Gérard Prêtre, Basle.

Renovation of residences in Basle (1988–89)
Rheinfelderstrasse 34/Hammerstrasse 9
Completed project. In collaboration with Gérard Prêtre, Basle.

Extension to residence in Basle (1988–90)
Gundeldingerstrasse 137
Completed project. In collaboration with Gérard Prêtre, Basle.

1989
"Luzernerring" residential development in Basle
Competition, second prize.
In collaboration with Gérard Prêtre, Basle.

Local authority residence in Basle (1989–93)
Müllheimerstrasse 138–140
Competition, first prize. In collaboration with Gérard Prêtre, Basle.
Completed project.

Claraschulhof in Basle (1989–approx. 96)
Competition, first prize.
In collaboration with Gérard Prêtre, Basle.

1990
Renovation of "Zülle les Coiffures" in Basle
Pfluggässlein 1
Completed project. In collaboration with Gérard Prêtre, Basle.

Design for west boundary area of Obermumpf (Canton of Aargau)
Competition, purchased design. In collaboration with Gérard Prêtre, Basle.

Summer pavilion on the Seltisberg (Canton of Basel-Land)
Preliminary project.

Residential development in Schiers (Canton of Grisons)
Competition.

Extension of fire station in Basle
Study commission for the city of Basle.
In partnership with Ackermann Architekten SIA, Basle.

Extension to residence in Basle (1990–91)
Arabienstrasse 27
Completed project.

1991
Hotel "Park im Grüene" in Rüschlikon (Canton of Zurich)
Competition, first prize. In partnership with Ackermann Architekten SIA, Basle.

Renovation of residence in Basle
Strassburgerallee 88
Completed project.

Renovation of residences in Basle
Im Sesselacker 26 and 46
Completed project.

Renovation of rectory of St. Joseph in Basle (1991–approx. 96)
Preliminary project.

Development of "Frauenhof" site in Altstätten (Canton of St. Gallen; 1991–approx. 96)
Competition, first prize.
Preliminary project.

Triple-purpose gymnasium, school extension and residential development in Basle (1991–approx. 96)
Final project. Now being executed.

1992
Day centre in Basle
Preliminary project.

Potential for extension of school buildings in Basle
Study.

"Melchrüti" residential development in Wallisellen (Canton of Zurich)
Competition.

Co-op site in Basle
Competition, second prize.

New library and renovation of exhibition rooms 4,5,6 and 7 in the Kunsthalle in Basle (1992–93)
Steinenberg 7
Completed project.

Renovation of interior of Elisabethenkirche in Basle (1992–94)
Elisabethenstrasse 14
Completed project. In partnership with Ritter/Nees/Beutler Architekten, Basle.

1993
Extension of Stadtkeller restaurant in Aarau
Competition, second prize.

Keppler Grammar School in Freiburg im Breisgau
Competition, purchased design.

"High rise block study"
Exhibition entry for Architektur Forum Zurich

Roof extension and new glazed veranda in Basle (1993–94)
Thiersteinerrain 132
Completed project.

1994
"Schlossmatte" residential development in Grenzach-Wylen, Germany
Competition, second prize.

Multiple residence in Binningen (Canton of Basel-Land; 1994–approx. 96)
Rottmannsboden 20
Final project.

Anbau Wohnhaus in Basel
1990–91

Auf einem engen, kleinräumigen Garten mußte ein bestehendes Wohnhaus aus den 40er Jahren durch zwei großzügige Räume ergänzt werden. Der Holzbohlenbau, innen mit weiß lasierten Sperrholztafeln, außen mit dreifach verleimten, grün gestrichenen Tannenplatten beplankt, ist auf einer anthrazit eingefärbten Betonplatte errichtet. Die Absicht bestand darin, die Konstruktion weder zu verstecken, noch sie bloß zu legen; eine Art Verhüllung – übrig bleibt die leise Ahnung. Die Realisation besticht durch ihre einzigartige Farbgebung sowie die Schönheit und Vielfältigkeit des ausschließlich verwendeten Materials Holz.

Extension to Residence in Basle
1990–1991

An existing house from the 1940s was to have two spacious rooms added within the area of a narrow, cramped garden. The planked wooden structure, lined inside with white-scumbled plywood panels and outside with triple-bonded, green painted pine boarding, is built on an anthracite-coloured concrete slab. The aim was neither to conceal the construction nor to expose it fully: a kind of veiling that gives a gentle hint. The implementation captivates the eye with its unique use of colour and the beauty and diversity of the material exclusively used, wood.

Anbau an das bestehende Wohnhaus / Extension to existing house

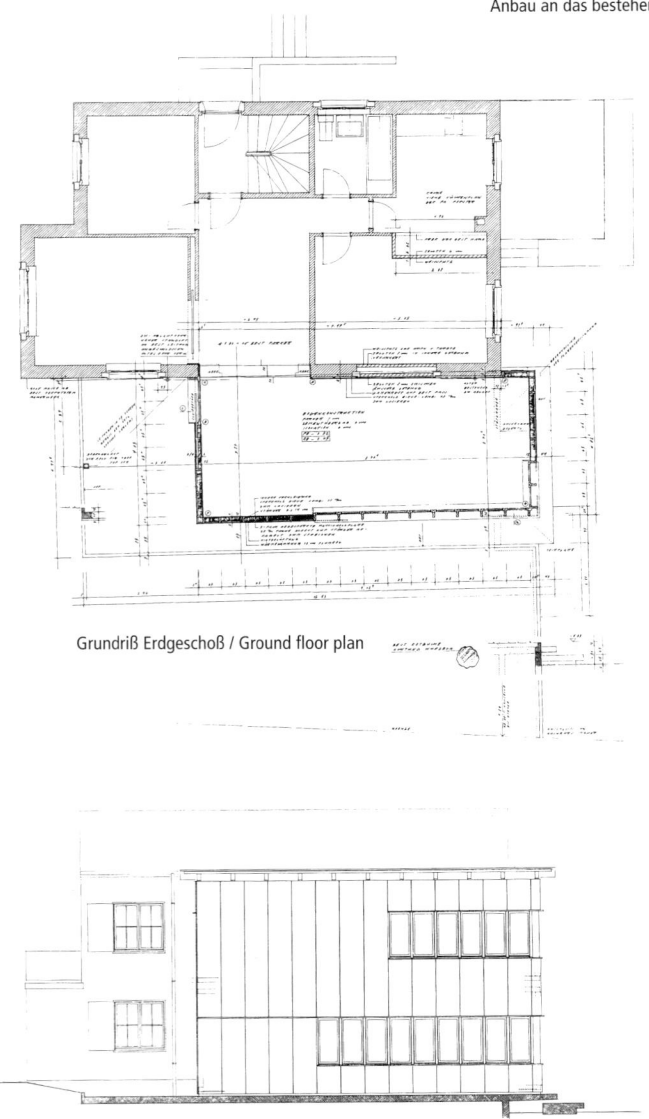

Grundriß Erdgeschoß / Ground floor plan

Südfassade / South façade

Überbauung Areal «Frauenhof» in Altstätten 1991–etwa 1996

Die historische Bedeutung des Ortes sowie der Ausblick von den umliegenden Anhöhen auf die Dächer, Gassen und Höfe waren wesentlicher Ansatzpunkt der Projektidee. Drei ungleich lange und hohe Baukörper, mit gemischter Nutzung, stehen in ihrer eigenen Ordnung parallel zueinander und definieren spannungsvolle Außenräume. Die alte, freigelegte Mauer faßt die Überbauung neu. Auffallend ist die Struktur des Fassadenaufbaus, die sich vom Sockel her nach oben verfeinert und durch ein extensiv begrüntes Flachdach abgeschlossen ist. Die vorgesehene Schichtung aus Holz zeigt mit aller Deutlichkeit die Reverenz an die regionale Baukultur.

Development of "Frauenhof" Site in Altstätten 1991–approx. 1996

The historical significance of the site and the view from the surrounding heights provided the starting point for the design concept. Three blocks of unequal length and height, with mixed uses, stand parallel to each other in a self-contained order, defining tension-charged exterior spaces. The old, exposed wall provides a new perimeter for the development. A striking feature is the structure of the façade, which is increasingly refined as it rises from the socle and is covered by a flat roof with extensive greenery. The planned laminated wood cladding very clearly shows the architects' reverence for regional architectural styles.

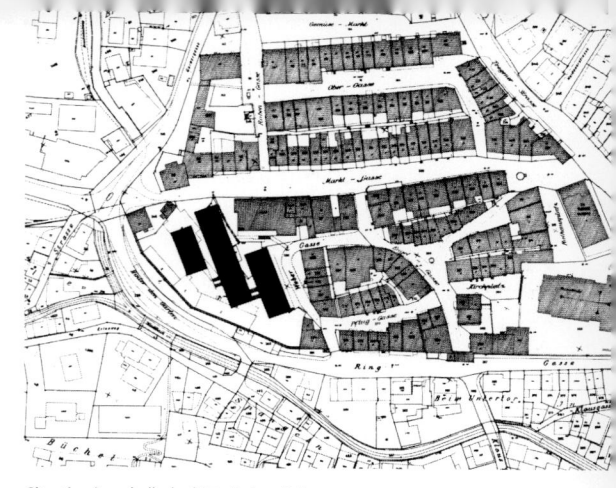

Situation innerhalb der historischen Bebauung
Situation within historic development

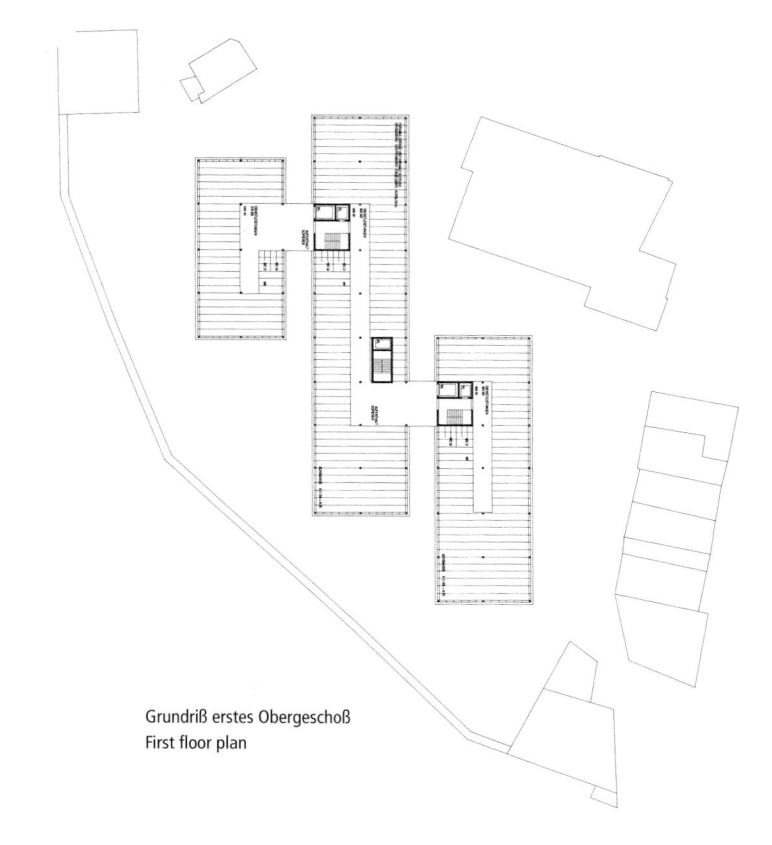

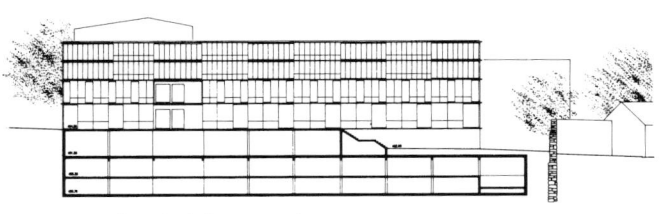

Grundriß erstes Obergeschoß
First floor plan

Längsschnitt durch die Untergeschosse
Longitudinal section through the basements

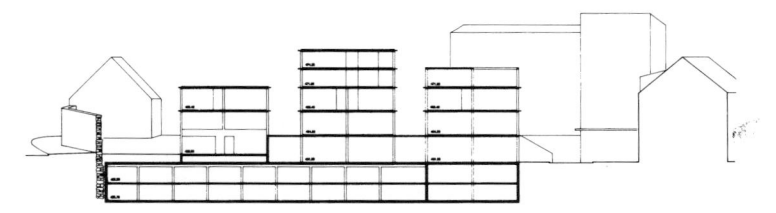

Querschnitt durch alle drei parallelen Volumen
Cross section through all three parallel volumes

Kommunales Wohnhaus in Basel 1989–1993

Bei diesem Wohnhaus für Familien niedrigen Einkommens war die städtebauliche Situation bestimmend für das Entwurfskonzept. Der Bauplatz, im Norden der Stadt gelegen, ist sowohl Teil einer strengen Blockrandbebauung als auch das letzte Glied einer vierzeiligen Reihenbebauung. Diese komplexe Rahmenbedingung haben Morger und Degelo architektonisch thematisiert: Das klar definierte Hauptvolumen, das sämtliche Wohnungen beinhaltet, liest sich als Zeile und als Teil des Blockrandes. Der rückwärtig angelegte Baukörper mit dem Kindergarten faßt den Hof, so daß die als Fragment dastehende Bebauung zu einem Ensemble aufgewertet ist.

Local Authority Residence in Basle 1989–1993

The town-planning context was decisive for the design concept of this residential building for low-income families. The site, situated outside the city centre, is both part of a strict block-edge development and the last link in a four-row terraced development. Morger and Degelo made these complex contextual conditions the theme of their building: the clearly-defined main block, containing all the apartments, is read as one row while the block at the rear with the kindergarten encloses the courtyard, so that the buildings, actually a fragment, appear as an ensemble.

Ansicht des Hauptvolumens mit durchlaufenden, auskragenden Balkonplatten
Elevation of main volume with continuous, projecting terraces

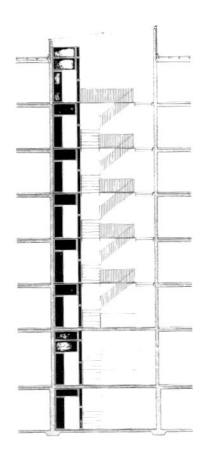

Schnitt durch das Treppenhaus
Section through stairwell

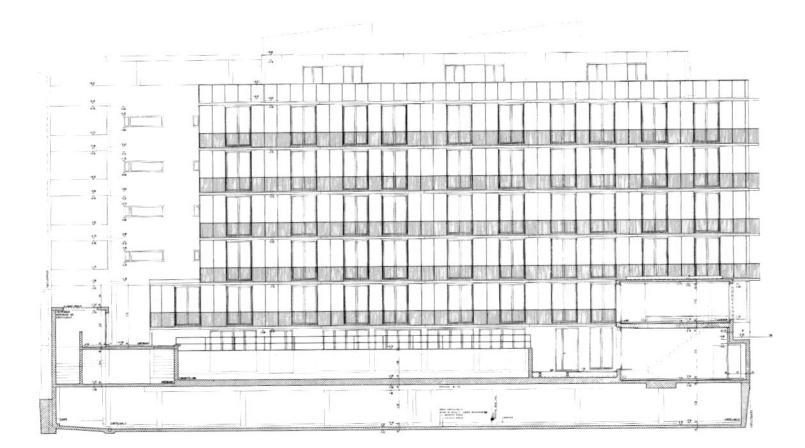

Ostfassade / East façade

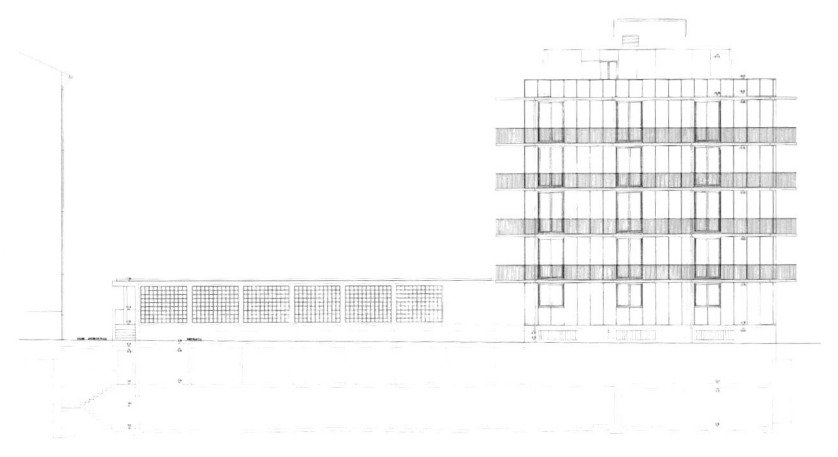

Nordfassade / North façade

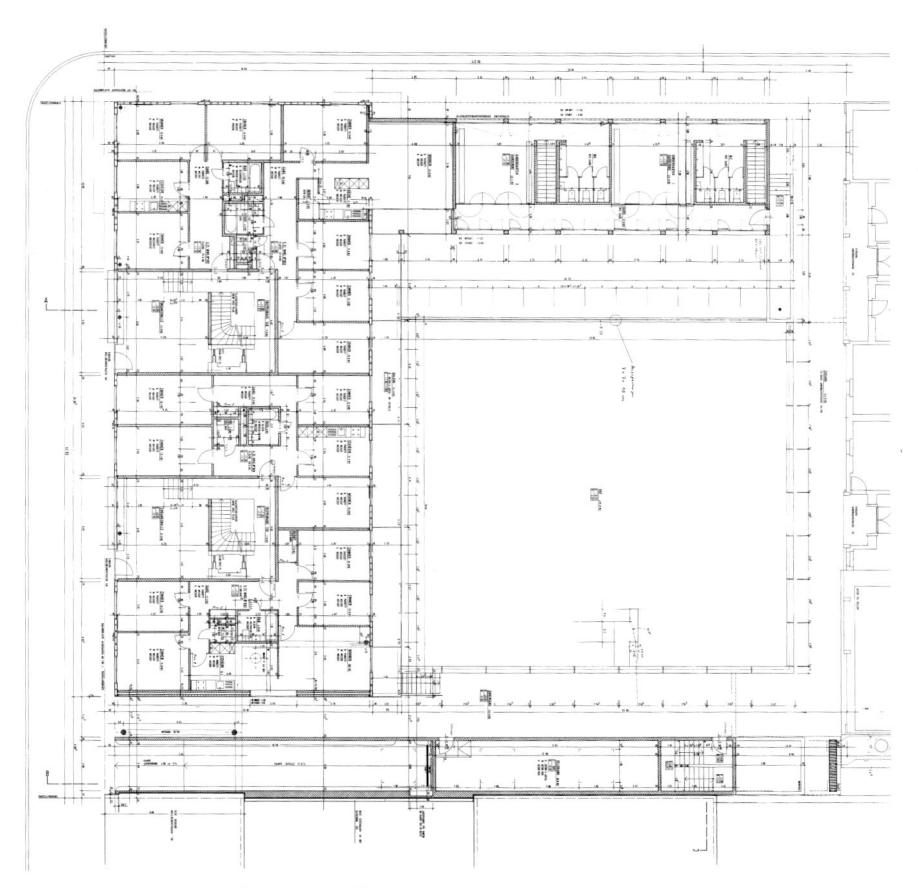

Grundriß Hochparterre / Plan of raised ground floor

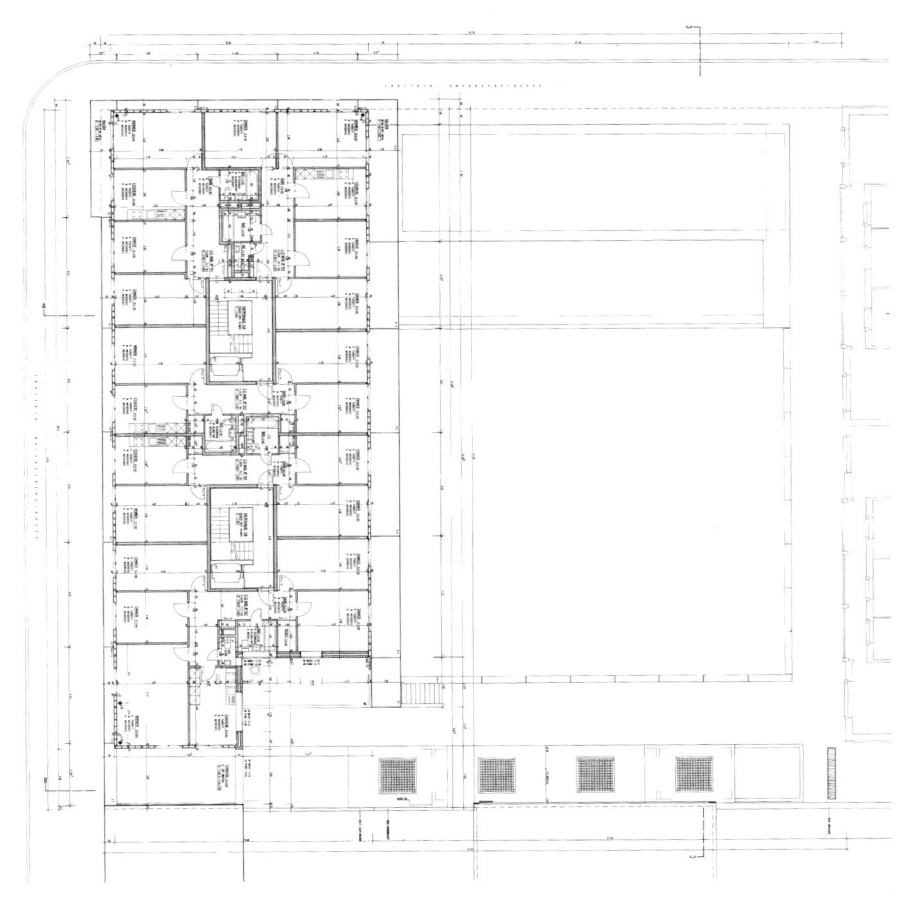

Grundriß erstes bis viertes Obergeschoß / Ground plan of first to fourth floors

**Dreifach-Turnhalle,
Erweiterung Schulhaus
und Wohnüberbauung in Basel
1991–etwa 1996**

Das in der Mitte der Parzelle liegende, bestehende historisierende Schulhaus wird von den drei neuen Volumen, die sich in Länge, Höhe und Tiefe klar voneinander unterscheiden, umfaßt. So reagieren die verschiedenen Baukörper auf ihre spezifische Umgebung und verleihen ihr ein kompositorisches Gegenüber. Um innen eine optimale Belichtung zu erreichen, weist die Dreifach–Turnhalle eine Decke aus Betonkassetten mit eingelagerten Glasbausteinen auf. Das Volumen ist völlig eingegraben. Ferner sind Schulräume als Erweiterung der bestehenden Anlage sowie 29 Stadtwohnungen geplant.

**Triple-Purpose Gymnasium,
School Extension and Residential
Development in Basle
1991–approx. 1996**

The existing school, in a historicist style in the middle of the plot, is surrounded by three new volumes, clearly distinguished from each other in length, height and depth. In this way the different buildings react to their specific environment, endowing it, with a kind of compositional counterpoint. To give optimum interior lighting the triple-purpose gymnasium has a concrete coffered ceiling with inlaid glass bricks. The whole building is recessed in the ground. A school extension and residential development with 29 apartments are planned.

Modell der Wettbewerbseingabe / Competition model

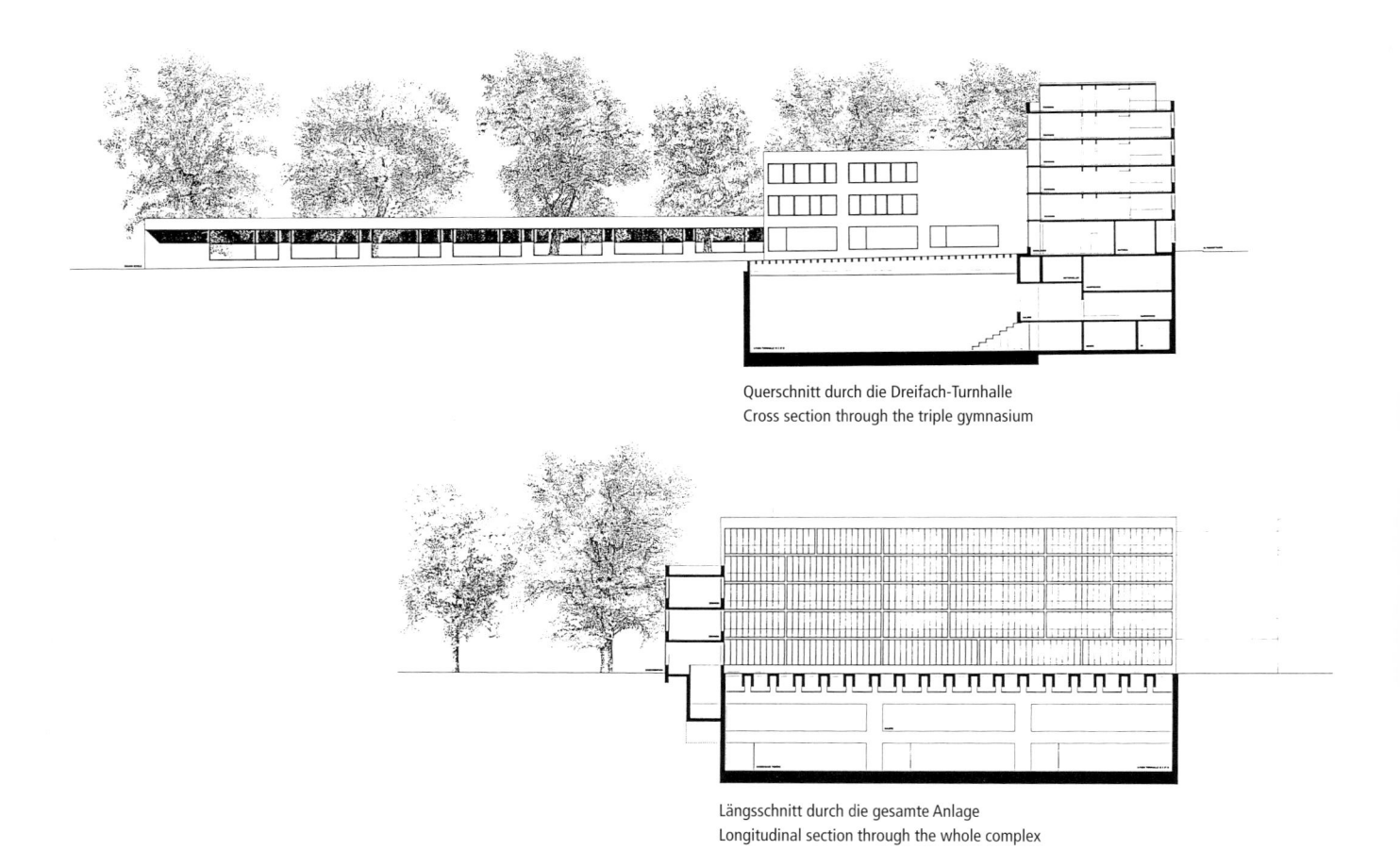

Querschnitt durch die Dreifach-Turnhalle
Cross section through the triple gymnasium

Längsschnitt durch die gesamte Anlage
Longitudinal section through the whole complex

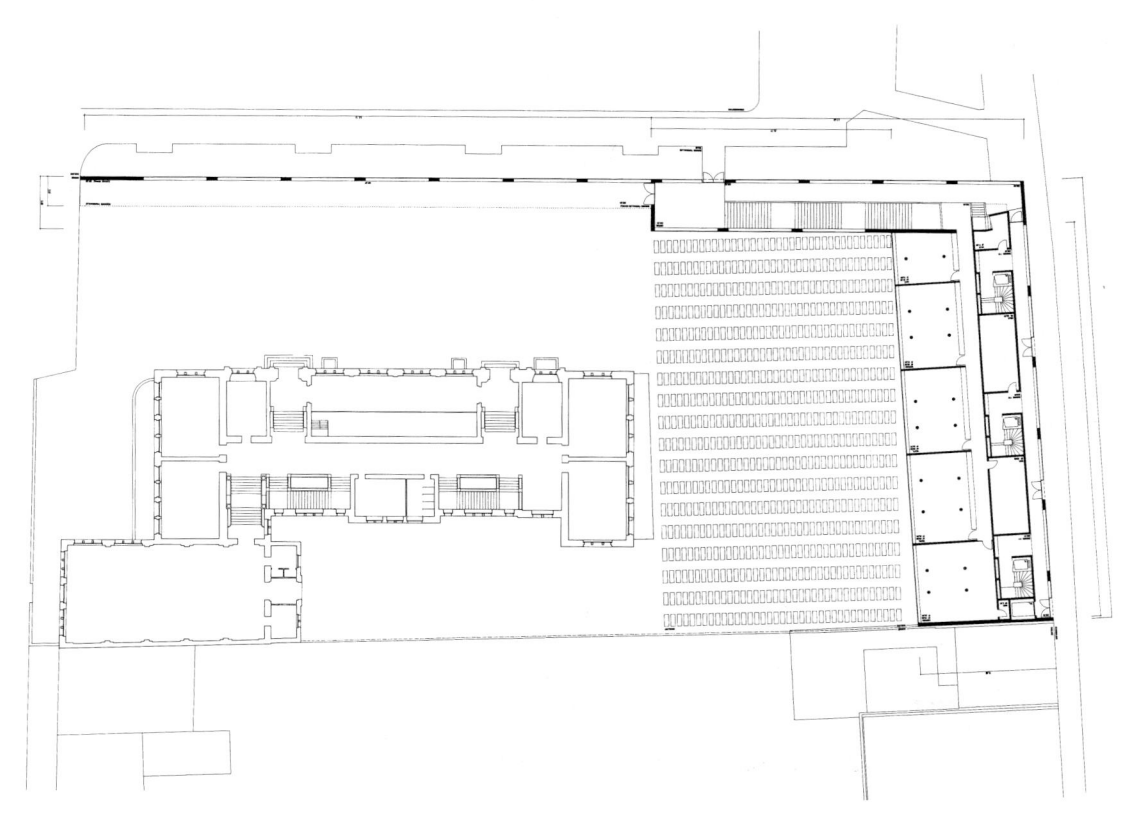

Grundriß Erdgeschoß / Ground floor plan

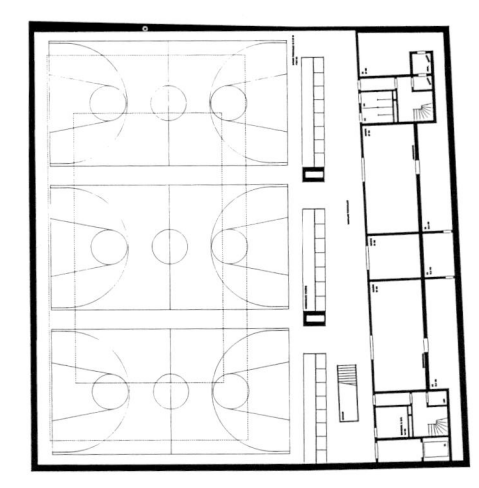

Grundriß drittes Untergeschoß / Ground plan of third basement

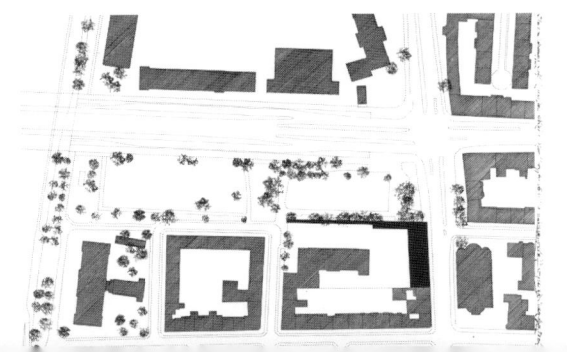

Situation / Situation

Wohnüberbauung «Melchrüti» in Wallisellen 1992

Die Architekten bezeichnen die zu bebauende Parzelle, irgendwo zwischen Autobahn, Kornfeld, Industrie, Bach und Mehrfamiliensiedlung, als ein «Ortloser Ort». Deshalb schlugen sie die Struktur eines geschlossenen, orthogonalen Blockrandes mit einem inneren ruhigen Hof vor. Die einzelnen Trakte erhöhen sich systematisch um ein Geschoß. Zuoberst jeweils befindet sich der begrünte, individuelle Dachgarten für Gemüse, Früchte oder Blumen. Die Grundrisse, bewährt und trotzdem weiterentwickelt, passen sich den spezifischen Bedürfnissen der Bewohnerinnen und Bewohner an und suchen eine intensive Beziehung zur Weite des Umlandes sowie zur Nähe des Innenhofes.

"Melchrüti" Residential Development in Wallisellen 1992

The architects describe the plot, situated somewhere between a motorway, cornfields, industrial buildings, a stream and a housing estate as a "placeless place". They therefore proposed a closed rectangular block with a quiet inner courtyard. The separate sections increase in height systematically by one storey at a time. At the top of each building is an individual roof garden for vegetables, fruit or flowers. The floor plans, which elaborate on a given configuration, are adapted to the specific needs of the residents, and are strongly related both to the expansiveness of their surroundings and to the closeness of the inner courtyard.

Modell der Wettbewerbseingabe / Competition model

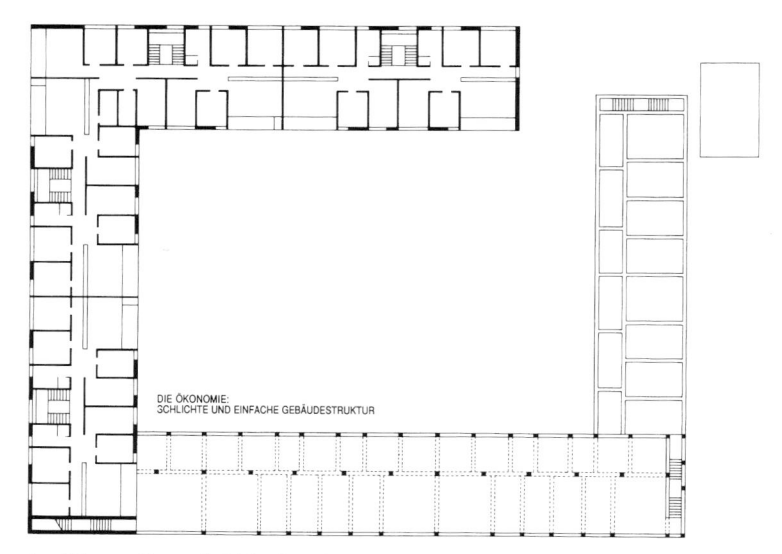

Grundriß erstes Obergeschoß / First floor plan

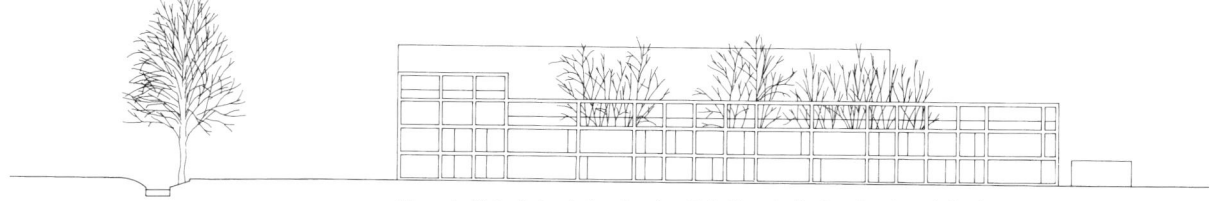

Längsschnitt durch den dreigeschossigen Trakt / Longitudinal section through the three-storey part

Keppler-Gymnasium in Freiburg im Breisgau 1993

Innerhalb der künftigen Siedlungsstruktur, aber außerhalb des Stadtzentrums existiert ein grüner Landschaftsraum, in den die Architekten vier verschieden große, solitäre Baukörper in freier Komposition einfügen, so daß sie sich deutlich von ihrer Umgebung abheben. Sie stehen zueinander und zur Parklandschaft in Beziehung. Allen neuen Volumen gemeinsam ist die Aufteilung in Schale, Kern und deren Dialog. Dies schafft eine Verwandtschaft und läßt gleichzeitig Raum für die unterschiedlichen Funktionen. Das Schulhaus ist offen und transparent gestaltet, während die Turnhallen von einem Ring von Nebenräumen umschlossen sind.

Keppler Grammar School in Freiburg im Breisgau 1993

Within the future built-up area but outside the city centre is an area of parkland in which the architects have placed large, free-standing buildings in a free composition, so that they stand out clearly from their surroundings. They are related to each other and to the park landscape. Common to all the new buildings is a division between the shell, the core and the dialogue between them. This interrelates the buildings while leaving scope for different functions. The school has an open, transparent construction while the gymnasia are surrounded by a ring of adjoining rooms.

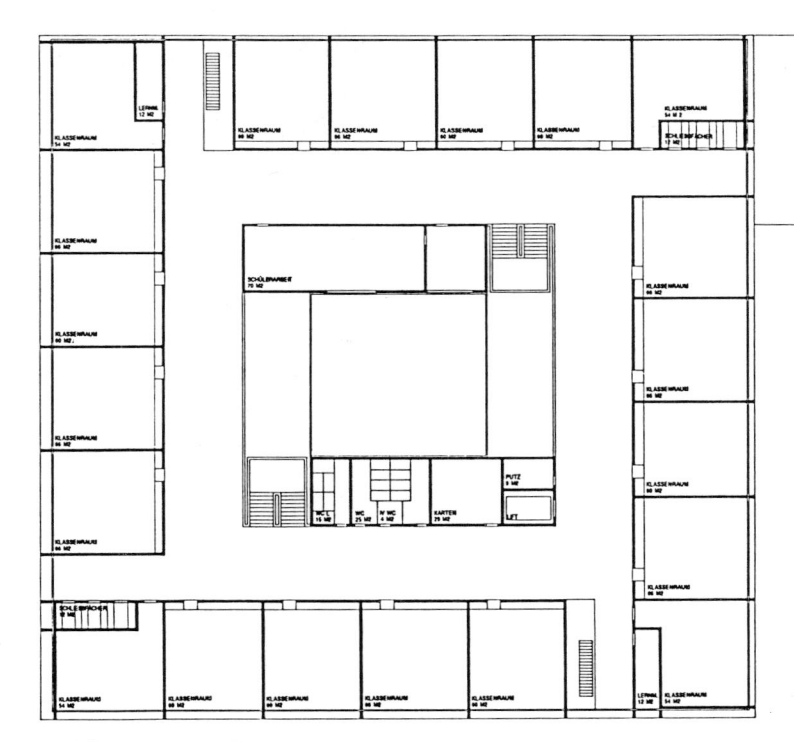

Grundriß erstes Obergeschoß des Schulhauses / First floor plan of school building

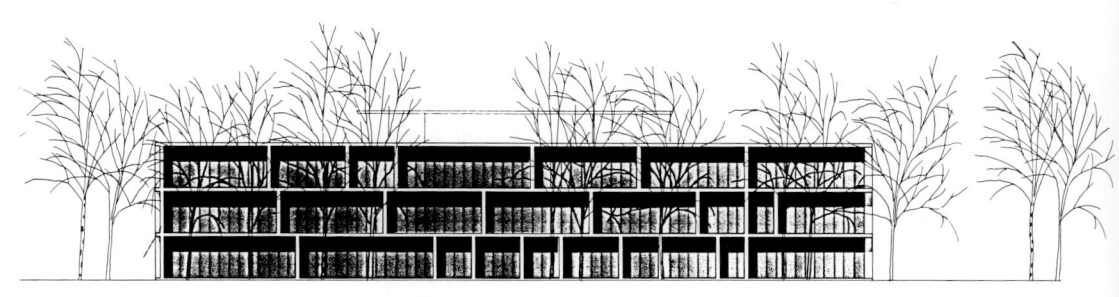

Westfassade des Schulhauses / West façade of school building

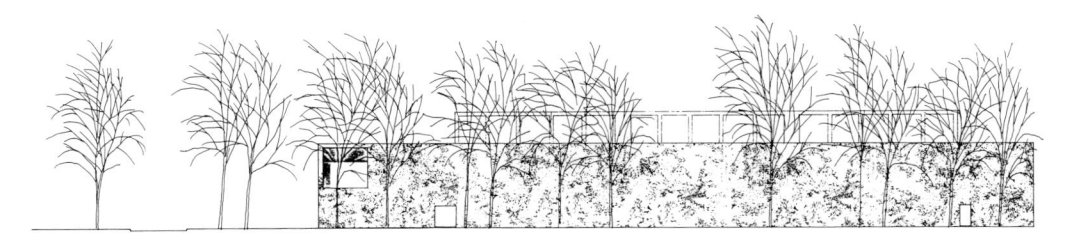

Nordfassade der Turnhalle / North façade of gymnasium

Situation / Situation

Wohnüberbauung «Schloßmatte» in Grenzach-Wylen
1994

Inmitten des zersiedelten Territoriums plazierten die Architekten dreizehn Wohnhäuser, die sich in lockerer Regelmäßigkeit über das ganze Areal verteilen. Zusammen mit den zu erhaltenden Bauten suchen sie eine schlichte, selbstverständliche Form, so als seien sie schon immer dagewesen. Die Baukörper bilden untereinander präzise räumliche Konfigurationen, die, stark durchgrünt, die benachbarten Parkanlagen und Gärten verbinden. Die Überbauung, eine einfache, nüchterne Architektur, sollte in fünf Bauetappen erstellt werden.

"Schlossmatte" Residential Development in Grenzach-Wylen
1994

The architects have placed thirteen apartment blocks, distributed in a loosely regular arrangement over the entire site, at the centre of the built-up area. In relation to the buildings to be retained, they have a simple, natural form, as if they had been there always. The buildings are interrelated in precise spatial configurations which, with dense plantation, link the neighbouring parkland and gardens. The development, in a simple, sober style, was to be completed in five stages.

Situation der gesamten Wohnüberbauung / Situation of whole residential development

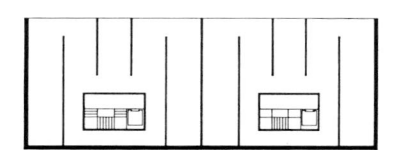

Gebäudestruktur / Building structure

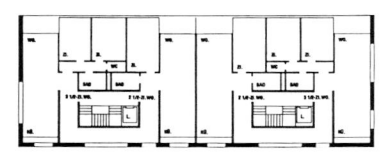

Grundriß Erdgeschoß / Ground floor plan

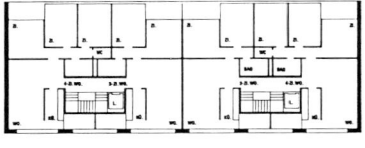

Grundriß erstes bis drittes Obergeschoß (Variante 1)
Plan of first to third floor (Variant 1)

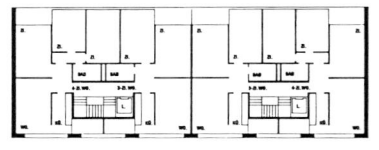

Grundriß erstes bis drittes Obergeschoß (Variante 2)
Plan of first to third floor (Variant 2)

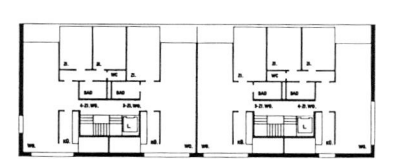

Grundriß erstes bis drittes Obergeschoß (Variante 4)
Plan of first to third floor (Variant 4)

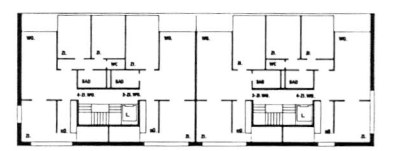

Grundriß erstes bis drittes Obergeschoß (Variante 3)
Plan of first to third floor (Variant 3)

Seitliche Fassade / Side façade

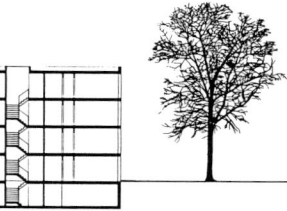

Querschnitt durch die Treppe
Cross section through stairs

Vordere Fassade / Front façade

Mehrfamilienhaus in Binningen
1994–etwa 1996

Die Parzelle, an einer Straßenecke gelegen, befindet sich in einem typischen Wohnquartier der Agglomeration. Der winkelförmige, dreigeschossige Baukörper bietet Raum für fünf Vierzimmer-Wohnungen mit dreiseitiger Orientierung. Die Erschließung, das Gelenk der beiden gegeneinander versetzten Volumen, erfolgt über ein gemeinsames, inneres Treppenhaus. Die Wohnungen im Erd- und ersten Obergeschoß verfügen alle über eine verglaste Veranda, jene im zweiten Obergeschoß über eine großzügige Dachterrasse. Der Bau ist mit Dorfbrandklinkerplatten, einem ortsbezogenen Material, verkleidet.

Multiple Residence in Binningen
1994–approx. 1996

The building plot, at a street corner, is in a typical residential district within the town. The three-storey, angled structure has space for five four-roomed apartments arranged in an east-west or a north-south configuration. At the junction of the two offset volumes a common, inner staircase area provides access to all the apartments. The ground floor and first-storey apartments all have a winter garden while those on the second storey have a spacious roof terrace.

Modell / Model

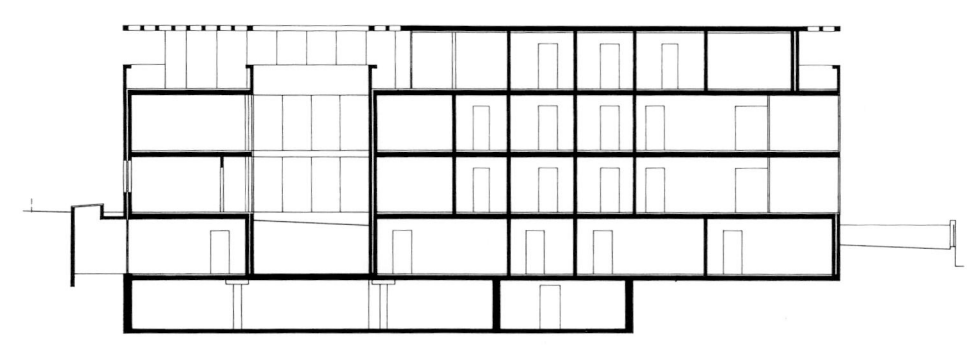

Längsschnitt durch das Entrée / Longitudinal section through entrance

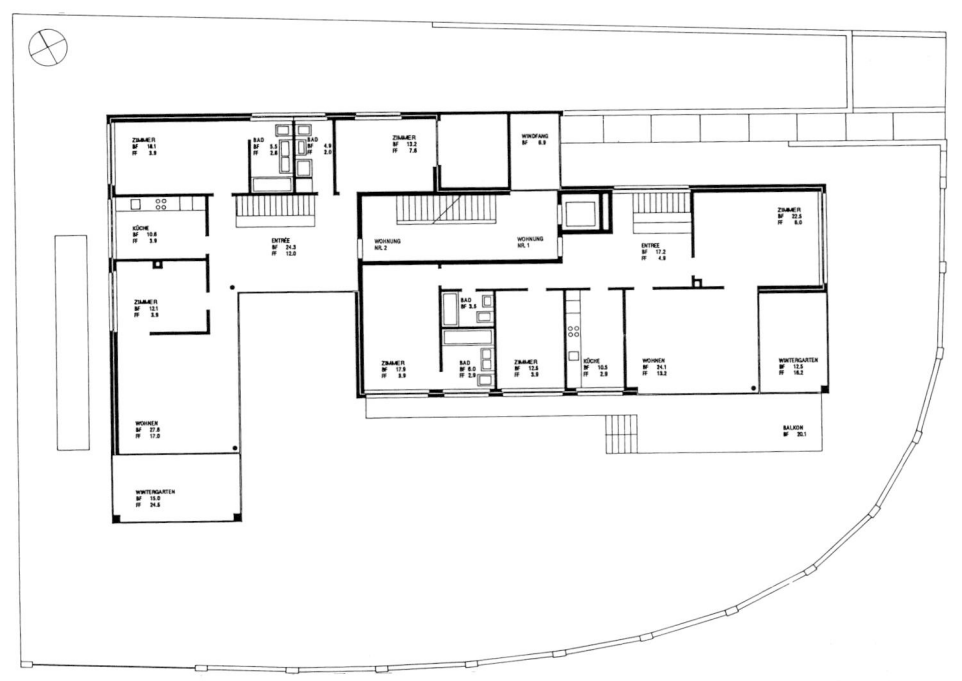

Grundriß Erdgeschoß / Ground floor plan

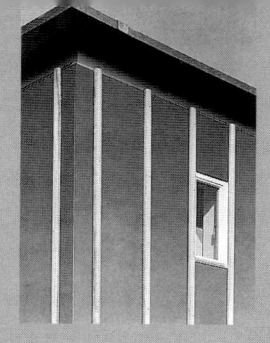

Pierre-André Simonet · Yvan Chappuis, Freiburg

Experimentelle Rohheit

Obwohl die beiden Architekten aufgrund verschiedener Ausbildungen in ihrem Büro eine strikte Arbeitsteilung von Entwurf (Simonet) und Ausführung (Chappuis) haben, fällt ihr architektonisches Werk durch das harmonische Zusammenklingen von Entwurf und Konstruktion auf. Diese Charakteristik kommt in ihrem fertiggestellten Bootshaus in Murten besonders gut zum Ausdruck. Ihre größtenteils in der näheren Umgebung von Freiburg geplanten und ausgeführten Arbeiten basieren nicht auf einer theoretischen Philosophie. Sie lassen sich aber deutlich in zwei zeitlich voneinander abgegrenzte Phasen einteilen; in die früheren, mit dem Attribut metaphorisch zu bezeichnenden Projekte, und in die späteren, die in freierer und unbeschwerterer Art und Weise sich mit dem jeweiligen Ort, dem Licht und den Materialien beschäftigen. In diese Kategorie gehört etwa die Erweiterung des Schulzentrums in Givisiez. Da das Gebäude in sehr kurzer Zeit gebaut werden mußte, hatten architektonische Entscheidungen schnell zu erfolgen, was eine besondere Herausforderung und eine einzigartige Erfahrung darstellte. Ihre Arbeiten, die sie selber als einen immer wieder von neuem anzufangenden Prozeß betrachten, bestechen durch ihre experimentelle Rohheit.

Experimental Brutalism

Although, in view of their different training, the two architects have a strict division of tasks between design (Simonet) and realization (Chappuis) within their office, the striking feature of their architectural works is the harmony between design and construction. This characteristic is especially well expressed in their completed boathouse in Murten. Their works, mostly planned and built in the immediate surroundings of Fribourg, are not based on any theoretical philosophy, but they can be clearly divided into two chronologically distinct phases. The earlier phase comprised projects that could be described as metaphorical, while buildings in the later one are characterised by a freer and altogether lighter touch in their treatment of the given place, the light conditions and materials. The extension to the school centre at Givisiez is an example of the latter. As the building had to be put up in a very short time, the architectural decisions had to be made quickly, which was a special challenge and a unique experience. Their works, which they themselves consider as a process that has to be started over and over again, attract the eye by their experimental brutalism.

Biographie

Pierre-André Simonet

1960
Geboren in Avry-devant-Pont
(Kanton Freiburg).

1979–85
Architekturstudium an der ETH-Zürich.

1985
Diplom bei Professor Dolf Schnebli
an der ETH-Zürich.

1986–87
Mitarbeit im Büro Hayoz und Bertoli
in Freiburg.

1987–88
Mitarbeit im Büro Michel Waeber
in Barberêche (Kanton Freiburg).

Seit 1989
Assoziiertes Büro mit Yvan Chappuis
in Freiburg für die Ausführung.

Yvan Chappuis

1959
Geboren in Corpataux (Kanton Freiburg).

1974–78
Lehre als Hochbauzeichner.

1978–79
Mitarbeit im Büro Maillart und
Pasquier in Bulle (Kanton Freiburg).

1979–82
Architekturstudium
an der HTL in Freiburg.

1982-86
Mitarbeit im Büro Michel Waeber
(Zoelly und Waeber) in Zollikon.

1986–88
Mitarbeit im Büro Michel Waeber
in Barberêche (Kanton Freiburg).

Seit 1989
Assoziiertes Büro mit Pierre-André
Simonet in Freiburg für die Projektierung.

Ausgewähltes Werkverzeichnis

1989
Gestaltung Bahnhofgebiet in Brig
(Kanton Wallis)
Wettbewerb, neunter Preis.

Spital in Riaz
(Kanton Freiburg; 1989–92)
Zweistufiger Wettbewerb, dritter Preis.

1990
Erweiterung Schulzentrum in Givisiez
(Kanton Freiburg; 1990–92)
Route de l'Epinay 7
Wettbewerb, erster Preis.
Teilweise ausgeführtes Projekt.

1991
Erweiterung Schule in Guin
(Kanton Freiburg)
Wettbewerb.

Ausstellung «11 sites, 1 itinéraire
pour des architectures de l'utopie»
in Neuenburg
Ausgeführtes Projekt.

1992
Bootshaus in Murten (Kanton Freiburg)
Am Mühlebach
Ausgeführtes Projekt.

Erweiterung Wohnhaus Chappuis
in Corpataux (Kanton Freiburg)
La Perrausa
Ausgeführtes Projekt.

Polizeiposten in Mont-sur-Lausanne
(Kanton Waadt)
Wettbewerb.

Raiffeisenbank, Post und Wohnungen
in Givisiez (Kanton Freiburg)
Wettbewerb, erster Preis.

Schweizerische Bankgesellschaft
in Delémont (Kanton Jura)
Wettbewerb, vierter Preis.

1993
Erweiterung Wohnhaus Allemann
in Corpataux (Kanton Freiburg)
Ausgeführtes Projekt.

Schul- und Sportzentrum in Murten
(Kanton Freiburg)
Wettbewerb.

1994
Freizeitzentrum in Châtel-St-Denis
(Kanton Freiburg)
Wettbewerb, erster Preis.

Erweiterung Wohnhaus Magne in
Corpataux (Kanton Freiburg; 1994–95)
Vorprojekt.

Gestaltung Wohnhaus Juvet
in Freiburg (1994–95)
Vorprojekt.

Wohnhaus Jeannet in Avry-devant-Pont
(Kanton Freiburg; 1994–95)
Vorprojekt.

Biography

Pierre-André Simonet

1960
Born in Avry-devant-Pont
(Canton of Fribourg).

1979–85
Studied architecture at the ETH Zurich.

1985
Graduated with diploma under
Prof. Dolf Schnebli at the ETH Zurich

1986–87
Worked at the Hayoz and Bertoli
architectural office in Fribourg

1987–88
Worked at the Michel Waeber architectural office in Barberêche
(Canton of Fribourg).

Since 1989
Associated architectural office
with Yvan Chappuis in Fribourg
for realization.

Yvan Chappuis

1959
Born in Corpataux (Canton of Fribourg).

1974–78
Studied architectural draughtsmanship

1978–79
Worked at the Maillart and Pasquier
architectural office in Bulle
(Canton of Fribourg).

1979–82
Studied architecture at the HTL
in Fribourg.

1982–86
Worked at the Michel Waeber
(Zoelly and Waeber) architectural office
in Zollikon.

1986–88
Worked at the Michel Waeber
architectural office in Barberêche
(Canton of Fribourg).

Since 1989
Associated architectural office
with Pierre-André Simonet in Fribourg
for design.

Selected list of work

1989
Design for station district in Brig
(Canton of Valais)
Competition, ninth prize.

Hospital in Riaz (Canton of Fribourg;
1989–92)
Two-stage competition, third prize.

1990
Extension of school centre in Givisiez
(Canton of Fribourg; 1990–92)
Route de l'Epinay 7
Competition, first prize.
Partly completed project.

1991
Extension of school in Guin
(Canton of Fribourg)
Competition.

Exhibition: "11 sites, 1 itinéraire
pour des architectures de l'utopie"
in Neuenburg
Completed project.

1992
Boathouse in Murten
(Canton of Fribourg)
Am Mühlebach
Completed project.

Extension to Chappuis residence
in Corpataux (Canton of Fribourg)
La Perrausa
Completed project.

Police station in Mont-sur-Lausanne
(Canton of Vaud)
Competition.

Raiffeisenbank, post office
and apartments in Givisiez
(Canton of Fribourg)
Competition, first prize.

Schweizerische Bankgesellschaft
in Delémont (Canton of Jura)
Competition, fourth prize.

1993
Extension to Allemann residence
in Corpataux (Canton of Fribourg)
Completed project.

School and sports centre in Murten
(Canton of Fribourg)
Competition.

1994
Leisure centre in Châtel-St-Denis
(Canton of Fribourg)
Competition, first prize.

Extension to Magne residence
in Corpataux
(Canton of Fribourg; 1994–95)
Preliminary project.

Design for Juvet residence
in Fribourg (1994–95)
Preliminary project.

Jeannet residence in Avry-devant-Pont
(Canton of Fribourg; 1994–95)
Preliminary project.

Erweiterung Schulzentrum in Givisiez 1990–1992

Die städtebaulich vorbildlich konzipierte Anlage befindet sich in der Mitte des Dorfes und ist gekennzeichnet durch die Nähe einer stark befahrenen Autostraße. Der Entwurf zeigt drei verschiedene Bereiche: Die Turnhalle, das Gebäude mit den Klassenzimmern und den beide Teile verbindenden Trakt, der den Eingang und die Umkleideräume sowie die Erschließung enthält. Von der Funktion her wirkt dieser Raum, der durch eine Säulenhalle definiert ist, zusätzlich wie ein Schutzraum gegen den Lärm der Straße. Das Projekt zeichnet sich ferner durch drei verschiedene Außenräume aus, von denen jeder seine Eigenheit besitzt. Die Anlage überzeugt durch ihre einfachen, rohen, sehr zweckmäßigen Materialien wie Holz, Beton und Eternit.

Extension to School Centre in Givisiez 1990–1992

The complex, exemplary from the town-planning aspect, is situated in the middle of the village and is characterised by the proximity of a main road carrying heavy traffic. The design shows three distinct sections: the gymnasium, the classroom building and the area linking these two parts and containing the entrance, the cloakrooms and access ways. Functionally, this area, defined by a columned hall, also act as a barrier to road noise. The project is also distinguished by three different outer spaces, each of which has its own individual character. The complex's charm lies in the expedient use of simple, materials in their natural form, such as wood, concrete and Eternit.

Ansicht der hinteren, offenen und zum Garten hin orientierten Fassade
Elevation of rear, open façade oriented towards the garden

Ansicht der vorderen, durch die Säulenhalle definierten Fassade
Elevation of the front façade, defined by the columned hall

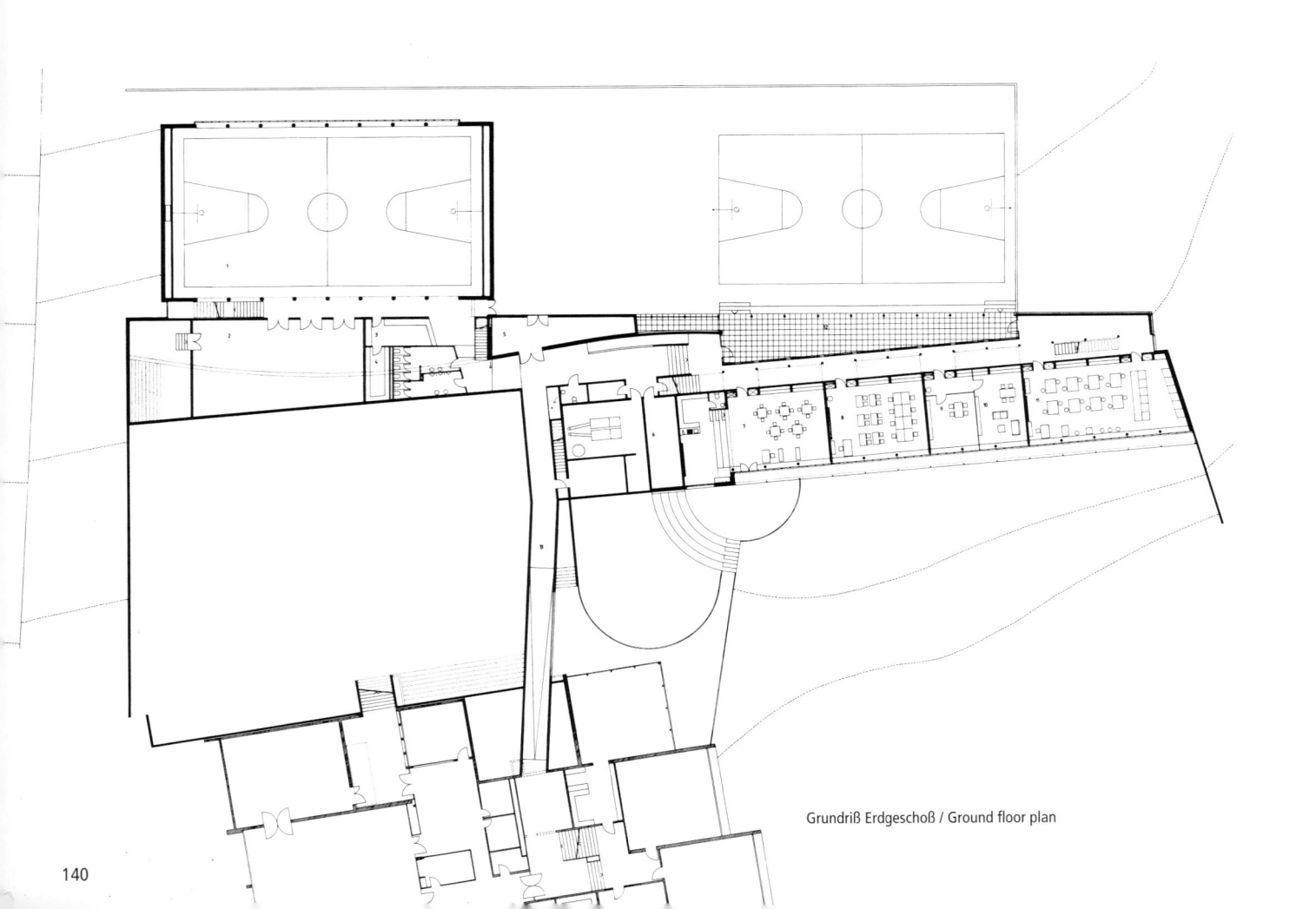

Grundriß Erdgeschoß / Ground floor plan

Längsschnitt durch die Klassenzimmer / Longitudinal section through classrooms

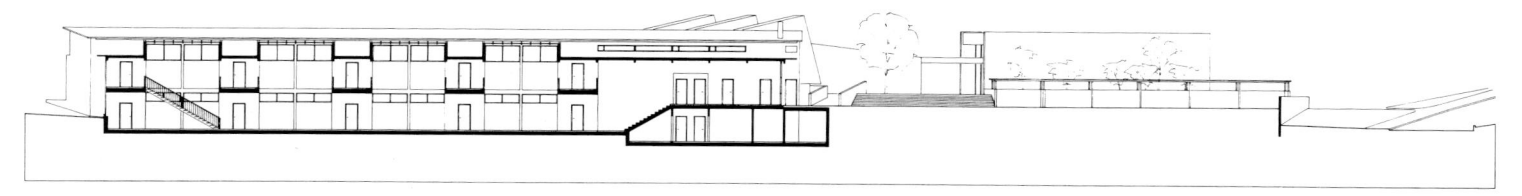

Längsschnitt durch die Pausenhalle / Longitudinal section through recreation hall

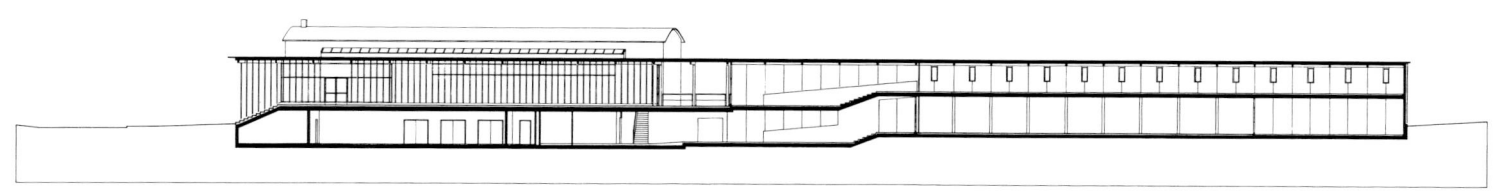

Längsschnitt durch die Erschließung / Longitudinal section of circulation

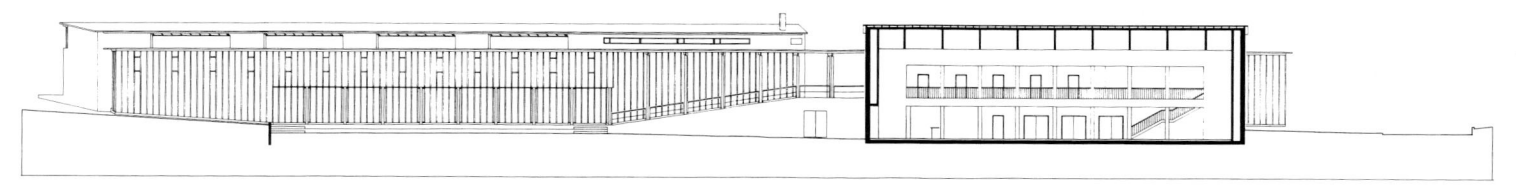

Nordostfassade / Northeast façade

Bootshaus in Murten 1992

Die Aufgabe bestand darin, direkt am See ein Gebäude für die Stationierung zweier Boote zu entwerfen. Der teilweise im Wasser stehende Baukörper, der vollständig aus Holz konstruiert ist, gefällt durch die elegante und ausdrucksstarke Formgebung, die unmißverständlich die dynamischen Linien von umgekehrten Bootsschalen assoziieren läßt. Die beiden kürzeren Fassaden – zum Wasser und zum Land – unterscheiden sich formal deutlich voneinander, sie sind einerseits mit einem flachen Steildach, andererseits mit einem ebenen Flachdach abgeschlossen. Das harmonische Zusammenklingen von Entwurf und Ausführung ist bemerkenswert.

Boathouse in Murten 1992

The commission involved designing a building for mooring two boats directly on the lake. The building, partly standing in water and constructed entirely of timber, has a pleasingly elegant and expressive form which unmistakably suggests the dynamic lines of inverted boat hulls. The two shorter façades – facing the water and the land – are clearly distinguished from each other formally, having a shallow pitched roof at one end and a flat roof at the other. There is a noteworthy harmony between design and realization.

Ansicht der vorderen, mit zwei Öffnungen und mit flachem Steildach versehenen Fassade
Elevation of front façade with two openings and gently sloping pitch roof

Seitlicher, gekrümmter Fassadenverlauf / Curved side façade

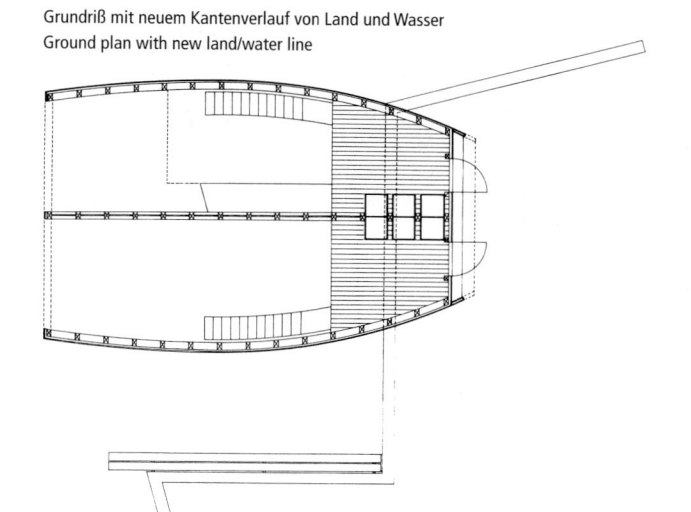

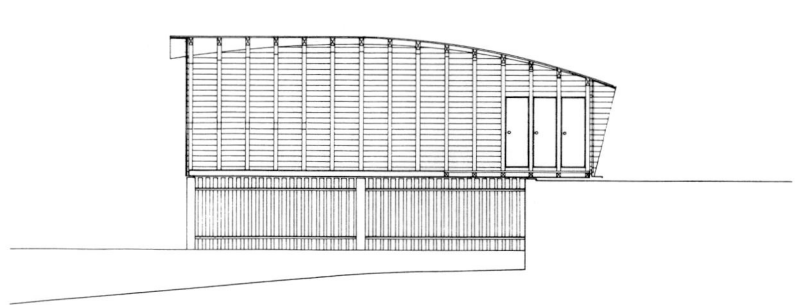

Grundriß mit neuem Kantenverlauf von Land und Wasser
Ground plan with new land/water line

Längsschnitt durch die eine Raumhälfte
Longitudinal section through one half of room

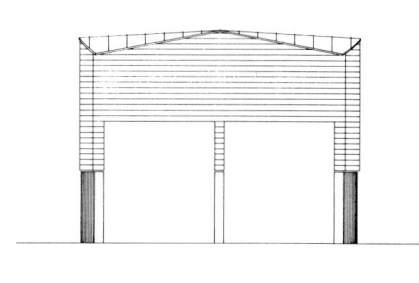

Nordfassade / North façade

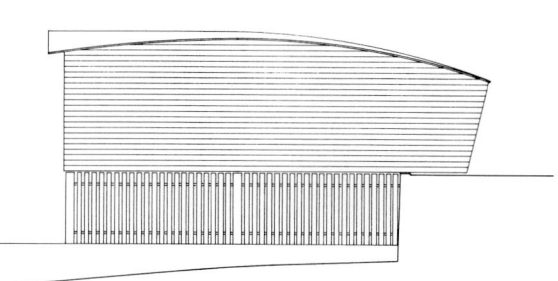

Westfassade / West façade

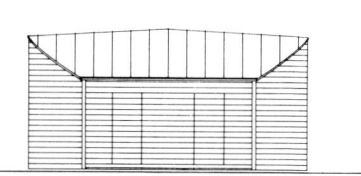

Südfassade / South façade

Erweiterung Wohnhaus Chappuis in Corpataux 1992

Die Erweiterung dieses Wohnhauses hebt sich klar von der alten Bausubstanz ab. Der neue quaderförmige, aus unverputztem Beton gefertigte, eingeschossige Baukörper ist präzise in die offene Landschaft gesetzt. Auffallend sind die tiefen, langen Bandfenster, die die ländliche Gegend, aus sitzender Perspektive, wie ein Bild rahmen, sowie die experimentelle Rohheit der Ausführung, die an die Maison Citrohan (1920) von Le Corbusier erinnert. Das Innere zeigt einen großzügig gestalteten Wohn- und Eßraum, der von einer zweckdienlichen Küche partiell abgetrennt ist, sowie ein Badezimmer.

Extension to Chappuis Residence in Corpataux 1992

The extension to this house stands out clearly from the old building. The single-storey, cuboid new part, made of exposed concrete, is placed precisely in the open country. A striking feature are the deep, long strip windows which, from a sitting position, frame the rural surroundings like a painting, while the experimental harshness of the execution recalls the Maison Citrohan (1920) by Le Corbusier. The interior contains a spacious living/dining room, partially divided from a functional kitchen, and a bathroom.

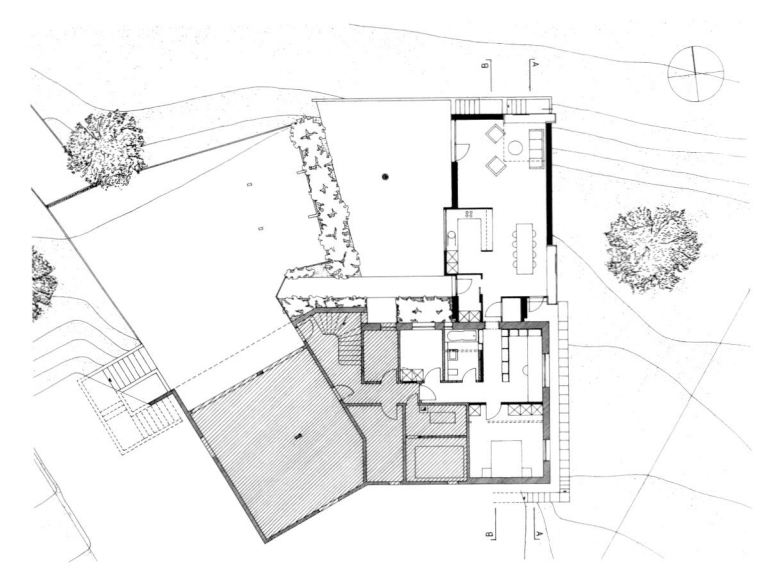

Grundriß Erdgeschoß / Ground floor plan

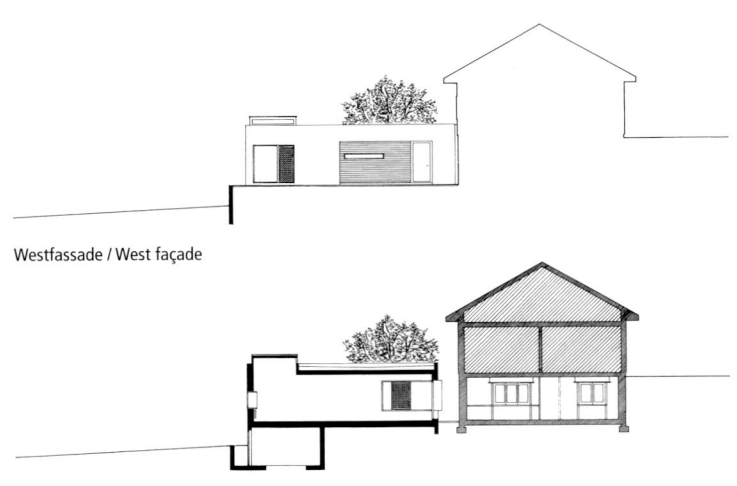

Westfassade / West façade

Längsschnitt durch die neuen und durch die bestehenden Räume
Longitudinal section through the new and existing rooms

Ansicht der seitlichen Nordfassade mit der experimentellen Anwendung des rohen Betons
Elevation of lateral north façade with experimental use of exposed concrete

Erweiterung Wohnhaus Allemann in Corpataux 1993

Leicht abgedreht zum bestehenden Gebäude, sucht das neue Volumen eine Beziehung zur umliegenden Landschaft. Der zweigeschossige, längsgerichtete neue Baukörper zeigt eine geschlossene, mit Wellblech verkleidete Eingangsfront und eine eher offene, aus Glas und Holz gefertigte, zum Garten hin orientierte Fassade. Die flexiblen Schiebetüren lassen den Innen- mit dem Außenraum verschmelzen. Beeindruckend sind die verschiedenen gutproportionierten Räume und deren spannungsvolle Abfolge. Deutlich voneinander geschieden sind die Wohn- und Aufenhaltsräume im Erdgeschoß sowie die Schlafräume im Obergeschoß.

Extension to Allemann Residence in Corpataux 1993

Turned slightly away from the existing building, the new structure seeks a relationship to the surrounding country. The two-storey, longitudinal new building has a closed entrance frontage clad in corrugated metal panelling and a more open façade, of glass and timber, facing the garden. Flexible sliding partitions allow the inner and outer spaces of the building to merge. The tension-charged sequence of different, well-proportioned rooms is an impressive feature. The living rooms and lounge on the ground floor and the bedrooms above are clearly distinguished from each other.

Ansicht der geschlossenen, mit Wellblech verkleideten Eingangsfassade
Elevation of closed entrance façade clad with corrugated sheet

Ansicht der offenen, mit Schiebetüren versehenen und aus Glas und Holz gefertigten Gartenfassade
Elevation of open, glass and wood garden façade with sliding doors

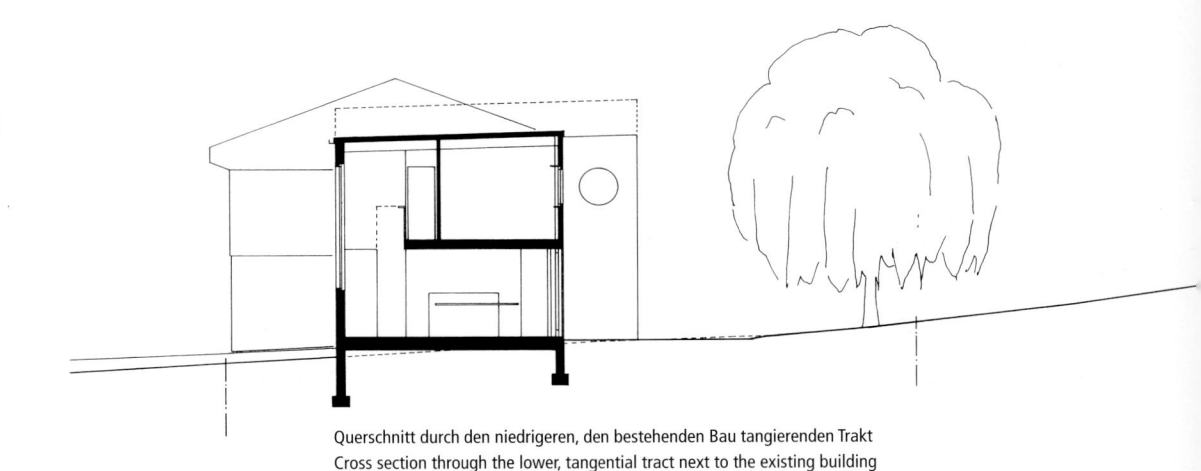

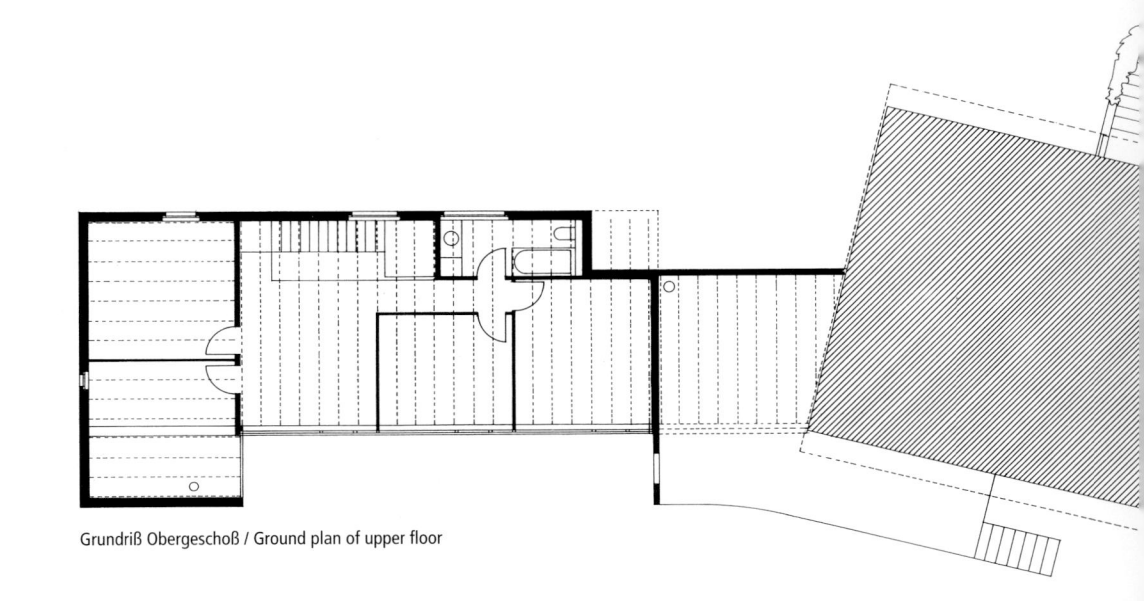

Querschnitt durch den niedrigeren, den bestehenden Bau tangierenden Trakt
Cross section through the lower, tangential tract next to the existing building

Grundriß Obergeschoß / Ground plan of upper floor

**Valentin Bearth
Andrea Deplazes
Chur**

Mitarbeiterinnen und Mitarbeiter
Collaborators

Timo Allemann
Christian Bandi
Adrian Christen
Michael Curdin
Paul-Duri Degonda
Sabine Fierschke
Seraina Gallmann
Isabelle Giger
Marlene Gujan
Caspar Hoesch
Markus Huber
Susanne Kipfmüller-Deiss
Daniel Ladner
Daniel Mettler
Reto Pahl
Barbara Perterli
Anita Reich
Bruno Sieber
Priska Signorell
Riccardo Signorell
Gion Simeon

Auswahlbibliographie
Selected Bibliography

«Tourismusarchitektur, zeigen oder verstecken?», in: Bündner Zeitung, 11. Mai 1989 – «Filipinis Garten», in: Bündner Tagblatt, 17. November 1989 – Marco Guetg, «Gartenhaus am Dorfrand», in: Hochparterre, 1991, Nr. 4 – Benedikt Loderer, «Neubeginn oder weitermachen», in: Hochparterre, 1991, Nr. 6 – «Internationaler Architekturpreis für Neues Bauen in den Alpen», in: Bündner Zeitung, 8. September 1992 – «Berg-Werke», in: Werk, Bauen + Wohnen, 1993, Nr. 1/2 – «Ecole et halle polyvalente à Alvaschein, Suisse», in: Le Moniteur architecture, 1993, Nr. 46 – Carmen Humbel, «Vielschichtigkeit durch Reduktion, Die Churer Architekten Valentin Bearth und Andrea Deplazes», in: Neue Zürcher Zeitung, 7. Januar 1994 – «Planen und Bauen in Chur», in: Hochparterre, 1994, Nr. 3 – «Schulhaus Tschlin», in: Werk, Bauen + Wohnen, 1994, Nr. 3 – «Schulerweiterung in Tschlin», in: Baumeister, 1994, Nr. 8 – «Schulerweiterung in Tschlin», in: Deutsche Bauzeitung, 1994, Nr. 8.

**Ueli Brauen
Doris Waelchli
Lausanne**

Mitarbeiterinnen und Mitarbeiter
Collaborators

Nicolas Bart
Laurent Bertuchoz
Valérie Cottet
Gabriele Gaiser
Daniel Gmür
Raphaelle Golaz
Renate Haueter
Franziska von Holzen
Stephan Kutschke
Nicolas Monnerat
Jean-Luc Torrent

Auswahlbibliographie
Selected Bibliography

«Ouchy-front de lac à Lausanne», in: Aktuelle Wettbewerbs Scene, 1989, Nr. 5 – «Maison d'étudiants et équipements sportifs ‹des Cèdres› à Lausanne», in: Aktuelle Wettbewerbs Scene, 1990, Nr. 4/5 – Florian Musso, «Géronde: Tausend rote Rosen», in: Hochparterre, 1990, Nr. 12 – Gilles Barbey, «Concours d'architecture pour le Centre Vuillermet à Lausanne», in: Habitation, 1991, Nr. 1 – «Aménagement du site de Géronde à Sierre», in: Aktuelle Wettbewerbs Scene, 1991, Nr. 6 – «Agrandissement de l'entreprise horlogère CORUM à la Chaux-de-Fonds», in: Aktuelle Wettbewerbs Scene, 1992, Nr. 4/5 – «Villa Suter à Montblesson», in: Architecture Suisse, 1992, Nr. 104 – «Repérages, tout béton, tout bois, oui mais...», in: Faces, 1992, Nr. 25 – «Eine anspruchsvoll-bescheidene Uhrenfabrik», in: Hochparterre, 1992, Nr. 11 – «Architekturpreis, Regard sur deux réalisations en bois: Contraste et harmonie», in: Archithese, 1993, Nr. 1 – «Habitation pour le personnel et poste de gardes frontière à Villeneuve», in: Aktuelle Wettbewerbs Scene, 1993, Nr. 4/5 – Charles-André Meyer, «Concours à Viège, Objectifs de la Lonza AG», in: Habitation, 1994, Nr. 1 – Lore Kelly, «Holzhaus für mobiles Wohnen», in: Raum und Wohnen, September/Oktober 1994, Nr. 5 – Carmen Humbel, «Strukturelle Leichtigkeit, Zur Architektur von Ueli Brauen und Doris Waelchli», in: Neue Zürcher Zeitung, 7. Oktober 1994 – Marco Meier, «Provokation der Leichtigkeit, Einfamilienhaus Suter in Montblesson, Lausanne», in: du, 1994, Nr. 11.

**Raffaele Cavadini
Michele Arnaboldi
Locarno**

Mitarbeiterinnen und Mitarbeiter
Collaborators

Alves Ferreira
Silvana Marzari
Fabio Trisconi
Mauro Malisia
Giovanni Realini
Nicola Romerio
Paolo Canevascini

Auswahlbibliographie
Selected Bibliography

«Rigore e semplicità nella periferia di Locarno», in: Casabella, Dezember 1989 – «Casa dell'architetto a Brissago 1989», in: Rivista Tecnica, 1990, Nr. 9 – «Casa Kalt a Locarno Monti 1990–91», «Casa Calzascia-Vairora a Gerra Piano 1991–1992», «Casa Svanascini a Tremona 1992», «Casa Juri ad Ambri 1991–1992», in: Rivista Tecnica, 1993, Nr. 1/2 – «1. Rango: Arch. Michele Arnaboldi e Raffaele Cavadini, Locarno, Arch. Paesaggista: Guido Hager, Zurigo», in: Rivista Tecnica, 1993, Nr. 10 – Carmen Humbel, «Geheimnisvolle Orte, Zur Architektur von Raffaele Cavadini und Michele Arnaboldi»,
in: Neue Zürcher Zeitung, 8. April 1994 – Lore Kelly, «Raffaele Cavadini, Architekt», in: Bau Doc Bulletin, Juli 1994.

**Jean-Pierre Dürig
Philippe Rämi
Zürich**

Mitarbeiterinnen und Mitarbeiter
Collaborators

Margrit Althammer
Roger Brunner
Carmen Campana
Desirée Cuttat
Eugen Eisenhut
Stefan Gisi
Jost Haberland
Jean-Claude Horlacher
Rolf Hörler
Marlen Hürzeler
Urs Keller
André Mathis
Wolfgang Maul
Michel Muhl
Stefan Müller
Maria Parrondo
Joao Penas
Barbara Rohner
Filippo Salmina
Thomas Schopper
Willi Schriber
Daniel Seitz
Michael Spoerri
Katja Steiger
Marion Sykora
Raffaella Taddei
Fredy Vogt
Urs Wäckerlig
Alexandra Walpen
Stefan Weber
Cordula Wigger
Rolando Zuccolo

Auswahlbibliographie
Selected Bibliography

«Bahnhof St. Gallen-Nordwest», in: Aktuelle Wettbewerbs Scene, 1988, Nr. 6 – «Das Ganze ist das Fragment», in: Hochparterre, 1992, Nr. 5 – holl. [Roman Hollenstein], «Eine neue Universität für Nikosia», in: Neue Zürcher Zeitung, 23. Juli 1993 – «Universität Nikosia», in: Bauwelt, 19. November 1993, Nr. 44 – «Drei Fragen an Architekten, Jean-Pierre Dürig, Philippe Rämi», in: Werk, Bauen + Wohnen, 1994, Nr. 3 – «Berufsschulanlage, Zürich», in: SIA, 31. März 1994, Nr. 14 – «Berufsschulanlage auf dem Areal Schütze, Zürich», in: Aktuelle Wettbewerbs Scene, 1994, Nr. 2 – «Der Wiederaufbau Beiruts», in: Neue Zürcher Zeitung, 2. September 1994 – «L'architecture suisse triomphe à l'étranger», in: Bilan, September 1994, Nr. 9 – Carmen Humbel, «Grosse Strukturen», in: Wohnen, 1994, Nr. 9.

Rolf Furrer
François Fasnacht
Basel

Mitarbeiterinnen und Mitarbeiter
Collaborators

Sascha Birrer
Roger Bolliger
Adrian Boss
Andreas Brantschen
Samuel Bünzli
Giovanni Ferrara
Mauro Filoni
Isabella Gaggini
Gaetano Gastiello
Ruth Giger
Susanne Greuter
Monika Isler
Raphael Loeliger
Astrid Mathatias
Barbara Rentsch
Stephan Rolli
Alix Röttig
Yvonne Rütsche
Dominique Soiron
Christina Steinegger
Dan Steiner
Lynette Widder
Thomas Zaugg

Auswahlbibliographie
Selected Bibliography

Werner Jehle, «Wartehallen für die Basler Verkehrsbetriebe», in: Archithese, 1986, Nr. 6 – Werner Jehle, «Informatikabteilung des Kantonsspital Basel-Stadt», in: Rivista Tecnica, 1992, Nr. 2 – «Wartehallen für die Basler Verkehrsbetriebe», in: Baumeister, 1993, Nr. 12 – Carmen Humbel, «Im Zentrum das städtische Detail, Die Basler Architekten Rolf Furrer und François Fasnacht», in: Neue Zürcher Zeitung, 4. März 1994 – «Bürohaus Steinenvorstadt 62 in Basel», in: Baumeister, 1994, Nr. 8 – «Augenklinik Inselspital Bern», in: Werk, Bauen + Wohnen, 1994, Nr. 9 – St. deMontmolin, «Augenklinik Inselspital Bern», in: Faces, 1994, Nr. 32.

Nick Gartenmann
Mark Werren
Andreas Jöhri, Bern

Mitarbeiterinnen und Mitarbeiter
Collaborators

Thomas Arnold
Mona Bangerter
Stephan Flückiger
Raphael Forny
Reto Giovanelli
Regina Glatz
Jean-Daniel Gross
François Guillermain
Marc Langenegger
Yvan Schneuwly
Donat Senn
Philippe Stübi
Christina Stucki
Daniel Ulrich
Adrian Weber

Auswahlbibliographie
Selected Bibliography

«Bankverein-Neubau in Ittigen: Der hörbare Schweiger», in: Der Bund, 18. Juni 1991 – Katharina Matter, «Berner Vision für Berliner Regierungsviertel», in: Der Bund, 20. Februar 1993 – Rudolf Stegers, «Lustwandeln im Kanzlergarten, Der Entwurf des Architekturbüros GWJ», in: Der Tagesspiegel, Berlin, 24. Februar 1993 – Fred Müller, «Für Berlin ist nur das Beste gut genug», in: Tages Anzeiger, 1. März 1993, und in: Berner Zeitung, 3. März 1993 – Christoph Luchsinger, «Formverzicht, Substanzgewinn», in: Werk, Bauen + Wohnen, 1993, Nr. 6 – «Eine Stadt, kein Regierungsghetto bauen», in: Der Bund, 10. Juli 1993 – «Stadtplanung, Erfolg für Berner Büro in Berlin», in: Berner Zeitung, 1. Dezember 1993 – «Hauptstadt Berlin, Parlamentsviertel im Spreebogen, Internationaler Städtebaulicher Ideenwettbewerb 1993», Basel, Berlin, Boston 1993 – Christoph Allenspach, «Mehr als einen Koffer in Berlin», in: Berner Zeitung, Kulturwerkstatt, 28. Mai 1994 – Carmen Humbel, «Integrales Denken, Zur Architektur von Gartenmann Werren Jöhri», in: Neue Zürcher Zeitung, 3. Juni 1994 – «Musterprojekt Wohnsiedlung Sonnegg in Langnau BE», in: Diane Oeko Baublatt, 1994, Nr. 2, Hrsg. Diane Oeko-Bau, Teilbereich von Energie 2000, Aktionsprogramm des Eidgenössischen Verkehrs- und Energiedepartements – Christoph Allenspach, «Neue Bären, Berner Architekturszene», in: Hochparterre, 1994, Nr. 10.

Christian Gautschi
Marianne Unternährer
Zürich

Mitarbeiterinnen und Mitarbeiter
Collaborators
Marco Bertoli
Mauro Colazzo
Wolfgang Latzel
Christopher Lim
Marco Rossi
Marie-Theres Stauffer
Sybill Tomaschett
Kurt Zweifel

Auswahlbibliographie
Selected Bibliography
Markus Friedli, «Denkgebäude», in: Werk, Bauen + Wohnen, 1992, Nr. 4 – Bea Goller, «renovacio», in: quaderns, Nr. 201 – Carmen Humbel, «Gesteuerte Interpretation, Zur Architektur von Gautschi und Unternährer», in: Neue Zürcher Zeitung, 6. Mai 1994 – Carmen Humbel, «Gesteuerte Interpretation», in: Archithese, 1994, Nr. 3.

Dieter Jüngling
Andreas Hagmann
Chur

Mitarbeiterinnen und Mitarbeiter
Collaborators
Rolf Berger
Serge Borgmann
Heinz Caflisch
Vincenzo Cangemi
Katja Dambacher
Monika Geissler
Alex Jörg
Urs Meng
Andrea Pfister
Evi Tharandt
Peter Walser
Alex Zoanni

Auswahlbibliographie
Selected Bibliography
Lutz Windhöfel, «Neue HTL in Chur: Und eine grosse Halle. Das Architekturbüro Jüngling und Hagmann baute die neue Ingenieurschule HTL in Chur», in: Bündner Zeitung, 31. Juli 1993; überarbeitete Fassung als: «Im Zentrum: Eine riesige Halle», in: Hochparterre, 1993, Nr. 12 – «Heterogene Einheit», in: Werk, Bauen + Wohnen, 1993, Nr. 12 – «Projektwettbewerb für die Gestaltung des Regierungsplatzes, Chur, 1992», in: Werk, Bauen + Wohnen, 1994, Nr. 3 – Carmen Humbel, «Experimentelles Schichten, Zur Architektur von Dieter Jüngling und Andreas Hagmann», in: Neue Zürcher Zeitung, 4. November 1994 – «Higher Technical School», in: A + T 1994, Nr. 4.

Claudine Lorenz
Florian Musso
Sion

Mitarbeiterinnen und Mitarbeiter
Collaborators
Francesco Della Casa
Philippe Ebiner
Annette Leiggener
Carine Mayor
Murielle Moret
Florian Werpelin

Auswahlbibliographie
Selected Bibliography
«Über den Wettbewerb zur Architekturdebatte, Fazit des Walliser Kantonsarchitekten Bernhard Attinger, Grimisuat: Home pour personnes agées ‹Les Crètes›», in: Archithese, 1991, Nr. 3 – «Pavillon Tabin-Darbellay in Savièse», in: Architecture Suisse, 1992, Nr. 103 – «Umbau des Bundeshauses, Machbarkeitsstudie», in: Werk, Bauen + Wohnen, 1992, Nr. 1–2 – Carmen Humbel, «Spannungsvolle Räume, Zur Architektur von Claudine Lorenz und Florian Musso», in: Neue Zürcher Zeitung, 2. Dezember 1994.

**Meinrad Morger
Heinrich Degelo
Basel**

Mitarbeiterinnen und Mitarbeiter
Collaborators

Dalila Chebbi
Lukas Egli
Philipp Esch
Danielle Fischer
Gian Fistarol
Adriana Georgieva
Alexandra Gübeli
Katrin Gügler
Aja Huber
Johannes Käferstein
Nadja Keller
Hermann Kohler
Barbara Lenherr
Raphael Loeliger
Urs Meister
Margot Meier
Simon Monnier
Albi Nussbaumer
Rebecca Rossi
Anja Snellmann
Regula Stahl
Donald Stählin
Hansueli Sutter
Othmar Villiger

Auswahlbibliographie
Selected Bibliography

«Kindergartenprovisorium an der Zähringerstrasse», in: Holzbulletin Lignum, 1990, Nr. 24 – «Alloggi comunali a Basilea», in: Rivista Tecnica, 1992, Nr. 4 – «La fin et les moyens», in: Techniques & Architecture, 1992, Nr. 404 – «Guardevia», in: quaderns, 1992, Nr. 195 – Walter Zschokke, «Basler Klima», in: Die Presse, 28. November 1992 – «Hinter dem roten Tuch wohnt es sich billig», in: Basler Zeitung, 17. Juli 1993 – «Ausgezeichnete Architekten», in: Hochparterre, 1992, Nr. 8/9 – «Kommunales Wohnhaus Müllheimerstrasse für die Stadt Basel 1989–93», in: Werk, Bauen + Wohnen, 1993, Nr. 9 – «Wohnhaus Anbau Basel», in: Holzbulletin Lignum, 1992, Nr. 30 – «Kommunales Wohnhaus, Müllheimerstrasse», in: Baumeister, 1993, Nr. 12 – Philippe Gueissaz, «Un prisme rouge», in: Faces, 1993, Nr. 28 – Matthias Ackermann (Hrsg.), Kommunales Wohnhaus 1993, Morger & Degelo Basel, Werkverzeichnis 1988–1994, Basel 1994 – Carmen Humbel, «Ästhetische Notwendigkeit, Die Architekten Meinrad Morger und Heinrich Degelo», in: Neue Zürcher Zeitung, 4. Februar 1994.

**Pierre-André Simonet
Yvan Chappuis
Freiburg**

Mitarbeiterinnen und Mitarbeiter
Collaborators

Marc-Antonio Antonio
Gaby Arriola
Christophe Berra
Martine Chenaux
Juan Carlos Milan
Isabelle Staub

Auswahlbibliographie
Selected Bibliography

«Agrandissement du Centre scolaire 1762 Givisiez», in: Schweizer Architektur, März 1993 – «Agrandissement d'un appartement dans la villa familiale La Perrausa, Corpataux (FR)», in: Schweizer Architektur, Mai 1994 – Carmen Humbel, «Material und Licht, Die Freiburger Architekten Simonet und Chappuis», in: Neue Zürcher Zeitung, 2. September 1994.

Bildnachweis / Illustration credits

Hans Baumann, Hünibach-Thun:
74 oben / above
François Bertin, Grandvaux: 32, 37
Ralph Feiner, Chur: 22, 26
Reto Führer, Chur:
18, 23, 24, 109, 110, 111
Heinrich Helfenstein, Zürich: 98
Robert Hofer, Sion: 116
Christian Kerez, Chur und Zürich:
20, 24, 106
Antonio Martinelli, Paris: 36
Thomas Rast, Zürich: 96
Bertrand Rey, Lausanne: 118
Marco Schibig, Bern: 88
Michael Schneeberger, Bern:
74 mitte und unten, middle and below
Filippo Simanetti, Como: 48, 50, 52
Andreas F. Voegelin, Basel: 70, 72, 73, 76
Ruedi Walti, Basel:
126, 128, 130, 132, 135
Umschlag oben, cover above
Jürg Zimmermann, Zürich:
140, 142, 144, 145

Alle Pläne und Fotos stammen, sofern nicht anders vermerkt, aus dem Archiv des jeweiligen Architekturbüros.
Unless otherwise stated, all plans and photographs are taken from the architects archives.

Carmen Humbel

1961 geboren in Zürich. 1978–82 Mittelschule und Matura an der Kantonsschule in Wohlen (AG). 1982–88 Architekturstudium an der ETH-Zürich. 1988–91 Mitarbeit in verschiedenen Architekturbüros und im Architekturmuseum in Basel. 1991–93 Geschäftsführerin im Architekturforum Zürich. Ab 1993 selbständige Architektin in Basel. Arbeitsgemeinschaft Ernst & Humbel seit 1995 in Zürich und Basel. Daneben publizistische Tätigkeiten für verschiedene Tageszeitungen und Fachzeitschriften; Dissertation mit dem Thema «Hermann Baur – ein Architekt im Aufbruch zur Moderne und mit ethischer Gesinnung».

1961 Born in Zürich. 1978–82 Secondary schooling at the cantonal school in Wohlen (Canton Aargau). 1982–88 Student of architecture at the ETH (Swiss Federal Institute of Technology) in Zürich. 1988–91 Work with various architecture offices and the Museum of Architecture in Basel. 1991–93 Manager of the Architekturforum Zürich. Since 1993 – free-lance architect based in Basel. 1995 Partner in the team Ernst & Humbel (Zürich and Basel). Journalistically active for diverse daily papers and trade journals; dissertation on the subject "Hermann Baur – ein Architekt im Aufbruch zur Moderne und mit ethischer Gesinnung" (Hermann Baur – An Architect of Ethical Conviction on the Verge of Modernism).